WOMEN AND THE CHURCH

Women and the Church

From Devil's Gateway to Discipleship

NATALIA IMPERATORI-LEE

Paulist Press
New York / Mahwah, NJ

"Word Made Flesh" and "Woman's Body" by Miriam Therese Winter used by permission of the author.

Cover image: STORY OF RUTH, copyright 1991, John August Swanson Trust, www.JohnAugustSwanson.com
Cover design by Sharyn Banks
Book design by Lynn Else

Library of Congress Cataloging-in-Publication Data
Names: Imperatori-Lee, Natalia M., author.
Title: Women and the church : from devil's gateway to discipleship / Natalia Imperatori-Lee.
Description: New York : Paulist Press, [2023] | Includes bibliographical references and index. | Summary: "A textbook designed for undergraduate courses in Women and Catholicism or Feminism and the Catholic Church, which looks at women's work, their questions and contributions to the study of theology, as well as the presence and sustained suppression of women's voices in both scripture and tradition"—Provided by publisher.
Identifiers: LCCN 2023016464 (print) | LCCN 2023016465 (ebook) | ISBN 9780809154708 (paperback) | ISBN 9781587688669 (ebook)
Subjects: LCSH: Women in the Catholic Church—Textbooks. | Women—Religious aspects—Catholic Church.
Classification: LCC BX2347.8.W6 I47 2023 (print) | LCC BX2347.8.W6 (ebook) | DDC 282.082—dc23/eng/20231122
LC record available at https://lccn.loc.gov/2023016464
LC ebook record available at https://lccn.loc.gov/2023016465

ISBN 978-0-8091-5470-8 (paperback)
ISBN 978-1-58768-866-9 (e-book)

Published by Paulist Press
997 Macarthur Boulevard
Mahwah, New Jersey 07430
www.paulistpress.com

Printed and bound in the
United States of America

For Elsie Miranda, Beth Johnson, and Cathy Hilkert,
who midwifed me into my vocation as a feminist and a scholar
And for my students, who teach me more than they know

CONTENTS

PREFACE

"I don't know how any woman can stay in the Catholic Church. It's so sexist!"

"Wait, are you religious? I thought you were a feminist."

"You're such a good example of a Catholic woman. Thank God you're not like those feminists."

Have you ever heard these questions or comments? What is your response? How do they make you feel?

Each of these statements has been uttered to me over the past twenty-odd years of teaching religious studies at a small Catholic college in a major metropolitan city. You may have heard them too or even had them directed at you. The sentences contradict each other and, like most sentiments, reflect the speaker's biases more than the reality of feminism or Catholicism, or the ways in which those ideas overlap.

As we embark on the third decade of the third millennium, we find ourselves as U.S. Catholics at several crucibles. We are still confronting the reality of the sexual abuse crisis, including especially the massive, systemic cover-up of sex crimes by the hierarchy of the church and the civil society that turned the other way. The #MeToo movement has exposed the ubiquity of sexual harassment in the workplace, on public transportation, in the most ordinary moments of life for women and girls. The midterm elections of 2018 ushered in more than one hundred women elected to the U.S. House of Representatives, and Pope Francis's commission to study the history and contemporary feasibility of women deacons finished its work this same year. The Women's March, the pro-life movement, the absence of women in decision-making roles in the church: all of these point to the overlap between religion and feminism. They also remind us that Catholic feminism isn't an oxymoron but a vein of rich theological reflection and experience that can, and should, be mined again and again.

The act of writing a book about women in the church is daunting because each of the realities this text sets out to describe exist in such variety and complexity that it seems impossible to do justice to feminism, Catholic Christianity, and women's lives. If we add in the massive, global church; intersecting racial/ethnic identities; privileges and oppressions of race, gender, class, sexual orientation, and more, the work seems even more difficult. But the imperative remains to tell a true story of how women have shaped and been shaped by their interaction with the church, the ways in which the church has tried and succeeded in marginalizing women, and the creative ways in which women's voices can be heard in the church. Though it may not seem obvious if one reads news headlines, women's work continues to buoy the church even in its most difficult challenges.

Those challenges are many. The first decades of the century has seen a rise in people who self-identify as having no religion, or "nones." The Catholic Church is among the religious communities that have seen the most de-conversion, that is, the most loss of members from the church to the nones. Whether because of social forces like anti-institutional sentiment or more acute causes like the sex abuse scandal, the church's membership is changing. Latines will soon make up most of the U.S. church, but these numbers are not represented proportionally in church leadership and governance. Increasingly, most of the church's thinking, its theology, is done by laypeople trained at universities, not priests trained in seminaries. All of these shifts mean that the Catholic Church must do some reevaluation of its mission and its goals. This reevaluation must include women's voices if it is to be legitimate.

But there are broader challenges as well. People have widely varied opinions on the value and usefulness of religion. Perhaps to study religion at all is to give it an importance that it doesn't necessarily have in people's lives anymore. To study religion with a particular focus on the role of women might seem biased or like a fool's errand, particularly in a male-dominated community like Roman

Catholicism. And what might it even mean to study religion, or to "do" theology?

The best analogy I've heard, which I use with my own students, has to do with driving. This text, as a work of theology, is not an exercise in catechesis. Catechesis, or religious formation, is one way to do instruction about religion. It is what the church does with new members through RCIA or with children in a CCD class. Catechesis is a bit like a driver's ed course: you learn the rules (of the religion, as in morality, or of the road), you learn how to operate the machine (how the blinker works, or what to do at Mass), and you learn how to share the road with other drivers (the life of faith). Theology, while also a type of instruction that has to do with religion, is not catechesis.

Theology is like being a mechanic. Students in a driver's ed course do not need to know how to change a tire to pass the class, much less how to change the oil in their car or replace the transmission, but mechanics do. Like a mechanic, a theologian knows the intricacies of the faith, why it does what it does, and how it developed into the reality we have before us. Moreover, rather than a goal of correct worship or enhanced faith (though these are certainly important side benefits of theology), theologians seek to optimize the faith in a variety of ways: by returning to the sources and reexamining scriptural translations, for example, to ensure that what believers hear is as close as possible to the original text of scripture. Or a theologian might, in her role as a mechanic, hear a funny noise coming from the tradition and look under the hood to figure out what has gone wrong. Sometimes we discover that practices or beliefs we thought to be ancient are actually later innovations. Other times, we realize, because we are a church in history, that previous positions held by the church (such as those about slavery or capital punishment) are no longer a faithful reflection of the Triune God and the dignity of humanity made in God's image. Theologians seek to optimize the faith through reinvigoration, correction, or development of doctrine. Where the goal of catechesis is ongoing growth of faith in persons, the goal of theology is to ensure that the faith remains faithful to the gospel.

This book is a work of feminist theology that seeks to uncover that which has remained hidden in Christianity, either deliberately or by omission: the role of women in creating, sustaining, and continuing to develop the church, its teachings, and its presence in the world.

About This Book

Designed as a text that can be used in a fifteen-week semester, *Women and the Church* examines the history of Christian feminism as a response to patriarchy, the ways in which women have been portrayed in scripture and women's hermeneutical strategies, and the seminal contributions of women to the subfields of systematic theology. To optimize its usefulness in a college setting, this text has fourteen short chapters, in addition to an introduction and pedagogical apparatus like discussion questions and activity prompts. The book focuses mainly, though not exclusively, on women in the Roman Catholic Church. I divide the work into three sections: Problematizing the Feminine; Women, Scripture, Tradition; and A Woman's Place Is in the Church.

The first section, Problematizing the Feminine, will lay out various methodological approaches in feminist theology, including some historical background on Christian feminism. It will explore the ways in which the church has understood women as inferior, then equal in dignity but not power, to men. This section will also introduce students to the contemporary discourses about gender, sexuality, and sexual orientation and the relationship of these to church doctrine and papal pronouncements, specifically John Paul II's *Mulieris Dignitatem* and *Ordinatio Sacerdotalis.*

Women, Scripture, Tradition, the second section, focuses on women and biblical literature. Chapters in this section will look at salient figures in the Hebrew and Christian scriptures, such as Eve, Ruth, Mary the mother of Jesus, Mary Magdalene, and women of the early Jesus movement, such as Junia. Using the work of feminist biblical scholars like Carol Christ and Elisabeth Schüssler Fiorenza, this section will demonstrate for students how the Bible has been used as a tool of women's oppression and also how it can become a source of liberation.

The final section, titled A Woman's Place Is in the Church, looks at systematic theology through a feminist lens and features the work of Elizabeth Johnson (on the naming of God and the purpose of theology), Susan Ross (on ecclesiology and sacraments), M. Shawn Copeland (on theological anthropology), and María Pilar Aquino (on method and interculturality). Beyond just getting "women's perspectives" on standard issues in systematic theology, though, this text also highlights the ways in which feminist theologians have pioneered subdisciplines in Catholic theology like ecological theology, theological anthropology, and intercultural methodologies. Where appropriate, this section includes incidents where women's theological work brought them into conflict with the institutional church in the contemporary period.

Most texts for undergraduate feminist theology courses are anthologies of essays written by multiple authors compiled into one volume. The benefit of that type of book is that it includes a variety of viewpoints, subfields, and contexts. This book, by contrast, is a monograph. Though I strive to incorporate a wide range of sources, inevitably the choices (and mistakes, especially those!) are mine. The benefit here, I believe, is a unity that cannot be achieved in an anthology. Similar to sitting in on a course with one professor, the consistent viewpoint and narrative voice helps synthesize a vast array of material into a coherent narrative. My hope is that readers will use this book as a jumping-off point for further research into the roles women have had and should have in the contemporary church. Further, I hope this book might be an entry point into the varied, intercultural world of contemporary feminist theology and help readers to rediscover faith and feminist solidarity, together.

ACKNOWLEDGMENTS

Like all worthwhile work, this book is the result of rich collaboration. My main coconspirator, cheerleader, and guide in this process has been the tirelessly optimistic Christopher Bellitto, my fantastic editor at Paulist Press. Together with the whole Paulist team, Chris was tenacious and patient through delays and freak-outs. I am grateful for his encouragement, his confidence in me, and his insight into the process of book writing. His edits throughout this text have strengthened and clarified my arguments, improving them at every turn.

I am also indebted to my colleagues at Manhattan College who supported me in this process. A sabbatical grant in the spring of 2020 allowed me to devote all my time to researching and drafting this book. When that sabbatical was interrupted by the emergence of the COVID-19 pandemic, David Shefferman selflessly agreed to serve as interim chair for a semester while I finished the manuscript. My colleagues Michele Saracino, Ashley Cross, and Jordan Pascoe all contributed sources, insight, and support during the process of bringing this text to life. Many colleagues and friends read and gave feedback on portions of this text. To Jim Keane and Rabea Ali: thank you!

For me, the writing process is a repeating pattern of crises and rewards, and my growth as a writer has largely depended on my ability to intersperse rewards into the process of research, drafting, and revision. Oftentimes, these rewards consisted of time with dear friends. My dear colleague and friend Rocco Marinaccio surprised me with an impromptu picnic on the day I wrote the last page of this text. My semi-regular lunches with David Witzling made the work easier to bear, as did my biweekly breakfasts with John Seitz. Both are terrific accountability partners. Brenna Moore, Maureen

O'Connell, Christine Hinze, and I were all in similar places with our writing, and they have served as selfless support for my work (and my life) in countless ways. Kristin Heyer's texts got me through many a long pandemic day. The support of my core group of "mom friends," Jennifer Petras, Lara Dua-Swartz, and April Brown, is now more than a decade long and unmatched in the preservation of my sanity. I must also acknowledge the help I got from prescription antidepressants along this journey. It is always ok to ask for help.

The main audience for this book is undergraduate students, and I have relied on the wisdom and insights of my students throughout the writing of this text: from conceptualizing it, to drafting it, to revising it. I am particularly indebted to the students in my Women in Western Religion seminar in the fall of 2019: Rabea Ali, Joselyn Castro, Sam Crutchfield, Alisse Fullerton, Livia Haven, August Kissel, Nora Nugent, Ireland Twiggs, and Meredith Taylor. In addition, much of my growth as an intersectional feminist is due to the conversations and venting sessions I've enjoyed with students at the Lasallian Women and Gender Resource Center at Manhattan College. These students and others, whom I now count as friends, include Christina Trichillo, Reilly Reibhan, Rose Brennan, Natalie Heinitz, Alannah Boyle, and Jo-Ann Mullooly. Rabea Ali and Fatoumata Saho, both of whom were fixtures at the LWGRC, in my classes and in my office, have cheered me with their infectious joy, coffee, and chocolate breaks.

Finally, I must express the depth of my gratitude to my family. My wonderful spouse, Michael Lee, has sustained me with physical nourishment (quite literally, as our family cook) as well as steadfast emotional and spiritual strength. It's a privilege to share life with you. Our sons, William and Benjamin, have grown into teenagers in the process of writing this, and I am grateful to them for their patience with their mom's anxiety as I struggled to meet deadlines. Ben has been such a good cheerleader, congratulating me at every milestone. Will took filial support a step further, helping me with formatting the "Read Further" sections that appear at the end of each chapter. Mostly though, I am grateful to these three Lees for the joy and laughter they bring to each of my days.

PART 1

PROBLEMATIZING THE FEMININE

In the first five chapters of this book, we lay the groundwork for our investigations. One important way to do this is to define our key terms: What is *feminism* and why do we need it? What do we mean by the word *church*, and how will we be using that term? We look at the history of the feminist movement both within and outside the domain of Catholicism. We explore the method of feminist theology: how these thinkers go about their work. A brief overview of different key thinkers on gender and sex in the Christian tradition rounds out the first section of this book and gets us ready to delve into scripture, tradition, and theological exploration in a feminist key.

1

WHY FEMINISM?

What do you think of when you hear the word *feminist*? For many years, the word has had a negative connotation. Some associate feminism with a very radical movement, an anti-male sentiment, or an angry, vengeful community. Feminists are seen as anti-family, anti-marriage, or anti-joy. Conversely, they might be caricatured as ugly, unhappy women with an axe to grind. A conservative political radio show host coined the term *feminazi* in the 1990s and it stuck surprisingly well. While it's normal to be skeptical of any "-ism" or ideology, feminism seems to provoke heightened emotions in people. Why?

Don't women already have equality? Women in the United States have it pretty great, why are they still complaining? Doesn't the Bible say that men and women are equal but different? Now that women can vote and work outside the home and even have viable presidential campaigns, the idea that women are somehow "oppressed" might seem silly. But while there are ways in which women's lives have dramatically improved in the United States (white women have been able to vote since 1919, and women have been able to have credit cards in their name since 1974), the systematic marginalization of women's voices, expertise, and even court testimony continues to shape our society.

In the world of religion, especially a male-dominated religion like Catholic Christianity, women's voices, their lives, and their testimony have been systematically undervalued and pushed aside. At times this marginalization has been intentional, and at times it has been the byproduct of secular cultural factors, but the marginalization of women's lives and their distance from access to and reflection on the work of God in the world remains a constant. But must it? Jewish feminist theologian Judith Plaskow argues in her foundational text *Standing Again at Sinai* that people cannot accurately speak of Judaism, since women's voices have been excluded from the Torah. Written and often interpreted only by men, the scriptures reveal themselves as only one half of the testimony to God's divine action in history. So, until women are able to tell the Torah that they have seen and heard and experienced, Judaism remains hobbled, incomplete.

The same is true of Christianity. The male-dominant perspective of scripture reveals itself in many ways, most obviously in the dearth of women who are identified by name. This does not mean that women were not present. After all, can we really say that God reveals the divine nature only to men? Or that only men knew Jesus? We know that women were among Jesus's followers, but we hear their stories only from the perspective of men. What's more, scriptural interpretation has long been the purview of men, who were deemed more capable than women of understanding things related to God (and, not coincidentally, were the ones taught to read and write, rendering them the only ones capable of reading scripture).

The result of this alienation of women from the work of theology—telling, retelling, and interpreting scripture; shaping and handing on tradition—is a hobbled faith, a partial response to God's self-giving invitation to participate in the divine life. The injury that women's marginalization has caused to Christianity is not the result of bad decisions by relatively few people in positions of power over the centuries. Neither is this absence an anomaly or an accident of history. The exclusion of women from participation in theological work is the result of systematic forces in our societies and our churches. These forces can be understood under the umbrella term of *sexism*. Within the category of sexism, we can identify several terms that describe how sexism functions in the world: through the ideology of patriarchy, the thought patterns of androcentrism, and the behavior of misogyny.

In any course I teach, I find it helpful to begin fruitful discussions by defining our terms. So let's do that:

Sexism is the term used for the preference of one sex over the other. But it is not, as some would say, a neutral or "two-way" term.

The meaning of words is rooted in their historical context, and historically *sexism* has operated as an ideology that prefers men and masculine identities over women and feminine identities. We can think of *sexism* as an umbrella term with specific manifestations. Some of these manifestations are clearly visible and easy to identify: the gender pay gap, the entire beauty industry. Others require more reflection if we want to unearth how they operate. For example, women who give birth (or adopt a child) are expected to take a leave of absence from their jobs. We know it as maternity leave. But if a man takes a leave, and parental leaves are increasingly becoming available to men, the response is either incredulity or adulation: "Wow, what an AMAZING dad." This stems from our propensity to view women as innate nurturers and men as lacking that inborn ability. But that assumption is sexist, since not all women are naturals at mothering, and since expecting women to bow out of the workforce puts them at a disadvantage whether they take advantage of parental leave or not. Because of this, we might say that sexism is pervasive—it forms a large part of what we consider to be "the way things are" or "the way it's always been done."

But women's experience, particularly the experience of women who do archival work or historical investigation, has shown that often "the way things are" has varied among historical eras, differing cultures, classes, and races. In fact, "the way things are" or the status quo is more dependent on who has power in a given society than on previous experience. All of this is to say that although sexism may characterize the status quo, it needn't. For centuries, women have said this. It is time to make that assertion a reality.

The system of sexism works in a variety of ways. The first of these is what we call *patriarchy* from a word meaning "father-rule." Some feminist theologians have expanded this notion to kyriarchy, which seems more appropriate, given the interplay of race and class in who gets deemed "dominant" in a society. *Kyriarchy* refers to the rule of a master or lord and therefore takes into account the intersecting oppressions that function to organize social groups into more and less central, more and less dominant, more and less marginalized.

A word about intersectionality will be helpful here. Kimberlé Crenshaw's groundbreaking work on intersectional feminism reoriented the movement for women's equality away from an exclusive focus on women's liberation, which had often amounted to white women's liberation, to a more comprehensive understanding of the ways in which race, class, gender, and other factors affect someone's privilege or marginalization in a society. Rather than claim that oppression should be tackled in a single-file line, where this week we defeat sexism and next week we can be free to move on to racism, intersectional feminism recognizes that complex, diverse societies wield power in complicated ways, and, as a result, marginalization cannot be compartmentalized. Black women suffer disproportionately lower health outcomes than white women not only because sexism conditions us to devalue women's bodies but also because the medical establishment's devaluing of the pain of Black people can be attributed to racial bias.

Kyriarchy, then, is the ideological manifestation of sexism. A kyriarchal society is one in which men, especially white, heterosexual, able-bodied men, run things, from corporations to families. These dominant men are seen as the adults, the decision-makers, the "breadwinners," and the serious actors in the public square. If men who all look alike are in powerful positions and decision-making roles in numbers that far outweigh women's roles, that is usually a sign of a kyriarchal society. Kyriarchy is also visible in wage gaps (e.g., the "mommy-track" where women's careers suffer once they have children either because they stop getting promoted or because the burden of childcare falls primarily on them, which prevents them from advancing in their careers) and in health and mental-health outcome disparities. The ideology of kyriarchy teaches us that some men are more rational, more logical, more brilliant than most other persons and are therefore more deserving of their role as dominant figures in society.

Androcentrism is an interior or mental manifestation of sexism. Androcentrism is the centering or making-normative of the white, heterosexual, able-bodied male and his worldview, preferences, and goals as the default of what it means to be "human." To put it bluntly: normal means what a straight, white guy says is normal. Everything and everyone that deviates from that white heterosexual able-bodied norm is "also-human" but slightly less so. It can be difficult to wrap our minds around something like androcentrism because it functions like a mental filter in a lot of ways.

Let's do an exercise to see androcentrism at work on Twitter. The most successful way I've found to help students see androcentrism at work in their everyday lives is to point them to a Twitter account that flips the gender script and reveals how differently men and women are addressed in society. The account is called "man who has it all," and a typical tweet reads as follows: "I don't know where any of my clothes came from because my husband buys them all for me. He buys the kids' clothes too. And he buys holiday clothes, sun cream, and swimwear. This is because he just happens to love shopping. Claire, CEO."

Here's another: "Men! Is having it all REALLY possible? Kids, wife, work outside the home, a Korean skincare routine, beach-ready ankles, and pH balanced forearms?" I love reading tweets like this because they sound utterly ridiculous, and precisely in that ridiculousness our own androcentric expectations are revealed. Of course not all women do all the shopping for their families, nor do all women strive to have it all. But that sort of language is rarely addressed to men, because we live in an androcentric, kyriarchal, and ultimately sexist society.

A third crucial term to understand why we need feminism is *misogyny*. If sexism denotes the systemic reality, kyriarchy the ideology, and androcentrism the epistemological structure of the dominance of white, heterosexual men; then misogyny is, as feminist philosopher Kate Manne has brilliantly noted, the behavior used to police the boundaries of male dominance. She writes, "Whereas misogyny upholds the social norms of patriarchies by patrolling and policing them, sexism serves to justify these norms, largely via an ideology of supposedly natural differences between men and women with respect to their talents, interests, proclivities, and appetites."[1]

We are all too familiar with church language that subjugates women to men. The theory of complementarity, covered later in this text, centers on the notion that men and women are a gender binary that is complementary—that is, each gender makes up for what the other lacks. From the biological connection of heterosexual, vaginal intercourse, the theory of complementarity extrapolates that just as men's and women's bodies fit together and do not overlap, so too their personalities, interests, and talents work together without overlapping. One prominent text where this features is in John Paul II's 1988 encyclical on women, *Mulieris Dignitatem*.

But the language and thought-patterns of gender complementarity are everywhere in Catholicism—from its theology to its art to its piety. Women are taught to emulate the Virgin Mary: nurturing, silent, accepting of God's will for her life, submissive to God's plan. Men are taught, more often, to model their lives on Jesus: self-sacrificing leadership, sonship, public ministry. The canon of saints, the exemplars of the faith, are mostly men. Of the relatively few women who are venerated as saints, virtually none lived outside of religious life or the convent. In the church even more acutely than in the culture, women are told that to please God they should obey their husbands (it's in the marriage vows, after all). Misogyny of the kind described by Manne seems baked in to the core of the church.

I used to recoil at the idea of misogyny, saving it for only the most extreme cases—intimate-partner violence, for example, or people who murdered their wives or killed women at random. That's probably because the term is derived from words meaning "hatred of women," and hatred seemed particularly reserved for graphically violent situations. Very few men openly admit to loathing all women, after all. But if we look at the term the way Manne sees it, the fullness of misogynistic behavior becomes more clear. The first step is to recognize that to view misogyny in that extreme way is to adopt the perspective of the perpetrator of misogyny. Thus, it's not really misogynistic behavior if I don't also express conscious, premeditated hatred of all women as I do the behavior.

What if, instead, we viewed misogyny from the perspective of its objects: women? When we look from women's point of view, we see that those of us who step out of prescribed roles have historically been singled out for punishment, sometimes harshly. It can be as simple as being called unlikeable when making simple requests at work, or it can be as fraught as the burning of witches in (whatever century). If women do not fulfill their prescribed role as nurturers, supporters, even admirers of men, they are cast as problematic or difficult, as crones or hags, as bitches. If women don't perform the adequate amount of modesty (determined by patriarchal societies in different ways), they are called easy or loose or sluts. When women dare to show ambition or not tolerate abuse, they are viewed as catty or vengeful. In short, women must adhere to strict gender roles or face scrutiny, punishment, or even violence and death at the hands of misogynistic enforcement.

Some of you may be thinking that sexism, kyriarchy, androcentrism, and particularly misogyny are not that widespread. Sure, there may be some exceptional cases here and there that show that women's worth is still less than men's, but women have recourse to the legal system, and the majority of people aren't actively trying to hurt women. And in many ways, misogynistic behavior can be difficult to pinpoint. This is why it is important to remember that the behavior of misogyny, its enforcement-character, exerts itself against women who refuse to conform to predetermined roles. Women are routinely punished (violently, emotionally, socially, economically) for failing to live up to and live into the patriarchal notions of what a woman should be: nurturing, oriented toward others, admiring of men, and supportive of colleagues whether or not that support or admiration is deserved.

Nor are women the only objects of misogynistic behavior. Let's look at an example from Catholicism. When Fr. Roy Bourgeois, a Maryknoll priest, participated in a Mass where a woman was ordained a Catholic priest in 2008, he was immediately subjected to a church trial, and he was removed from the priesthood just four years later, in 2012. The swift justice brought against Bourgeois, and the automatic excommunication of the woman priest (and any woman who calls herself a Roman Catholic woman priest), unfolded amid the scandal of the sexual abuse crisis. From 2002 on, when the *Boston Globe* broke the story of the system of abuse and cover-up of the sexual abuse of minors in the Archdiocese of Boston, the U.S. church has been forced to account for the inaction of priests, pastors, and bishops in reporting abuse to police and the complicity of many U.S. bishops (some of whom retain their episcopal sees to this day) in the cover-up and transferring of pedophile priests. Women and men who challenge prescribed roles (by ordaining women) are subject to near-immediate punishment, while mothers who pleaded for justice for their abused children were ignored. The difference is a matter of role-play. Mothers are supposed to care for their children and worry about them; this wasn't deemed strange or challenging since women lie outside the power structure of the Catholic Church. It is only when women attempt to become part of that structure that the law-enforcement branch of kyriarchy must be activated.

So far we have explored two answers to the question of the existence of feminism. The first answer to "why feminism?" is because Christianity has been told, retold, interpreted, and performed by men and for men. The second answer is because sexism, kyriarchy, androcentrism, and misogyny still exist.

But there are positive reasons why we need feminism as well. This movement, this method, this theology represents more than a reaction to marginalization: it is an elaboration of proposals, a vibrant sisterhood, a cross-cultural and gender-diverse community of solidarity. For decades, women have discovered bonds of unity based on shared experiences of marginalization at the hands of kyriarchal structures. In the 1970s this solidarity was discovered in consciousness-raising groups where women realized for the first time that they were not alone in feeling demeaned, undervalued, and ignored in their day-to-day lives, which Judith Plaskow describes as the "yeah, yeah" moment.[2] Other theorists have termed this the feminist "click," where the reality of marginalization clicks into place as more than an individual reality; it is a communal and structural reality shared by women as a group. More recently, thanks to the activism of Black, Latinx, LGBTQ, and Asian feminists, Euro-American/white feminism has been forced to decenter the experience of dominant women in order to allow intersectional feminism to flourish. In all this, the "yeah, yeah" experiences or feminist "clicks" when it clicks into place that we are not alone in our experience of marginalization, or the "oh wow" when we are presented with the compounding oppressions that intersectionality reveals, have built up a life-giving community where many people of all genders feel seen, affirmed, and enlivened to do the work of liberation. This book is for people engaged in that work.

Feminism is important because the systematic exclusion of women's voices impoverishes every community, every discipline, and every discourse. This is especially true in theology, which is faith seeking understanding. To limit the insights of theology to those deduced or produced by men reflecting on their experience of faith impoverishes our understanding of God's presence and action in the world.

Let's take for an example something as basic as the way we talk about and imagine God. Imagining God exclusively as male closes off the fundamental mysteriousness at the heart of the doctrine of God—God's fundamental incomprehensibility precedes any and all images, words, sacraments we might use to imagine and relate to the divine. But when we use particular images repeatedly and to the exclusion of others, we become accustomed to these particular images. We get into a rut with some of them, and we become so comfortable that any different sort of image (of God as a mother hen, e.g., or a woman looking for a lost coin) makes us wince uncomfortably. Even if we know, on some level, that God is not exactly like a shepherd (or a rock, or a stream, or a father), when we come to rely on these images to the exclusion of other, equally valid and biblical ones, our familiarity can slip into idolatry. We begin to worship the image and not the God that the image is meant to evoke. We forget God's mysterious nature. We become overfamiliar. This is a sin.

Feminist theologians seek to broaden our language about God to include images from women's experience not as a competition or in order to create a balance sheet of images for God such that there are an equal amount of "male" and "female" and "nature" ones but so that we use the entire repertoire available to us, feeling both comfortable and uncomfortable to some degree with the images, and thereby protecting the incomprehensibility of God. In this way, the church needs feminist theology to keep it honest to its own principles, even the most fundamental ones, like the notion that God is beyond our understanding.

We can see even in this short example that feminism is vital to religion. But we should be wary of the word *feminism* in the singular as if all feminists think the same way and go about their work the same way. This is not even true of feminist theologians. The next section will tease out different strands in the tapestry that is feminism, including religious and nonreligious (even some antireligious) feminisms.

Feminism Should Always Be Plural

Feminism is not monolithic. As generation after generation of women has tried to defy the expectations placed on them by sexist social structures, women and their allies have explored varying approaches to reclaiming their full humanity. There are a variety of ways of understanding these different movements within feminism: as waves, as generations, as ideological schools. However we classify them, it is important to understand the variety that exists within feminism if we are to properly grasp both the progress feminists have made and the challenges that they have faced. Interestingly, movements for women's rights have long been entangled with theological reflection and production. From the first wave of suffragists like Lucretia Mott, Lucy Stone, and Elizabeth Cady Stanton (who wrote *A Woman's Bible*), feminists have grappled with both the content of the scriptures and the way in which the text has been interpreted in mainstream Christianity. More on that in chapters 6 through 10.

One important way we can tease out the variety of viewpoints that can be placed under the term *feminism* is historically. This has usually been done by referring to at least three "waves" of feminism. The first wave occurred in the United States in the late 1800s and early 1900s, and centered on getting (white) women the right to vote and own land. Many of these early feminists were also abolitionists, fighting to end slavery. Their focus, however, and the one they eventually unified behind, was access to the ballot box for white women. Major figures at this time included Lucretia Mott, Elizabeth Cady Stanton, Lucy Stone, and Abigail Adams. Sojourner Truth, a former slave who escaped in the early nineteenth century, can be described as a precursor to feminism's first wave. A version of her famous speech at the Ohio Women's Convention noted the disparities in how white and black women were treated—for all the chivalry and deference shown to white women, black women's bodies were brutalized in the slave trade. Women's supposed physical weakness was never allowed of slave women, who performed backbreaking labor while suffering sexual assault, the decimation of their families, the sale of their children. Truth's speech, as published more than a decade later by Frances Gage (a colleague of Stanton and Moss, and an early suffragist herself), reads powerfully:

> That man over there says that women need to be helped into carriages and lifted over ditches and to have the best place everywhere. Nobody ever helps me into carriages, or over mud-puddles, or gives me any best place! And ain't I a woman?...I could work as much and eat as much as a man, when I could get it—and bear the lash as well! And ain't I a woman? I have borne thirteen children, and seen most all sold off to slavery, and when I cried out

> with my mother's grief, none but Jesus heard me! And ain't I a woman?[3]

Truth is not the only precursor to the first wave of feminism, however. One of my favorite precursors was a woman religious (a nun) who lived in Mexico during the era of colonization. A *criolla* (a woman of European descent born in the Americas) and a child of privilege who entered the convent, Sor Juana Inés de la Cruz was a poet and a theologian. While her work is vast, her feminist poetry clearly indicates that feminism is not a recent phenomenon or a modern project—women have been dissatisfied with kyriarchal structures and strictures, probably for as long as the kyriarchy has existed. Her famous poem "Hombres necios" ("You Stupid Men") calls out the double standard that expects men to "court" women, pressuring them into relationships and marriage, and then excoriates women who aren't virginal. She chastises men who view women as "a Thaïs" when they are courting her and "a Lucretia" after they have gotten her. It seems the double standard of wanting women to be pure while demanding that they give in to sexual pressure and then looking down on them for having sexual relationships is as fresh today as it was hundreds of years ago.

The twentieth century witnessed a huge swell of feminist consciousness, writing, and creative production in the arts. Women across the globe were once again publicly clamoring for equality, spurred by the notion of sexual liberation (and the advent of reliable ways to control fertility), and a growing awareness of the intersecting sexist, racist, and economic systems that functioned to keep women subordinate to men. In 1949, French philosopher Simone de Beauvoir published *The Second Sex*, which became the inspiration for many women to examine their social, economic, and spiritual positions vis-a-vis men. Repercussions from de Beauvoir's text began in the United States with the publication of Betty Friedan's *The Feminine Mystique* and continued into the 1970s and 1980s with projects like Gloria Steinem's *Ms.* magazine, popular music like "I Am Woman (Hear Me Roar)" and "These Boots Are Made for Walkin'," along with marches and demonstrations demanding women's liberation from oppressive sexist structures.

Many caricatures of "feminists" are rooted in imagery from the second wave: the exaggerated notion of angry "women's libbers" who burned their bras in the name of "free love" or "consequence-free" sexuality dovetails with the very real increasing visibility of lesbians and bisexual women, the frustration of women who were tired of being underpaid and harassed in the workplace, and the ebullience of women who were able to control the size of their families reliably for the first time. Second-wave feminists championed the Equal Rights Amendment to the U.S. Constitution, which would guarantee equal treatment for women and men under federal law (it has yet to be ratified, more than fifty years later). They pushed for coeducation, and many colleges and universities began admitting women students during the second wave. Feminists of this time fought for women to have equal access to quality education, to resources for sports, and to health care.

Where the first wave of feminism focused on issues of access—to rights, to property, to the ability to vote—the second wave's signature issues were more personal. In fact, one of the big mantras of second-wave feminism was "the personal is political." What feminists meant by this is that women's lives, even the parts of their lives that are private, like marriage, relationships, and sexuality, are not oppressive individually, but systemically. In other words, people might be tempted to think that once a woman has the right to vote, and her vote counts as much as a man's, then her "political" equality is achieved. But the reality is much more complicated and intertwined with institutions and realities that had been deemed "personal" or "private," like sex and marriage.

A watershed moment for second-wave feminism was the invention and widespread availability of oral contraception. The pill (as oral birth control came to be known colloquially) allowed, for the first time in the modern era, for women's sex lives to be separated from their fertility. With the pill, a heterosexual couple could have sex without worrying about pregnancy; provided that a woman took her medication faithfully, she would not conceive. While contraceptive methods didn't originate in the 1960s, the ease and availability of the pill, coupled with its relative privacy (a woman could get it from her doctor, her husband did not need to consent or even know), a woman could finally exercise some control over the number and timing of the children she had. This changed many women's lives, allowing white women, for example, to pursue career opportunities that the responsibilities of large families had precluded them from seeking. Other personal-political issues that second-wave feminists embraced were to make visible the realities of domestic violence and marital rape, of harassment in the workplace, and of the reality of abortion. In 1973, the Supreme Court legalized abortion in the United States, which second-wave feminism regarded as a major victory for women's health, in particular the health of poor women.

Along with Steinem and Friedan, who advocated for women to emphasize their equality with men while reclaiming the power of their womanhood, feminists of color like Alice Walker and Audre Lorde worked to forge ties of solidarity between white feminists and feminists of color. Lorde, Walker, and other nonwhite activists frequently felt marginalized by a movement that was often represented as a white, middle-class women's fight for more freedom. When cast in that light, second-wave feminism seems less like a struggle for liberation and more like a collection of niche issues meant to make white women's lives easier. This is particularly true when the focus of the second wave is deemed to be the rights of women to pursue careers and work outside the home. Black feminists eagerly noted that nonwhite women had never had the luxury of stay-at-home motherhood in numbers like their white sisters. Thinkers like Angela Davis reminded white feminists that while they were fighting to secure abortion rights for white women, many women of color were sterilized against their will. Black and Latina feminists were also active in movements for civil rights and gay rights that overlapped with the beginning of the second wave.

As with the first wave of feminist consciousness, second-wave feminism also overlapped with Christianity in important ways. Feminist theology grew into a discipline in its own right in the 1970s and 1980s, spearheaded by pioneers like Mary Daly, who wrote *The Church and the Second Sex* in 1968. Daly, profoundly influenced by the work of de Beauvoir, critiqued the Roman Catholic Church's all-male power structure, the glorification of the virginity of Mary, and the masculinization of God as patriarchy in bold form. Though she would eventually leave Christianity behind, Daly was the first Catholic woman to write forcefully about the intersection of ecclesial and social issues in the second wave. In the following decades, more women would explore how the church's structure, mission, and priorities had historically been antifeminist. These figures include Black, Asian, and Latina feminists who highlight the intersecting oppressions of race, class, and sex in Christianity, particularly the church's role in colonial violence. Riding the wave of coeducation, Catholic institutions of higher education would begin admitting (mostly white) women as undergraduates and eventually to graduate degrees in fields like theology, which had traditionally been reserved to men. As more women were trained to be theologians, the field changed. All this was set in motion by second-wave feminism.

But the second wave of feminism was not merely a string of progressive accomplishments. Feminists of color disrupted the "platform" of second-wave feminist thought that centered the experience of white, middle-class women at the expense of a more thoroughgoing analysis of the double- and triple-marginalization brought about by the confluence of race, class, and sexual orientation. A Latina was not merely oppressed because of her sex but also because of her race. She was more likely to be the victim of racial discrimination, underemployment, and domestic violence. As just one example, Puerto Rican women were used as experimental recipients of new contraceptive methods, in many instances against their will and without their consent, and suffered terrible health consequences as a result. The racial tensions were not the only fault lines that became visible in second-wave feminism, though. There were disagreements even among the white women about, for example, whether pornography should be made illegal. Eventually the movement splintered, though women's voices in the public square and the academy became more common.

Historians date the third wave of feminism to the 1990s, coinciding with the emergence of the "riot grrrl" movement. The riot grrrls were feminists who were involved in Washington State's punk subculture. They pushed against feminism being defined as a single issue or single goal movement, preferring more freedom to define what feminist goals meant for each woman. One defining moment of the third wave was the growing acceptance of the term (and the reality of) sexual harassment, particularly workplace harassment. Third-wave feminists watched Anita Hill testify against Clarence Thomas and watched the Congress confirm Thomas to a Supreme Court seat anyway. This generation of feminists took on unfair working conditions for women, hypersexualization, beauty standards, and environmental degradation. The third wave of feminism is also marked by Kimberlé Crenshaw's coining of the word *intersectionality* to describe how different oppressions compound to marginalize women along the lines of race, class, and sexual orientation, and so the feminist response must also be intersectional—taking these layered oppressions into account.

The third-wave feminists, like the two before them, were bold in the public square, reclaiming objectionable language like *bitch* and *slut* into liberating terms that women could wield freely. One feminist magazine was named *Bitch* (it has now evolved into *Bitch Media*). A galvanizing moment of activism was the first "Slut Walk," protesting the idea that women who dress provocatively deserve rape. Eve Ensler's *The Vagina Monologues* presents the issues third-wave feminists cared about—repressive beauty standards, sexual assault, the divergence of sex and gender, and sex positivity (among others)—as a popular play that continues to be performed in theaters and on college campuses to the present day. Where lesbians and bisexual women's visibility were hallmarks of second-wave feminism, the visibility of trans women increases in the third wave.

Even this very brief historical overview demonstrates that women have been organizing for their liberation for generations. If you have ever felt underestimated or marginalized because of your sex, your sexual orientation, or your gender identity, you have something in common with decades, even centuries, of women who have voiced their displeasure and demanded to be treated as full human beings with rights and dignity. Far from being a small group of angry women who burn undergarments and hate men, feminists have historically been a diverse, multinational coalition of activists, scholars, artists, and thinkers who fought and continue to fight for a better world for all persons. In the process, feminist thought has enriched the lives of women and men, the discourse of the academy, and even the theology of the church. The next chapter will turn to this theological enterprise.

DISCUSSION QUESTIONS

1. Can you think of other examples of sexism, androcentrism, and misogyny? What are some gendered expectations that let you know how you are supposed to behave in the world?

2. Are there some gender roles that you embrace? Is it a better idea to get rid of them all? Are there expectations of people who don't fit comfortably into the gender binary, like members of the LGBTQ+ community?
3. How is gendered language standard in church? Can you think of some examples? Are there workarounds that you think might work for most people?

DELVE DEEPER

There are many pioneering women who were not featured in this chapter. Delve deeper into the stories of Pauli Murray, Sr. Thea Bowman, or Sr. Theresa Kane. Each of these women pushed the boundaries in church and society.

READ FURTHER

Crenshaw, Kimberlé. *On Intersectionality: Essential Writings*. New York: New Press, 2017.

de la Cruz, Juana Inés. *Sor Juana Inés de la Cruz: Selected Works*. Translated by Edith Grossman. New York: W. W. Norton & Company, 2015.

Lorde, Audre. *The Selected Works of Audre Lorde*. Edited by Roxane Gay. New York: W. W. Norton & Company, 2020.

Manne, Kate. *Down Girl: The Logic of Misogyny*. Oxford: Oxford University Press, 2017.

———. *Entitled: How Male Privilege Hurts Women*. New York: Crown Publishing Group, 2020.

Plaskow, Judith. *Standing Again at Sinai: Judaism from a Feminist Perspective*. San Francisco: HarperOne, 1991.

2

WHY THE CHURCH?

Since this book deals with women and the church, and the previous chapter looked at the situation of women in contemporary society, this chapter turns our attention to the second big pillar of the book, which is the church. What do we mean by "the" church? In different ways it can be a building, a community, or an idea. Christians have struggled with, and even fought viciously about, what it means to have a church and to be a church. It's worth a bit of our time to look at how thinkers have defined the church historically and theologically and then to consider how feminist thinkers approach their relationships to the church.

Many people I encounter in my classes and public lectures have very specific ideas about why Christians are organized into a church at all. "Because of Jesus." On the one hand, this is of course true! Christianity would not exist without Jesus, and without Jesus's disciples, and without the community of believers that they left in their wake, so of course we have a church "because of Jesus." If we really want to understand how we got from Jesus to the church, this would be a whole other book. We can say with certainty that the origins of the church lie with Jesus and the community of disciples gathered around him. Does this mean that Jesus left architectural designs for St. Peter's Basilica?

One ecclesiologist, Fr. Frederick Cwiekowski, helpfully outlines two paradigms of, or ways of looking at, the foundation of the church.[1] The first paradigm, and a very popular one among Catholics, is what he calls the "blueprint" approach to the church. This view claims that Jesus set up the church, its structure and offices, as it currently exists. Those who see the church this way believe the Bible to be saying that Jesus intentionally founded a new religion, entirely separate from the Judaism in which he was raised, in his lifetime. Further, Jesus gave special knowledge, and ordination, to some apostles—making Peter the first pope in a public and official way. What's more, Jesus instituted both the sacrament of the Eucharist and of Holy Orders as they exist right now. The blueprint also extends to Jesus's apostles, who, according to this view, definitely saw themselves as priests of a new religion. This approach also holds that even if something isn't explicitly established in the gospel narratives, at least the seeds for development are there. So, even if there is no explicit mention of the college of cardinals, since Peter is surrounded by eleven other apostles, the college of cardinals is an inevitable legitimate development that is seeded or foreshadowed in the New Testament.

In contrast to the blueprint approach, Cwiekowski lays out what he calls the "historico-critical" approach. This understanding of the church takes modern biblical scholarship into account and sees both the life of Jesus and the writing of the Gospels in historical context. This approach, in line with Bible scholars, highlights what we can know about Jesus's life and death and about the writing of the Gospels according to historical, literary, and other methods of investigation. From these studies, scholars have concluded that Jesus was definitely an itinerant preacher who spoke with unusual authority about his close relationship with God. We can also say definitively that Jesus gathered disciples around him. Dining together, or table-fellowship, was definitely a hallmark of Jesus's life and ministry. Through that table fellowship, and particularly at the Last Supper, Jesus laid the groundwork for a continuation of his ministry among his disciples. Scholars have found no evidence that Jesus intended to start a new religion that was set apart from Judaism. The gospel texts reveal Jesus's desire to reform Judaism.

Many of my students get very worked up when they learn about the historical-critical approach to the church. It seems to them (and to me, when I first learned it!) that the existence of the church is now somehow a sham, an invention or unnecessary innovation on the part of Jesus's followers that somehow "contradicts" Jesus's own motives. But this is not the case.

Underlying the blueprint approach is a simplistic view of the church as it exists in history—an idealized vision where the church cannot change or else everything the church teaches is potentially not true. But let me put a challenge to you: can you think of instances where sometimes things have to change in order to stay true? I want to contend that precisely because the church is trying to say something that is true (the good news), and to protect something that is true (God's revelation in Christ), sometimes change is not only good but necessary. When contexts change, language has to change too.

Let's look at an example: If, in 1940, I were to say "Jesus was gay" it would be evident to people that I was saying that Jesus was a generally happy person. In 1940, *gay* generally meant "joyful." (Think of the Judy Garland inviting you to "make the yuletide gay.") On the other hand, if this week I were to propose a paper to the American Academy of Religion titled "Jesus Was Gay," the meaning would be completely different. If I want to say that Jesus was joyful, I have to change my sentence. Sometimes you have to say something different if you want to say the same thing. Sometimes you have to change in order to stay the same.

The church works like this. Because the church exists in history, and history is constantly changing (our language, our technology, our understanding of events), the church is called to change in order to stay the same. Yes, that's a paradox. We don't have to look further than the church's stance on slavery to realize that the church can change, dramatically at times. Slavery is mentioned in the Bible repeatedly, and the Catholic Church participated in the trafficking, buying, and selling of enslaved persons all over the world. In the United States, several religious orders, including the Jesuits, have begun to come to terms with their legacy of slave ownership and reliance on the labor of enslaved persons. In fits and starts and through small and larger gestures, including papal bulls, encyclicals, and decrees from the Holy Office (which is now known as the Congregation for the Doctrine of the Faith), the church eventually moved from viewing the owning of persons in servitude as a matter for civil law to legislate, to viewing it as a violation of human dignity. By Vatican II, the Catholic Church definitively held that slavery, along with torture and subhuman living conditions, was evil, with *Gaudium et Spes* (The Constitution on the Church in the Modern World) referring to these things as "infamies" that dishonor God.

We can name several other examples: the concept of limbo, which is nonbiblical but was created in response to a pastoral need to comfort parents who had lost infants before they could be baptized. Limbo was a place where the unbaptized experienced an afterlife of contentment and peace: it wasn't heaven (which was doctrinally reserved for baptized Catholics), and it wasn't hell (because who can look a grieving parent in the eye and say their child is in hell for not having received a sacrament?). Eventually, however, the concept of limbo was itself deemed superfluous, almost abhorrent. It doesn't appear in the *Catechism* after the 1980s. Another example: priestly celibacy was not made mandatory until the twelfth century. Was marriage always considered a sacrament? Not unless your church history starts with the Council of Trent! In every case, we must be careful to avoid the notion that things as we know them have always been this way.

So let's return to the blueprint versus historical-critical paradigms and nuance them a little bit. To say that Jesus didn't leave a plan for where the bathrooms should go in St. Peter's Basilica is not the same thing as saying that the church did not legitimately grow out of Jesus's life and ministry. The important thing to acknowledge is that the church is both rooted in Jesus's paschal mystery (his life, death, and resurrection) and guided throughout its own history by the Holy Spirit. This is why Christians affirm that the church is the sacrament of salvation, that the church is one, holy, catholic, and apostolic, or any number of other ways in which we describe the church theologically.

Let's turn to how theologians talk about the church. We can do this in three categories: the church as mystery, the church's marks, and the church in metaphors.

The Church as Mystery

The bishops at the Second Vatican Council (1962–1965) affirmed that the church is first and foremost a mystery. Indeed, the first chapter of the Dogmatic Constitution on the Church (*Lumen Gentium*) is titled "The Mystery of the Church." In doing this, they acknowledge a dynamism, a movement, at the heart of the institution. It is a kind of ironic movement: needing to change in order to stay the same, or having to say something differently in order to preserve the same meaning. By affirming that the church is mysterious at its core, a sacrament of salvation (LG 9), Vatican II invites us to struggle with what a mystery really is. A mystery is something we can never fully understand but are nevertheless moved to investigate and probe. Mysteries are different from problems: a problem has a solution, even if we don't know it yet. A problem has an answer. A mystery invites more questions the more you delve into it.

Here are some examples to illustrate the difference. Arithmetic, like 2 + 2 = 4, is a series of problems. They have answers that are discoverable with the right skill set. That we can use mathematics to make stable predictions about the universe's size and scope, so much so that we can fly rockets and land on the moon or Mars, is a mystery. Why does math work? That's the mystery. Another one: we pretty much know how life began on earth. Scientists have a good idea about how humans came to be. So the origins of life are, it's safe to say, a problem. What about the purpose of life, though? The why-are-we-here that can accompany the how-did-we-get-here? When we think about life's purpose, many other questions come to mind: What do we mean by purpose? Does life have to have a purpose? Is it joy? Is it sacrifice? Fulfillment? Can any of those be defined? That litany of questions comes from the mystery, the unknowability, of our original question about life's purpose. Every solution we propose just causes more questions to come to mind.

Can you think of some examples of problems or mysteries? The meaning of life? (Mystery!) The cause of illness? (Problem, usually!) The purpose of suffering? (Mystery!) The origin of hope? (Mystery!) The cause of my teenager's morose attitude? (I don't know.)

Let's take an example about Jesus and mystery. How is it that Jesus is fully human and fully divine but still just one person? How can 100% + 100% = 100%? The church had to face just this question in the first few centuries of its existence. It's not that Jesus wasn't fully human and fully divine, just that it took time to come up with the right words to express that mystery. Through trial and error, which in the church is frequently called battles with heresy, eventually we came up with the right language for the unique nature of Christ. That's called "the hypostatic union," and it was developed in stages. "Hypostatic" was used by Cyril of Alexandria to combat the

Nestorian heresy that Mary was the mother of Jesus the man but not of Christ the Second Person of the Trinity. This was doctrinally affirmed at the Council of Ephesus in 431. The notion of the two natures (divine and human) in one person came from the Council of Chalcedon, twenty-five years after Ephesus. This formulation, which we still use, developed in response to the monophysite heresy, which claimed that Jesus looked human but did not have human nature; only the divine nature existed in him. Through these (sometimes painful, always dramatic) processes of disagreement, Christians developed the language to explain what they believed to be true about the mystery of what happened in Jesus Christ.

To say that the church is a mystery at its root is to claim that we cannot know exactly what the church is or how the church saves, but we cannot help but struggle with these realities and try to make them make sense, however imperfectly, in our own contexts.

Needless to say, the mysteries of the church, of salvation, of Christ, require a great deal of discernment and reflection. After all, Christianity as a whole is a story of humanity's effort to understand what happened in Jesus and how we are supposed to live as a result of Jesus's life, death, and resurrection. The work of reflecting on what happened in Jesus's incarnation and as a result of it has been ongoing for centuries. Each historical age understands Jesus according to the linguistic and philosophical categories of its time. For example, the idea that the bread and wine truly become Jesus's body and blood has always been there, but it took medieval philosophy and theology, and the categories and language developed in those disciplines, to come up with "transubstantiation" to describe the eucharistic mystery in a satisfactory way. The ideas, the inklings, and the intuitions many times exist before we can adequately describe them in language. It doesn't mean the truth has changed. It means we can make better sense of it. In other words, Christians have been trying to make sense of Jesus, in communities, using their own words and experiences as lenses through which to understand the message of Jesus. How else could we make sense of anything except by using language and imagery that makes sense to us?

Because our language and history are constantly changing, we have the opportunity to probe the mystery of the church, its nature and its mission, from new angles all the time. Moreover, when we broaden our perspective and allow new voices into the conversation reflecting on God, Jesus, and the church, we are treated to new ways of seeing and understanding the nature and mission of the church. This is why women's voices, which have habitually been excluded from theological discourse, are vital. Women's perspectives improve our understanding of the imagery of God as mother, of wisdom, of the sacredness of the everyday. Women's voices have sharpened our understandings of the violation of Bathsheba, the bravery of Queen Esther, and the outspokenness of Mary, as we will see in future chapters.

The Church's Marks

Despite its fundamental character as a mystery, thinkers, theologians, and even the Christian creeds have described the church as having certain characteristics, or "marks," that identify it across historical contexts. You may recognize them from hearing them at the end of the creed that Catholics proclaim each Sunday at Mass: the church is "one, holy, catholic, and apostolic." These are the four marks of the church: unity, holiness, catholicity, and apostolicity.

But how can we say that the church is one, when we know there are so many Christian denominations (Methodists, Greek Orthodox, Southern Baptists, Melkite Catholics, Roman Catholics, to name only a few)? There is a tension between the belief we profess in the church's unity and the visible plurality of churches we see even driving down the street. Moreover, we know that many denominations have deep differences in how they understand scripture, liturgy, leadership, and other important issues. How, then, can we claim any unity?

The clearest image that works for me is an organic one. Think of a mature tree with many branches. It starts out as something small and seemingly unified (even if it is unified underground in its roots and therefore out of sight), and then with time it grows, and branches shoot off from the main trunk. In many trees, it can be difficult to discern which is the central or first trunk and which are the offshoots. But we know it is one tree. Another way to conceptualize the unity of the church is philosophically: we can think of the church(es) we see, or the churches as we see them in history (distinct, separate), versus the ideal church, or the church as God sees it—unified. As Christians, we may even think of the church in history as something temporary and that the divisions among the churches will cease to exist when the world ends. This, in fact, is what we pray when we say, "thy kingdom come." Theologically, Christians believe that the church of any place or period will eventually pass away and be replaced by the eternal kingdom. However we envision it, we have language and imagery to help us hold the visible and invisible realities of the church together in productive ways.

When I was growing up, I assumed the "catholic" in the creed meant that we were professing that Roman Catholicism was the only real church. I would wager that this is true of many young Catholics still today. But the word *catholic* in the creed isn't capitalized—it's not the proper-noun name of one church but rather a characteristic of the universal church. In fact, the Greek word *catholic* means just that: universal. What might this attribute mean about the church? The universality of the church means something beyond the geographic availability of Christianity throughout the globe. The church is universal because the Christian message of salvation is available to all, regardless of race or sex or nationality or century. This message of salvation is also inculturated throughout the world. Probably my favorite understanding of the universality of the church has to do with how this characteristic acknowledges that Christianity looks different in different cultures, and that is a good thing. The cathedral in Cuzco, Peru, has a last supper featuring a local delicacy, guinea pig (known as cuy), as part of the meal on the table. Japanese depictions of the Virgin Mary look like the population; so do Nigerian ones. The music at the cathedral of San Fernando in San Antonio is different from what you hear at St. Patrick's in New York City. In all these places, with all these differences, the same truth about Jesus is being celebrated. Christianity is capable of inculturation—of a variety of expressions in prayer, liturgy, and song, without losing the central message of Jesus.

A third mark of the church mentioned in the creed is that the church is "holy." This is a particularly difficult one in our contemporary world because we know that sin exists in the church—in its members and in the institution itself via clericalism, insular cover-ups, and so on. The sex abuse and cover-up scandal in the Catholic Church really challenged our notion of how we might be able to call the church "holy." The Pennsylvania Grand Jury Report of 2018 gave us a snapshot of the scope of abuse in just a few dioceses: 301 priests abused over one thousand children in six dioceses. They were shuffled around by several bishops to "avoid scandal." Since the *National Catholic Reporter* began reporting on sex abuse by priests in the 1980s, followed by the explosive stories in the *Boston Globe* in the early 2000s, several studies have exposed the horrifying number of abusers and survivors, the even more scandalous inaction by bishops, and the depth of the damage to the church. Sadly, this is not the first time in the church's history that priests and leaders have been implicated in terrible acts. But we should not despair. Instead, we can turn to an early episode in the life of the church, the conflict between St. Augustine and the Donatists, a group who were eventually recognized as heretical, to see that the church has faced horrible circumstances in the past and emerged stronger for it.

The Donatists were a group of Christians who were dismayed that during the Roman persecution (when it was illegal to be a Christian and one had to worship the emperor), many Christians had denied their faith to spare their own lives. When Christianity became legal in the Roman Empire in the fourth century, these leaders returned to their roles in the Christian church, prompting a strong reaction from some Christians, who had lived through the persecutions and seen many of their fellow Christians martyred. For the Donatists, it seemed inconceivable to allow apostates (people who had left the faith) to administer sacraments. They felt that the sacraments depended on the holiness of the priest, and a corrupt priest would result in corrupted sacraments. Consequently for the Donatists, the church could not include such terrible sinners because the church was a community of saints.

Augustine countered with a vital lesson for all Christians. He said that the church is a mixed body. That is, the church contains sinners and saints, all at once. It is not a club for the perfect. Like the biblical metaphor of the wheat and the chaff (Matt 3:12) for Augustine, the separation of the sinners from the saints occurs at the harvest (after death), not on earth. The church's holiness is not made up of the holiness of Christians, added together (that wouldn't get us very far!). Instead, the holiness that belongs to the church is Christ's holiness. This is important to remember as we are increasingly polarized. Our communities are mixed bodies made up of saints and sinners. As Pope Francis reminds us in his 2018 exhortation *Gaudete et Exsultate*,

> Do not be dismayed, for the power of the Holy Spirit enables you to do this, and holiness, in the end, is the fruit of the Holy Spirit in your life (cf. Gal 5:22–23). When you feel the temptation to dwell on your own weakness, raise your eyes to Christ crucified and say: "Lord, I am a poor sinner, but you can work the miracle of making me a little bit better." In the Church, holy yet made up of sinners, you will find everything you need to grow towards holiness. (15)

Even the pope knows we rely on Christ's holiness!

The last mark of the church mentioned in the creed is *apostolicity*—not a common word. We can take a clue from the word itself that this means that the church is somehow related to the apostles. This relationship exists in several ways. First, we can trace the origins of the church to the faith of the apostles. Everything we know about Jesus and about God's revelation in Jesus comes from the faith of the people who surrounded Jesus and the good news they spread to others. Second, like the apostles, the church is sent out on a mission to save others by sharing the good news. Third, the church continues the pastoral work of the apostles: bringing good news to the poor, visiting the sick, clothing the naked, and the other works of mercy are the work of the church as well. We see this apostolicity alive today when we witness the work of Christians on behalf of social justice—whether they are marching in the streets protesting police violence, serving meals at a soup kitchen, visiting a nursing home facility with a group of high schoolers, raising money for refugees, or welcoming migrants at the border.

The marks of the church aren't the only tool we have to describe or analyze the church's nature and mission. But they are an important data point because they appear in the creed. Since the creed is a list of beliefs professed by so many Christian communities, there is a certain weight to what appears there. We can be confident that Christians throughout history have thought the church to be one, holy, catholic, and apostolic. This has been true in a history that is sometimes filled with evidence to the contrary: of disunity, sinfulness, exclusion, and inward focus. Thus, the marks of the church also point us toward the mystery of the church. We don't fully understand how these realities apply, and we can recognize that God is at work in the church in ways we may not completely understand. The mysterious nature of the church and our desire to investigate it and continue discovering more about it is what makes theology fun (for nerds like me, anyway).

The Church in Metaphors

While we understand the church fundamentally as a mystery, we nevertheless need ways to imagine the church, to engage with it. Historically, religious thinkers have turned to metaphors for this work. (We also just think this way, all of us. We use images to understand things more clearly. For example, we give kids manipulables, or props, to count and put into groups when they are learning math for the first time. Counting on our fingers helps us add and subtract; thinking in pictures helps us understand complex things.) A metaphor, as you may have learned in your English classes, makes a comparison between two things without the use of "like" or "as." "I am a rock" is a classic metaphor. Metaphors use analogical thinking: that is, they are a mixture of similarity and dissimilarity and need both to work. We know that a person and a rock are different, so our minds work to bridge the gap. What might that metaphor mean? It can mean that a person is strong, or unchanging, or stable, or hardened. Most theological language is also metaphorical, and metaphors figure greatly in the study of the church.

Like all imagery, metaphors are drawn from human experience and expressed through language. That's not all they share with human experience, though. Metaphors also have what you might call a lifespan: they are born, they thrive, and then they die. A metaphor dies when it becomes irrelevant or when the historical context (or the word usage) has changed so much that it no longer expresses what the image was meant to convey. For example, unless you are a crossbow enthusiast, you may not realize that when Lady Macbeth encourages her husband to "screw your courage to the sticking place" she was referring to pulling the string on a crossbow taut using the wooden screw, so taut that the screw would stick (to its sticking place!) and be ready for the battle ahead. When Lin Manuel Miranda sampled this line in his contemporary Broadway hit *Hamilton*, viewers like me needed a refresher. A more contemporary, and maybe devastating, example from the tech world: I recently read about a child who happened upon their parent's collection of floppy discs from the late 1990s. The child asked how the parent had gotten "a 3-d printed 'save' icon." In the case of the floppy disc, the place we used to save our data became the image shortcut for "save your data" and, once those discs became obsolete, the thing itself, "in the wild," as it were, was puzzling to a child.

Many theological metaphors are rooted in scripture. Jesus spoke in parables, using metaphors for the reign of God drawn from his own historical experience. We know that there are many agricultural images in the Gospels. For example, "If you have faith as small as a mustard seed," or, "I am the vine and you are the branches." God is compared to a shepherd looking for a lost sheep, or a farmer who separates lambs from goats or wheat from chaff. I often ask my students, "How many of you have seen a mustard seed?" Sometimes if you have a grainy mustard you might, but otherwise, we rarely see it. I teach in New York City. None of my students have ever separated wheat from chaff. If you've never seen a mustard seed or winnowed wheat, the metaphors lose some of their power. You know a mustard seed must be small, and you know that the wheat is the good part and the chaff is garbage, but otherwise you're in the dark. If you grew up on a farm with sheep and goats, you may have a bit of insight, but few of us in the United States know shepherds that sleep outside with their sheep, so the kind of care and attention of the shepherd toward the sheep in that biblical image is a little lost to us. Because metaphors are rooted in human experience, as your experience varies, your mileage with a metaphor will also vary.

So where do church metaphors come from? The answer is that they originate in a variety of places. Most are from scripture, philosophy, or mysticism. But the commonly used metaphors for the church tend to be taken from the Bible. Let's look at four metaphors recently used to describe the church. Since the mid-twentieth century, the church has been described as a perfect society, a mystical body, the people of God, and the bride of Christ.

Of these four, the first we'll look at is the church as a *societas perfecta*, or perfect society, which is what some of those Donatists were thinking in the fourth century. When we hear "perfect" we tend to think "flawless," but in this case perfect is closer to the meaning in grammar, like "past perfect." The past perfect tense means something that was completed in the past. Similarly, the church as a perfect society didn't mean to convey that the church was 100 percent without mistakes but rather that it was a complete society. The church was a fully functioning community on its own and didn't need input from outside. Everyone in the church, because of its hierarchical structure, had a role to play, and this functioned smoothly.

Taken from Aristotelian philosophy, the church as perfect society was a dominant image in the papacies of Pius IX and Leo XIII. The phrase appears in Leo XIII's encyclical *Immortale Dei* (1885), which deals with the rights of the church in countries with secular governments. In an effort to carve out a kind of independence for the church as European governments were moving toward secular rule, Pope Leo described the church as its own complete society. Paragraph 35 of *Immortale Dei* reads in part as follows: "It is to be understood that the Church no less than the State itself is a society perfect in its own nature and its own right, and that those who exercise sovereignty ought not so to act as to compel the Church to become subservient or subject to them, or to hamper her liberty in the management of her own affairs, or to despoil her in any way of the other privileges conferred upon her by Jesus Christ." Leo XIII was concerned that the church be viewed as its own complete unit, founded by God, not to be interfered with by civil authorities. This metaphor of the perfect society was useful for a while, but completely disappeared at the Second Vatican Council.

A second pre–Vatican II metaphor is that of the mystical body. In 1943, Pope Pius XII published an encyclical by that name: *Mystici Corporis*. The origin of this image is not Aristotle but Paul. In the First Letter to the Corinthians, Paul says that the church is the body of Christ, that each Christian is a member of Christ's body. This imagery expresses the church as an organic whole despite its differences. So Paul says that each part of the body has an important function, and all parts rely on one another for health. "The eye cannot say to the hand, I do not need you" (1 Cor 12:21). Like a body, all of us make up the church, and though we have different roles (clergy and laity, bishops and priests, deacons and the pope) we are united into one thing. Pius XII extols the virtue of his preferred ecclesiological metaphor in the thirteenth paragraph of *Mystici Corporis*: "If we would define and describe this true Church of Jesus Christ—which is the One, Holy, Catholic, Apostolic and Roman Church—we shall find nothing more noble, more sublime, or more divine than the expression 'the Mystical Body of Christ'—an expression which springs from and is, as it were, the fair flowering of the repeated teaching of the sacred scriptures and the Holy Fathers." For Pope Pius XII, the mystical body image highlights the unity and the multiplicity of the church, the mutual benefit of each member for the other, the diversity of missions and unity of purpose of all members of the body of Christ.

The idea of the church as Christ's mystical body remains somewhat popular because it conveys important truths about the unity and diversity of the church. It is also an accessible image because all of us have bodies and so the metaphor is something we can relate to in an intimate way. The church as mystical body hinges on the idea that Christ is the head and Christians are the rest of the body. Do you think this metaphor still works given what we know about human biology? What happens to the metaphor when we say, for example, that what governs our actions isn't only our brain, but our hormonal chemistry, which is located throughout our bodies? Does that change what the metaphor is saying at all? It's worth thinking about how our changing scientific knowledge about the world and ourselves affects the imagery we use for the divine mystery. My favorite example of this has been the resurgence of interest in Hildegard of Bingen, particularly in her notion of God as *viriditas*, or greening. For Hildegard, a medieval mystic, God's grace was evident in the greenness of things, in their moisture, which gave life to plants and trees and verdant things. Ecological concerns have once again spurred interest in Hildegard's mysticism, as we look toward more eco-friendly, "green" ways to live in harmony with a suffering planet.

THE CHURCH AS PEOPLE OF GOD: A PARADIGM SHIFT

One of the most common metaphors for the church, and the preferred image of the bishops at Vatican II, is the church as the people of God. A quick glance at *Lumen Gentium*, the Dogmatic Constitution on the Church, reveals this preference plainly. The term "people of God" appears forty-one times. The other metaphors mentioned above don't come close: eight mentions of "mystical body," and the word "society" appears only ten times. Clearly, the council wanted to affirm that the church is first and foremost a mystery and that this mystery is structured in the world as the people of God.

This shift to the church as people of God tells us several things about the church at the time of Vatican II. To begin, the bishops at Vatican II display a new appreciation for the scriptures and a historical-critical approach to God's word. In "people of God" we have a deeply biblical image. The notion of God choosing a people out of God's gracious nature runs throughout the Old and New Testaments. From God's covenant with Abraham in Genesis through the annunciation in Luke, the story of salvation echoes the theme of God choosing people in history as God's own, to do God's work. This move reveals the deep appreciation for scripture that had been growing in Catholic circles through the 1940s and 1950s. Many experts at the council had studied scripture with non-Catholic scholars in Europe and had learned biblical criticism methods. These more modern approaches to scripture gave scholars an appreciation for the biblical text as books embedded in history that nevertheless point to truths that transcend history. As such, *Lumen Gentium* and the other decrees produced by Vatican II reflect less of the prooftexting that one sees in so many official church documents and more sophisticated biblical analysis, as one sees in the use of "people of God."

A second fact about the church that this preferred metaphor reveals is the increasing historical consciousness of the church's hierarchy. In the wake of the Second World War, the bishops at Vatican II were aware of the evils of anti-Semitism, and most likely they were also aware of the role the church's own rhetoric had played in anti-Jewish sentiment. Even more fundamentally, though, Vatican II understood the relationship of the church and the world in a new way. According to Karl Rahner, a German Jesuit priest and one of the most influential Catholic theologians of the twentieth century, the bishops at the council recognized that there had never been a preexistent church without human beings or without some interaction with social contexts. Understanding that historical events take time to fully comprehend, the bishops are more cautious about their proclamations. Having witnessed the horrors of the Holocaust, the council fathers also wanted to affirm in a special way the close ties between Christianity and Judaism. To use the term *people of God* to describe the church echoes the Hebrew scripture's understanding of Israel as God's chosen people. Might council documents be accused of appropriating a Jewish symbol and thereby erasing the experience of Jews? While this is certainly a possible interpretation, many scholars agree that the bishops' intent was not to co-opt the image of chosen people but rather to affirm the continuity of God's grace between Judaism and Christianity. A later decree, *Nostra Aetate* (On the Relationship of the Church to Non-Christian Religions), backs up this interpretation.

Finally, shifting to people of God as the main metaphor for the church displays a democratizing impulse on the part of the council. An earlier draft of *Lumen Gentium* listed a chapter on "the church is a hierarchy" before "the church as people of God." When the draft came to the bishops for a vote, this structure was rejected and the hierarchy chapter was swapped with the people of God.

While these may seem like a quick editing changes, the effect is profound. The bishops were making a statement about what the church fundamentally is: a whole people, equal in dignity by virtue of their baptism.

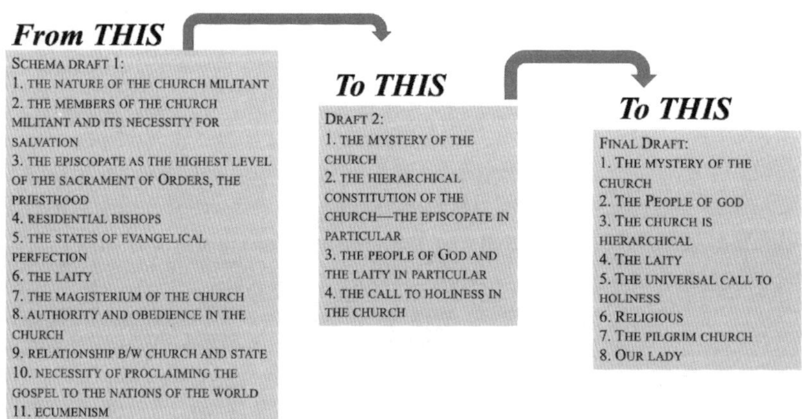

Only after they affirm this basic equality do they go on to discuss the different functions of the members of the church: the hierarchy (bishops, priests, deacons), the laity. Had they gone with the original structure, with hierarchy appearing first, it would appear that the church has two parts: a hierarchy and a people. That the council rejected this is evidence that it wanted to affirm the baptismal dignity of all people who made up the church before it differentiated the roles each of us plays within the people of God. This is an example of the church changing the way it was talking: a new era needed a new way of expressing an ancient mystery.

What the council did was to acknowledge the complexity of history, affirm an intuition that we don't always know all the facts of a story as it occurs, and demonstrate that some humility about our abilities is always a wise course of action.

THE BRIDE OF CHRIST: A PROBLEMATIC, DYING METAPHOR

The final ecclesial metaphor we will examine in this chapter is the spousal or nuptial metaphor for the church. This image has deep roots in the Bible, appearing in different contexts in both the Hebrew and Christian scriptures. Old Testament authors refer to Israel as a bride, and many interpretations of the Song of Songs and Hosea liken God to the bridegroom and God's people to the bride in these texts. In the Christian scriptures, the notion of Jesus as the bridegroom appears in the Gospel of John (3:29) when John the Baptist refers to Christ as such. The more direct source of the metaphor for the church-as-bride to Jesus, the bridegroom, is Paul's letter to the Ephesians. The relevant verses in chapter 5 (22–28) read as follows:

> Wives, submit yourselves to your own husbands as you do to the Lord. For the husband is the head of the wife as Christ is the head of the church, his body, of which he is the Savior. Now as the church submits to Christ, so also wives should submit to their husbands in everything.
>
> Husbands, love your wives, just as Christ loved the church and gave himself up for her to make her holy, cleansing her by the washing with water through the word, and to present her to himself as a radiant church, without stain or wrinkle or any other blemish, but holy

> and blameless. In this same way, husbands ought to love their wives as their own bodies. He who loves his wife loves himself.

Here, Paul is presenting the relationship between the church and Christ as one modeled on marriage in the first century: the husband is the head, and while the wife should obey the husband, both parties should love each other. The image conveys an intimacy and closeness between God and the church. Readers could easily infer that Christ and the church were "one flesh" as Jesus described spouses. In this way, the image also conveys the importance of the body—both Christ's body and the church's physical presence on earth.

The notion of Christ being the husband of the church and the church as Christ's bride, therefore, has deep biblical roots. It appears in theological reflection throughout history and even makes an appearance in the documents of Vatican II. Still, the metaphor was never a dominant one, until the pontificates of Paul VI and especially John Paul II, who championed the spousal metaphor as a cornerstone of his theological anthropology (his views on the human person) and ecclesiology (views on the church).

To what can we attribute the increased interest in the spousal metaphor? It's possible that this image was simply one preferred by some popes, that it spoke to one or another of them in a profound way, and surely this is true of any metaphor. Inevitably, some images resonate with us more than others. But theologian Susan Ross points us to some historical context that might also have affected the rise in usage of the spousal metaphor to describe the relationship between Christ and the church. In her text *Extravagant Affections*, Ross notes that the spousal metaphor coexisted with many other ecclesial and anthropological imagery for many years, until the 1970s. That was the decade when other Christian denominations (mainline Protestants, for example) began to grapple with the idea of ordaining women to ministry. These movements for women's ordination prompted Catholic thinkers to reflect on the nature of the priesthood, what priesthood meant in the church, and who could fulfill this role. Once women's participation increased in the public sphere—through employment, voting, activism, and increasingly important ministerial roles in the churches—Catholic thoughts on ministry, on the church, and on what it means to be a human person came to rely more and more on explanations of gender. And the spousal metaphor is one ecclesial image that hinges on gender, on a female bride and a male bridegroom.

The magisterium of the church (its teaching arm, which includes the popes' writings, the writings of church offices like the Congregation for the Doctrine of the Faith, and other material) took up the notion of spouses in earnest in 1968 with Paul VI's encyclical prohibiting birth control, *Humanae Vitae*. Because it dealt with sex in marriage, *Humanae Vitae* focused a lot of attention on what marriage means and how spouses should view and act toward each other. But the spousal imagery in magisterial documents really picks up steam in the writings of John Paul II, especially his encyclical on the "special nature" of women, *Mulieris Dignitatem*. Here, John Paul II outlines his ideas about the complementary nature of women and men, femininity and masculinity. This complementarian theology, where each sex completes the other biologically but also emotionally, socially, and spiritually, is a cornerstone of his papal magisterium.

While we don't want to do a line-by-line analysis of *Mulieris Dignitatem*, we should indicate the major themes that contribute to the complementarian theology found there, as it pertains to how some Catholics understand the church, the ministerial priesthood, and God. The overall theme of the letter is the role of women in church and in society. For John Paul II, this role is two-dimensional: women are mothers and/or virgins (17). It is important to note at the outset that in this letter (and in understandings of sex and gender in the Church generally) there is no distinction made between biological sex and gender: "men" and "masculinity" are used interchangeably, as are "women" and "femininity." Beyond this, men are viewed as the persons who initiate and women as the ones who receive. This is based on understandings of heterosexual intercourse.

So, if women are fundamentally receptive, they have two vocational options in the church's eyes: they can be mothers or virgins. In either case, women are united to an Other: either to a husband (and then they become mothers) or to Christ (as vowed religious women, in which case they are mothers according to the spirit) (21). From this understanding of the relationship of women and men, *Mulieris Dignitatem* extrapolates to the relationship between the church and Christ. Paragraph 23 reiterates that the church is the bride of Christ and that Christ is the bridegroom. "The bridegroom loves us first," and the church responds to that love in return (25). Thus, the church is receptive and feminine, and Christ is initiatory and masculine. Redemption also "flows from the bridegroom to the bride" (26), revealing once again that initiative (in this case the initiative to redeem) is a masculine trait and responding to initiatives is a feminine one.

Ross points out that this imagery for the church depends on a specific, first-century understanding of marriage. That is, the bride-bridegroom relationship described in the spousal metaphor is a relationship of two persons of unequal status. And indeed, men (bridegrooms) did have higher status than women (brides) in the first century and for many centuries after that. Women were given as brides or bought with dowries. A bride was viewed as the property of her father who was transferred to her spouse. We can still see this in contemporary wedding vows. The language of "to have and to hold from this day forward," which so many interpret romantically, also appears on deeds of sale for cars, land, and other goods. What we think of as a sweet sentiment, of the bride and groom embracing each other forever, is actually the language that transfers property in perpetuity after a payment. Now, contemporary marriage no longer involves the metaphor of a spousal relationship between Christ and the church takes this inequality into account. In fact, this inequality is a fundamental part of how the metaphor works, according to Ross. After all, we would never assert that the church is equal in stature to Christ, because Christ is God and the church is not. Christ is the bridegroom because he is the head of the church, its boss and owner. If, when we hear the spousal metaphor, we are considering it an image of marriage as we understand it in the present, a relationship of two equal partners, we are distorting a central truth that the spousal metaphor is trying to convey.

What happens when a metaphor's foundation has shifted so dramatically that the image essentially projects something contrary to what was intended originally? Let's return to an insight at the beginning of this section about metaphors. Because they are rooted in human language and human experience, metaphors and imagery also have a lifespan. It's possible that the spousal metaphor is reaching the outer limits of its lifespan. This does not mean that it is useless and ought to be thrown out. Nothing in the church ever really changes in that dramatic way. Instead, it will just stop being as relevant and will fall out of use. Think of how many people you know who refer to the church as the perfect society. That image had a lifespan and is no longer in use. It may happen that a reinterpretation of perfect society will lead to the re-invigoration of the image, but for now, it lies dormant. What about the bride of Christ?

First, we should acknowledge, with Ross, that the metaphor does contain important insights into the relationship between God and the church. For example, the image of Christ married to the church dignifies the institution of marriage. It reminds us of the importance of the incarnation, of God taking on a body because bodies and physicality are important in Catholicism. We are not merely souls trapped in flesh. The incarnation shows that our flesh is part of our salvation, not merely our downfall. To talk about Christ as a bridegroom and the church as his bride emphasizes the importance of physical relationality. It also reminds us of the intimacy between God and God's people. The spousal relationship is emotionally, physically, spiritually intimate, and that is central to not viewing the church as a merely worldly institution, a sociological reality without a theological component. So the metaphor isn't entirely off base; it reveals important aspects of the God-church relationship.

A second reality we must acknowledge is that the notion of marriage as a union of equal partners, while enshrined in Catholic teaching, is nevertheless not universally accepted. Sexist thinking about marriage, where men exercise more power and women use their "special gifts" to work behind the scenes, still abounds. Stereotypical thinking about women as more natural caregivers, that ties their social, emotional, and spiritual capacities to their biological capacity for gestation, is also a feature of magisterial teaching, as *Mulieris Dignitatem* shows. So while popular thinking may quickly agree that a marriage is a romantic partnership between two equals, church teaching, social structures, and misogynistic activism show us we have a long way to go before this equality is a reality. Perhaps the spousal metaphor's understanding of marriage as an unequal partnership has life in it still.

The great thing about studying theology is that the topic is inexhaustible. This is true even of the church, a human institution that functions in history but is nevertheless animated by the presence of the Holy Spirit. Ecclesiology, the study of the church, reminds us that the church is first and foremost a mystery, something that prompts us to ask more questions with every answer it offers. The church is also characterized by its historical marks of unity, catholicity, holiness, and apostolicity. And throughout its history, Christians have used metaphors to make sense of God's work in and through the church. But this is a book about women in the church. Now that we have outlined some productive ways of talking about the church, we can turn our attention to how women interact with this complex, sacramental institution.

DISCUSSION QUESTIONS

1. Which metaphor for the church do you find most compelling or least? Can you think of new metaphors for the church, drawn from your own experience, that might speak to people in your generational or geographic context?
2. How did the sex abuse scandal get presented to you, if at all, in your schooling? Was it discussed? Did it affect your relationship with family, with community, with institutional religion? How?
3. Which of the marks of the church is most difficult to see in the present day? Which is the most obscure or least obvious, and why?
4. Given the rise in disaffiliation, or moving away from the institutional church, among young people, can you think of any strategies that might spark interest in the church? Or is it a lost cause?

DELVE DEEPER

Compare how movies like *Doubt* or *Spotlight* portray the sex abuse crisis versus documents like the John Jay Report or the

Pennsylvania Grand Jury Report. What accounts for these differences? Consider genre, audience, timing, and other factors.

Many Catholics were not on board with the reforms of the Second Vatican Council. Today, some see Pope Francis as fulfilling the vision of Vatican II. Investigate the overlap between groups who rejected Vatican II and those who oppose Francis's initiatives, like the move toward a synodal church.

READ FURTHER

Cwiekowski, Frederick. *The Beginnings of the Church*. Mahwah, NJ: Paulist Press, 1987.

Hahnenberg, Edward. *A Concise Guide to the Documents of Vatican II*. Cincinnati: Franciscan Media, 2007.

McBrien, Richard. *The Church: The Evolution of Catholicism*. San Francisco: HarperOne, 2009.

Norris Jr., Richard. *The Christological Controversy*. Minneapolis: Fortress Press, 1980.

Rahner, Karl. *Concern for the Church*. Theological Investigations XX. New York: Crossroad 1986.

3

THIS IS HOW WE DO IT

Do you remember as a child hearing the parental mantra: "You get what you get and you don't get upset"? This is one of my favorite ways of, say, handing out Halloween candy or birthday cupcakes in one of my kids' classrooms. And surely my parents taught me when I was growing up that if we were ever having dinner at someone else's house, we should eat (and praise) whatever we were served, even if we didn't like it. To complain was extremely rude. This may play a part in why feminists, especially in the church, are viewed as troublemakers: We are complaining about our treatment. Shouldn't women just be satisfied with what they get? The answer, of course, is that all members of any organization or family—in this case, the church—should never settle for anything less than justice, even if they must demand it. After all, in our baptism we all take on Christ's roles as priest, prophet, and ruler, regardless of our gender. But in order to make our demands heard, we must feel like we belong. In the church, women's experience can include intense feelings of alienation alongside a sense of belonging. Women are excluded from ordination in the Catholic Church. This means that they cannot be deacons, priests, or bishops. Because the hierarchy of the church is made up of ordained men, women's voices are excluded from participation in high-level decisions of the church. Research tells us, however, that most of the labor of the church, the day-to-day work of staffing schools, hospitals, and parishes, is done by women. These workers, some of whom are vowed religious (nuns) and some of whom are laywomen, tend to be underpaid and overlooked in their roles that essentially keep the church running.

Women belong in the church. They are the church. Women were the first witnesses to the resurrection, as attested in all four canonical Gospels. And yet, women's experience and insight have been marginalized throughout a Christian tradition that is male-dominated. Because Christianity has existed in patriarchal societies (and propped these societies up with its own patriarchal rhetoric), women have been sidelined, systematically, from theological production, from theological education, and even in extreme cases from being viewed as full human beings. We saw in chapter 1 that women have not tolerated this marginalization, historically. But how do women who consider themselves feminists deal with a sexist church? This chapter will map out different strategies women have used in navigating their relationship to Catholicism. The strategies range from accommodation to the structural status quo while demanding some changes to absolute renunciation of the institutional church. And within that spectrum of strategies there are all manner of ways in which feminist theologians seek to revise doctrine, structures, interpretations, and practices that harm women and men and people from dominant and nondominant cultures. After this mapping, we will look at how feminist theologians go about their work, which we call the methods of feminist theology.

In chapter 1, we mapped feminism into historical "waves" that happened almost consecutively (there are always gaps and overlaps in history). We now turn to how Catholic feminists understand their relationship to the institutional church. Broadly speaking, we can identify three categories of feminist-church relations: the resisters, the revisers, and the renouncers.

Strategy I: Resist

Historian Kathleen Sprows Cummings uses a helpful image in a 2018 *New York Times* op-ed.[1] There, she speaks about her conversion from a "seat at the table" feminist to a "reset the table" feminist. A feminist who wants a seat at the table is advocating for the inclusion of women into the already-established structures of the church. This is what I am calling the strategy of "resistance." Rather than advocate for a revision of church structures (away from hierarchy and toward a more egalitarian power structure, for example), these feminists advocate for women to have a voice in church matters as the structures currently stand. One contemporary example would be the international group Voices of Faith. After the 2015 Synod on the Family, where the head of the Conference of Major Superiors of Men was given a vote at the synod, Voices of Faith began organizing to request that the head of the Conference of Major Superiors of Women be given the same right to vote. Previously, only bishops could vote at a synod. The inclusion of the head of the Conference of Major Superiors of Men and the exclusion of his counterpart in the group representing women religious did away with the expectation, however, that one had to be a bishop to vote. Since that synod, Voices of Faith has written letters and delivered petitions to the Vatican requesting that women be allowed to vote at future synods. They received no response.

Voices of Faith is just one example of an international group of Catholics who seek to resist the church's sexist structures by advocating for the inclusion of women's voices. In other words, they employ the strategy of resistance, asking for a seat at the Catholic table. Other groups also employ this strategy. In the United States, initiatives like Catholic Women Preach create online videos of women preaching on the Sunday Mass readings; FutureChurch prioritizes international collaboration with women seeking more robust inclusion in decision-making in the church. These groups, consisting of laywomen and laymen, vowed religious, and even some clergy, believe that the church should cast its net wider and allow women to participate more fully in its structures. Give women a seat at the table, they say.

In theological circles, many scholars employ this strategy as well (though the scholarly angles tend to employ the strategies of both resistance and revision, and fluctuate between the two or use them simultaneously). One example would be Elizabeth Johnson, who taught at Fordham and writes award-winning books on the theology of God. One of her texts, *Quest for the Living God*, got the attention of the U.S. Bishops' Committee on Doctrine. This committee claimed that Dr. Johnson was going against church teaching by advocating that we stop relying on male metaphors for God exclusively. Her arguments in that book, however, are parallel to Thomas Aquinas's understanding of God's incomprehensibility. In other words, Johnson was using Aquinas's thought (in which she is an expert, having written her dissertation on Aquinas and taught his thought for many years) to say that reliance on one kind of imagery for God amounts to idolatry. Because we cannot fully know God, which is a tenet of faith attested throughout scripture and tradition, a plurality of images is better than over-reliance on one kind. By framing her argument in the Thomistic tradition, Johnson is not arguing for a complete revision of the way we think about God. Rather, she wants an intellectual seat at the table for a more robust variety of images. Nowhere does Johnson advocate for changing the words of scripture or doing away with any kind of male language and imagery for God entirely. Instead, she wants us to cast a wider net with the imagery we use, not only because it is more just but, most important, because it reminds us of God's fundamental incomprehensibility. It is a great irony that she relied on one of the leading thinkers in the history of Christianity but still came under suspicion from Vatican authorities—and we note that even some of Thomas's positions were considered suspect shortly after his death.

The strategy of resistance extends to activism on a local and global level as well. Resistance focuses on the inclusion of women, the widening of the net of possibilities within a fundamental structure that already exists in Catholicism. The example of Voices of Faith organizing petitions for a vote for women at Vatican synods is one example. But even at the diocesan level when people demand that girls be allowed to be altar servers or that parish staff (more than half of whom are women) be paid a living wage, they are also using the strategy of resistance. Theologian Phyllis Zagano has made it her life's work to argue that women should be ordained to the diaconate. In 2017, Pope Francis named Zagano to a commission investigating whether women deacons existed in the church's history. An expert on the matter, Dr. Zagano has been very vocal in her findings that not only is there liturgical and historical evidence that women served as deacons in the early church but that this means we could once again have women deacons, should the pope allow it. When asked whether women should be ordained to all offices in the church, not just the deaconate, Zagano is quick to limit her findings to just women deacons. She does not wish to discuss women priests. She wants to work within structures that have clear historical precedents. This is her strategy of resistance at work.

Like all strategies, resistance has strengths and weaknesses. One strength is the belief that to be heard, one needs to be "in the room" so to speak. Change comes to institutions from within, from voices pushing boundaries from the inside out. The most effective ways to make change are to stand one's ground, affirm one's place at the bargaining table. You have to be at the table in order to make demands, after all.

Resistance has its drawbacks too. It can be exhausting to fight an institution that seems designed to work against change. Feminists who employ the strategy of resistance are sometimes viewed as too conciliatory, not going far enough in their desire for reform or their tactics to achieve it. Why demand a seat at a table that is exclusive already? Why work for access to a flawed system? Isn't that just capitulation? Do the problems faced by the church get solved by merely adding women and stirring? Or does real reform require a more intentional approach?

Strategy 2: Revise

In her *New York Times* article, Dr. Cummings notes that she has moved from being a "seat at the table" feminist to a "reset the table" feminist. When she read the grand jury report detailing the cover-up of sex abuse in the Archdiocese of Philadelphia, where she grew up, she was horrified. "We need to rip off the tablecloth, hurl the china against the wall and replace the crystal with something less ostentatious, more resilient, and for the love of God, safer for children."[2] She calls for a thorough reimagining of how the church is run and for bishops to renounce power and repent for having failed to protect the children entrusted to the church's care. To reset the table acknowledges that the church's structure is somehow flawed and that only adding women to the mix doesn't really fix things as much as we would like to think. Resetting the table—revision—is a call to dramatic action: flinging the china against the wall is pretty dramatic! Revision involves cleansing the church of its erroneous, hurtful, or sinful structures and having the courage to imagine something new.

As with the strategy of resistance, many women in the church are employing the strategy of revision in the ministerial and academic spheres. One prominent example is the Women's Ordination

Conference (WOC), a group that was founded in the mid-1970s to advocate for the ordination of women to the Roman Catholic priesthood. Through activism and worldwide partnerships, WOC has lobbied the church for its vision of a renewed sacramental ministry where women serve alongside men. On the surface, that seems like a "resistance" strategy. The Vatican has been very strong, however, in its denial of the possibility of ordaining women. Pope John Paul II, in his encyclical *Inter Insignores* in 1994, even declared the conversation closed. That is, even to want a continued dialogue about women priests put WOC on the outs with the church's hierarchy. Their persistence, and that of its affiliates worldwide, demanded a reenvisioning of what is possible in the church. Questions about ministry, sacraments, and even something as fundamental as being in the image of Christ animate the revisionist strategy of WOC. Their argument was and remains that there is nothing inherent in ordination limiting it to men. If we wish to live in a renewed, egalitarian church, allowing women to be priests is an absolute requirement.

In the academic sphere, it's always fun to talk about the strategy of revision because we get to talk about a pioneer of Catholic feminist theology: Mary Daly, who will make another appearance in the next section on renunciation. Daly's early career is a fantastic lens through which to view the sort of "smash the china against the wall" feminism described by Cummings. A professor at Boston College from the 1960s through the 1990s, Daly's life and writings are radical, exhilarating, and an all-around great read. My students' encounters with her early work, from *The Church and the Second Sex* to *Beyond God the Father*, open their eyes to the seemingly limitless creativity that existed in post–Vatican II Catholic theology.

Daly was born in 1928 in upstate New York and died in Massachusetts in 2010. Her career at Boston College was marked by controversy, both because of her feminist writings (radical in the sense of wanting to change things down to the roots) and because of her eventual policy to exclude men from her classes. She was willing to teach the male students in independent study formats, but they were, for Daly, inhibitors of class discussion. So she refused to have them register for her course. Professor Daly was in no way a shrinking violet.

From a theological perspective, Daly was deeply influenced by Simone de Beauvoir. While de Beauvoir ushered in second-wave feminism, Daly inaugurated contemporary Catholic feminist theology. Daly's strategy of revision is primarily one of what she calls "iconoclasm." Iconoclasm means the smashing of idols. As we know, idolatry happens when we worship something that is not God as if it were God. It is a sin—it's right there in the first commandment: You shall have no gods but me. What does Daly mean by iconoclasm?

Her first book, *The Church and the Second Sex*, hits at the sexism inherent in the church's theology and ministry, even in the exciting years after Vatican II. It is in this text where she wrote the famous phrase, "If God is male then the male is god." The maleness of God is an idol, for Daly and many other feminist theologians. It's not supported by biblical evidence, and it hampers women's full flourishing. When we envision God as male, then the qualities we think are more masculine will seem more appropriate for God, and feminine qualities seem less appropriate. It becomes a reinforcing circle—people who have those god-like qualities are viewed as closer to God. If God were always, in every case, imagined as having freckles, then freckles would start to seem like a semi-divine quality. Now imagine if we only ordained people with freckles.

But Daly's problems with Christian sexism don't stop at the notions of God we imagine by default. In her writings she takes aim at the ideas (taken from Christianity's adoption of some Greek philosophy) that changelessness is ideal, that revelation is closed, that doctrine cannot change. All these principles, for Daly, are symptoms of an androcentric bias at the heart of Catholic Christianity. That is, they reveal a bias toward understanding the "default human" as a white male—perfect with no need for change or conversion. All these characteristics and principles also rest on the maleness of God.

Her proposal is dramatic. Daly claims that theologians must begin "the process of cutting away the Supreme Phallus."[3] Surely this gives you a sense of the vivid language Daly uses to communicate her points. We find ourselves at quite a distance from Elizabeth Johnson's Thomistic arguments about divine unknowability. Daly advocates for divine castration but then moves beyond even this. Not only is God not a male being. For Daly, God is not a being at all. She will come to define God not as a noun but as a verb: Be-ing. In addition to her quite provocative observations about the hierarchy ("the clergy are about the only male professionals who still wear skirts"[4]), Daly makes radical suggestions about the nature of God and reality, about the usefulness of Greek philosophy for Catholic theology in the twentieth century, and about the church's limited understandings of nature that lead to a "natural law" with blinders to reality. She discusses ordination and birth control, revelation, and the human subject. The scope of her theology is vast, and the revision she suggests is robust and thorough.[5]

We may be tempted to think divine castration is pretty far along the road to a radical strategy of revision. I mean, it's quite an image! In recent years, however, thinkers from nondominant cultures have emerged to pose a challenge to mainstream feminist theology. Many early feminists, including Daly, were blind to how race, class, and immigration status work together to keep women from full participation in the church and from visibility in feminist theological communities. Latinas, Black women, and women from Asian backgrounds have been producing feminist theology since the 1970s. These thinkers represent a wave of the strategy of revision that takes more than sex and gender into account. Or maybe it's more accurate to say that these thinkers recognize that sex and gender are only one aspect of marginalization. Frequently these theologians are from groups that are doubly or triply marginalized: for their race, their sex, and their sexual orientation, their immigration status, or their class.

As second-wave feminism was getting off the ground in the United States, around the late 1960s and 1970s, a new theological movement began in Latin America that would become known as liberation theology. Its starting point is the perspective of the poor, and champions of this theological movement include priest-academics like Gustavo Gutierrez from Peru, Jon Sobrino in El Salvador, and Dom Helder Camara in Brazil. Inspired by these thinkers from the Global South, U.S. theologians from non-European backgrounds began to draw on their experiences of marginalization to reflect on revelation. This is how Latino theology, Black theology, and Asian theologies came to prominence in the late twentieth century.

Latino theology appeared on the contemporary academic scene with the publication of Virgil Elizondo's *Galilean Journey* in 1978. Black theology came to prominence at this time with figures like James Cone, who published *A Black Theology of Liberation* in 1970. These movements were headlined by men, usually clerics, with women working in the background, when they were allowed to study theology at all. The voices of women theologians from these communities eventually come to the fore with figures like Ada María Isasi-Díaz and Diana Hayes in the 1980s. But resistance to these women's insights came not just from the sexism in Latino and Black theological circles but from the mainstream feminist movement's racial blindness and bias.

Many of the issues raised by second-wave feminists do not acknowledge the experience of nonwhite, non-middle-class women. Let's take the example of working. The second wave of feminism was all about women embracing the ability to work outside the home, to have careers thanks to the invention and mainstreaming of reliable contraceptives. This was, wisely, lauded as a huge step forward for women. But was that the case for all women? Do all women have to break away from stay-at-home-motherhood to embark on a self-defining career? What about single mothers? What about poor women?

One of my favorite ways to illustrate this is by recalling the Montgomery Bus Boycott during the Civil Rights movement here in the United States. After Rosa Parks declined to give up her seat, activists continued by organizing a boycott of all buses to put pressure on bus lines to end segregated seating. Most bus riders were Black men and women. The boycott had some unlikely allies, though: white women in Montgomery were outraged and pleaded for the protesters' demands to be met. Was it out of solidarity with their fellow Americans? Perhaps. But many were upset that their maids, nannies, and cooks could not get to work during the boycott.

Staying at home, which felt like prison to white women of privilege (the same people who have access to education, publishers, etc.), feels like a great privilege to those who have no choice but to work outside the home. Poor women, especially women of color, do not experience staying at home as a barrier to their freedom. Instead, being forced to work in low-paying, backbreaking jobs inhibited these women's ability to decide the direction of their lives.

And let's talk for a minute about the development of a reliable contraceptive pill. The developers of the first birth control pill to hit the market in the 1960s conducted clinical trials on poor Puerto Rican women, many of whom did not know how to read. These women did not volunteer to be subjects of a drug trial. They were told the pills they were being given prevented pregnancy and not informed of the side effects of this pill. Why Puerto Rico? There was no legal ban against birth control there, unlike the mainland United States. But there are also racial and colonial factors that allowed these women to be viewed as suitable experimental objects—they were devalued, marginalized, poor women. Viewed as desperate to stop having children, they seemed an easy, even ethical choice. Their lives were quite literally worth less than the lives of women on the mainland. And so, the gateway to white women's liberation came about through the bodies of nonwhite women.

This complex history is important. It can be easy to think of feminism as a monolithic entity, a kind of cool-girl sisterhood of #bosslady and "you go girl" activism. Feminists of color remind us to check our "we"—who is the "we" who is empowered by work, and who is the "we" who doesn't have the option to stay home and raise her children, ever? Which "we" saw the birth control pill as a great escape from mandatory motherhood and which saw that same pill as a drug that brought horrific side effects? Too often, nonwhite bodies pave the way for white "progress" and liberation, at huge, unrecognized expense.

Out of this sense of being marginalized even from the women's movement, nonwhite feminists write theologies that focus on double and triple marginalization, on the compounding injustices of sexism and racism, and on the invisibility of being a nonwhite woman. Let's look at the feminist theological approaches of two groups of nonwhite feminists: womanists/Black feminists and mujeristas/Latina feminists.

Not all Black feminists self-identify as womanist theologians, but the movement is broad nevertheless. *Womanist* is a term coined by black feminists after "womanish," a word that comes from novelist Alice Walker, the author of *The Color Purple*. To be womanish means to be acting grown up, concerned with adult things, audacious, outrageous, courageous, or willful. The opposite would be girlish, concerned with childish things. Womanist theology takes the experience of Black women as its starting point. From the outset, womanist theologians seek not only to work against sexism but to work against how racism intensifies sexism for nonwhite women. Additionally, this mode of analysis refuses to leave behind nonwhite men, who are also victimized sexually in a racist society.

How? Nonwhites of any sex/gender tend to be viewed as hypersexual and therefore dangerous. Nonwhites are more likely to be incarcerated or to come into contact with the police. As movements like Black Lives Matter have brought to our national attention, Black persons are far more likely to be killed by police or while in police custody. So womanist theologies refuse to ignore the ills of racism and how racism and sexism work together to marginalize and dominate Black bodies.

For womanist theologian Delores Williams, the two goals of this theological perspective are survival and community building. Womanism encourages the exploration of Black women's history and culture, their folk wisdom and art, as sources for theological wisdom. In addition, the exploration of these sources allows womanist theology to avoid being defined by what white feminism determines to be "women's issues."

Mainstream (typically white) feminism can sometimes cast men as an enemy, and womanism refuses this binary. By focusing on the experience of nonwhite women, experiences that include slavery and Jim Crow, poverty, low wages, institutionalized racism, and incarceration, womanism offers a vision of liberation that refuses to leave Black men behind. Stated positively, womanism celebrates Black joy and loves Black women and men. Womanists promote the power of Black women to work for their own liberation and leave no one out. Womanist theologians believe that the liberation of Black women cannot come either as an afterthought to white women's liberation or as a corollary to Black men's freedom. It is, above all, a movement rooted in solidarity against the combined forces of racism, sexism, and classism.

In terms of its method, Williams describes womanism as having three intents: multidialogical, liturgical, and didactic. Multidialogical simply means that womanists engage in dialogue with all kinds of communities that are committed to the liberation of the oppressed. Womanists don't engage only with other Black communities, or only with white feminism, but with Asian, Latin American, Latinx, and other persons who are working for similar goals. Liturgical intent refers to the importance of the Black church in womanist thought both positively and negatively. Positively, the Black church is a space where women exercise authoritative leadership and where the Spirit is expressed and celebrated. Negatively, the Black church has been a space where respectability and homophobia have been promoted, and womanist theology rejects these tropes. So liturgical intent refers to a constant back-and-forth between prayer and theology. The third part of this method, didactic intent, means that womanist theology stresses the teaching function of theological reflection. Most important perhaps, the teaching function of theology must incorporate Black women's moral wisdom, Black art and folk wisdom, and the experiences of Black communities.

In a similar fashion, some Latina feminists coined the term *mujerista* to describe their mode of feminism that takes race, class, and colonialism seriously alongside sex and gender. Ada María Isasi-Díaz, a Cuban-born theologian who later lived and worked in the New York area, coined the term *mujerista* after bumping up against the unacknowledged racism of Euro-American feminists in the Women's Ordination Conference and the Womanchurch movement in the 1970s and 1980s. For Isasi-Díaz, Euro-American feminists, like many progressives, believed that because they were feminists it was impossible that they were racist. But in fact, in adopting a vision that for Isasi-Díaz modeled the power-over model that is so problematic in sexism, these feminists were doing violence to their own movement. They denied nonwhite women the power of self-determination. The Euro-American feminists were willing to welcome nonwhite women but unwilling to let these women set the direction of the movement. In other words, nonwhite women were welcomed, but not as equals; instead, they were considered workers in the movement with a subordinate role.

So Isasi-Díaz and others stepped away, sketching out a different kind of vision of women's liberation that focused on self-determination and what she calls "liberative praxis." Drawing on her own experiences of migration, bilingualism, and multiculturality, Isasi-Díaz's mujerista theology critiques not only sexism, but racism, capitalism, and the legacy of colonialism. Like womanist theology, mujerista theology holds that liberation for women cannot come at the expense of Latinx men or of anyone. Her goal is a society where power is shared in mutuality.

Here's a confession. When I first read Isasi-Díaz as an undergraduate, I cringed. Because I grew up in a part of the United States where light-skinned Latinos/as like myself were the dominant culture, I found Isasi-Díaz's attacks on Euro-American feminists exaggerated, and her solidarity with economically poor and struggling Latinas seemed strained. After years of living away from South Florida, however, I experienced the kind of racism to which I thought I was immune given my privileged background (I am a light-skinned, educated, economically privileged woman, and certainly embodied that mindset when I arrived at college). In light of this, mujerista theology has started appealing to me more and more. It didn't help that when I first encountered it, I was the only Latina theology major at my university and was frequently looked to for "commentary" on this sort of text. (Note to professors: never do this!) In my career, I've found Isasi-Díaz's work incredibly helpful, especially when trying to do justice to the lived reality of marginalized communities.

Isasi-Díaz was an activist as well as a scholar. When her parish church was closed by the Archdiocese of New York, she and some other parishioners celebrated street liturgies outside the church in protest. She used her voice to amplify the voices of Latinas, who had been caricatured as docile and incapable of serious self-reflection. She refused to settle for anything other than the transformation of church and society in a more just direction. And she did all this in Spanglish—introducing Spanish phrases and new words like God's *kin-dom* into her work. Because of Ada Maria Isasi-Díaz and thinkers like her, feminist theology lost some of its colonial impulse, and for that we should all be grateful.

Ultimately, womanist theologians and mujeristas remind us that the project of dismantling sexism in the church has to be an intersectional effort. We cannot bracket or leave aside questions of racism, classism, or colorism in the fight for an egalitarian world. Part of this work means that those of us who come from more privileged backgrounds must interrogate our own biases, the way we grew up and thought the world worked, in order to be able to see the world from the point of view of the most vulnerable. This is what thinkers like Copeland, Hayes, Isasi-Díaz, and others are pushing us to do. A women's movement that doesn't take nonwhite women into account is not worth taking part in. A feminist theology that only utilizes nonwhite voices to add to its number but never to set its agenda is not a genuine movement for liberation.

The revision that womanist and mujerista thinkers seek from the church is one that takes compounding marginalization seriously.

They ask questions about the church's complicity in slaveholding. They remind us that the church was a tool of colonialism and frequently took the side of oppressive colonial powers against native movements for independence. These revisionist feminists ask us to broaden our view of how power is used in the church and to envision a different power structure, one that goes beyond "add women to the hierarchy and see how it changes."

Whether by radically reforming our God-language, as Mary Daly did early in her career, or by radically reframing what we mean by liberation, as womanist and mujerista scholars do, the strategy of revision is powerful. Revising the church invites us to step back and consider what we want the church to be, not merely what the church is. Feminists use the strategy of revision to create a more inclusive church, one that is, in their view, more faithful to the gospel. This strategy goes beyond resistance because it calls for structural change, even a change of vision. It is more radical in the sense that it makes changes closer to the root of the church—not merely who is holding office, for example, but what sort of power structure is most appropriate in the church. The revisers are not merely asking where women can function in the church or how they can exercise some decision-making. The revisers want the church to make more liberating decisions and to make these decisions in a more inclusive way.

Some drawbacks to the revising approach are the feasibility of this project: Can a church that is so thoroughly kyriarchal in structure and power, and has been for so long, really be changed? How much should people sacrifice in order to change it? Is it worth a lifetime of struggle, often at personal and professional cost? Given the global nature of the church, any kind of structural change is bound to come up against resistance in all manner of unforeseen ways. Revisers have a tough row to hoe, and some give up the fight before they lose themselves in the process.

Strategy 3: Renounce

A third strategy feminists use to define their relationship to the church is the strategy of renunciation. That is, some feminists choose to walk away from the church. This can be done dramatically or quietly, publicly or in private. Some women walk away to other Christian denominations. A great many women walk away from institutional religion altogether, and this section will touch on the phenomenon of the disaffiliated generation. Some, like Mary Daly, walk out with a bang. In November 1971, Mary Daly delivered a sermon in Harvard Memorial Church. She was the first woman to preach there in its history, and at the end of her remarks, she led a ceremonial "exodus" from that church, and, for her, from Christianity entirely. By the early 1970s, Daly had given up on the possibility of reforming the thoroughly patriarchal Catholic Church. For her, it was impossible to remain in an institution that women had no part in, trying to reform a theology that had excluded women's voices on scriptures where women were routinely viewed as objects, not subjects. She claimed she could no longer "sing sexist hymns to a male god who tells us we [women] do not exist."[6] That dramatic action began a new phase of her career. From then on, Daly identified as a feminist philosopher, an ecofeminist thinker, and a radical lesbian feminist, but never again as a Catholic theologian.

Not all renunciations are announced with an article in Boston College's student newspaper. Far more women walk away from the church in quieter, less public ways. A couple of years ago, at an event at the college where I work, I spoke to a woman in her sixties whose son (a writer) was speaking at the college. She was born and raised in the Bronx, the child of Italian immigrants. She married a former priest. She raised kids who now work for progressive causes in politics and beyond. And she confessed to me that she no longer went to church. "I just couldn't do it anymore," she said. "I had taught my kids that we didn't want any part of any institution that wouldn't allow Black people, and there I was in an institution that refused to ordain women. It was hypocritical. So I stopped going."

My sense is that Mrs. X's story resonates with a lot of Catholics. The data show that in the last decade, the United States has seen a sharp rise in people who no longer identify with any religious tradition. The Pew Research Center identified this group as the "nones." Within the "nones," a large percentage are former Roman Catholics. In fact, approximately 10 percent of the U.S. population are former Roman Catholics. Think of it this way: the largest Christian denomination is Catholicism, with 24 percent in the United States identifying as Catholic. The next largest, the Baptists, make up roughly 17 percent of the population. Former Catholics are the third largest. Third!

We cannot say that all the disaffiliated, or even all the former Catholics, left because of sexism. But in Pew's research, almost 40 percent of the formerly Catholic disaffiliated claimed they disagreed with the Church's treatment of women. Larger numbers disagreed with teachings on homosexuality and/or birth control, issues feminists care deeply about.

Critics of the path of renunciation claim that one cannot change an institution from outside, that one must remain in the trenches to have one's voice heard. While this may be true, the numbers of Catholics who have walked away from the church are troubling to all of us who remain affiliated. We cannot fault people for walking away from a church that ignores their needs, diminishes their humanity, or overlooks their baptismal dignity. For Daly, and many others, to remain a part of the church is to support, in some way, the kyriarchal structure (remember: *kyriarchal* means "ruled by the lords or masters") of that church. It involves continuing to listen to magisterial teachings about male-female complementarity. It may include giving, via the collection basket, to lobbying efforts aimed at making gay marriage illegal. For many Catholics this is untenable and not worth compromising on.

Smaller groups of Catholics have created spaces where those who wish to walk away from the church can find some community. Groups like Roman Catholic Women Priests (RCWP) and the Independent Catholic Churches can be a sort of middle path between renunciation and revision. Rather than wait for the institutional church to approve women's ordination, Roman Catholic Women Priests ordains women and celebrates women-led liturgies all over the United States (where the movement began) and internationally as well. Independent Catholicism is not as uniform as RCWP. Any group can declare itself independent of Rome, including groups that have been excommunicated (like some right-wing groups after Vatican II). Therefore, it's possible to find an independent Catholic Church that aligns with any doctrinal or ideological leanings. Because the movement is less centrally organized and therefore more diffuse, these communities can be harder to engage.

Women have worked to make a place for themselves in Roman Catholicism, to have their voices heard, to honor the dignity of their baptism. For some feminist thinkers, the key to being heard in the church is a posture of resistance. Others, especially those from non-dominant communities, believe that wanting a seat at the table is not enough. For these thinkers, the table has been set in such a way that it ignores and erases the central concerns that intersectional analysis demands. And so they advocate for a revision of the power structure, of the language we use for God, of the way we envision the church's ministries and moral teachings. Still, for others, the church's misogyny is too much to bear. The work of reforming the church is soul-crushing, and so they renounce their affiliation to Catholicism, either publicly or quietly, with fanfare or with a shrug. All these postures should concern us. If we truly believe that women belong in the church, that the people of God is incomplete without the witness of women, then the witness of the resisters, the revisers, and the renouncers should matter to us all.

DISCUSSION QUESTIONS

1. This chapter examines resisters, revisers, and renouncers. Many Catholics don't fall neatly into one of these categories; rather, they find themselves in a mix of all three. What aspects of culture—whether ecclesial culture, school culture, or some other institutional culture of which you are a part—require strategies of resistance, revision, or renunciation? Are there examples of people who are doing this type of work?

2. Can all aspects of cultures be revised, or are there instances (racism, other kinds of abuse or violence) where renunciation is the only option? Give examples from current or historical events.

3. Recent demographic analyses are revealing a new kind of religious disaffiliation—among older women specifically and older people of all genders—who are tired of trying to change institutions that refuse to budge. How do these movements away from religion after a lifetime (the "dones") compare to the motivations of the younger disaffiliated crowd (the "nones")? Are their motivations different? Their goals? Their decision-making processes?

DELVE DEEPER

This chapter examined Black theology, womanism, Latinx theology, and mujerista theology. What about Asian theologians and their relationships to the institutional churches? Investigate the work of Agnes Brazal, Diana Macalintal, and Kwok Pui-lan. South Asian voices include Marianne Katoppo, Swarnalatha Devi, and Sumitra Mukherjee. Or investigate on your own. How do these thinkers negotiate their relationship with the institutional church, particularly in light of questions raised by postcolonial and decolonial thought?

READ FURTHER

Cummings, Kathleen. "For Catholics, Gradual Reform Is No Longer an Option." *New York Times*. August 20, 2018.

Daly, Mary. *Beyond God the Father: Toward a Philosophy of Women's Liberation*. Boston: Beacon Press, 1973.

———. *The Church and the Second Sex*. Boston: Beacon Press, 1986.

Flanagan, Barbara. "Mary Daly Leads Exodus after Historic Sermon." *Heights* 62, no. 11 (November 22, 1971).

4

THE WOMAN PROBLEM IN CHURCH HISTORY

There's no easy way to say it, so let's just say it: the Christian tradition is filled with sexism.

This is not to say that Jesus was sexist. In fact, scholars have made quite compelling cases as to why Jesus was very different from many men in his day. He welcomed women as disciples, as we see in Mary and Martha of Bethany. He defended women who were on the verge of being killed by a mob. Jesus spoke to women who were deemed unclean, like the Syrophoenician woman. His prohibition on divorce can be read as a move toward justice for women, who were frequently left destitute by divorce and were unable to demand a divorce from their husbands, for any cause.

As good as Jesus was to women (that we know from the Gospels), the same cannot be said of many of Jesus's followers. The sexism that runs through the Christian tradition is deep and thoroughgoing. Some of the thinkers the church elevates as its greatest lights (maybe most of them) held intensely misogynistic beliefs. It makes sense since a kyriarchal and patriarchal social order has been in place for centuries.

But here's one important question for those of us interested in women's place in this tradition: Are the sexist ideas we find among theologians, biblical scholars, clergy, and saints pervasive enough to be disqualifying? Should we not listen to those who are harsh toward women when they talk about other topics? Or can we find ways to revise, resist, and reframe problematic aspects of the tradition so that all persons might find a liberating word in Christianity?

When I was in graduate school, I did a comprehensive exam (a big test that is like writing a paper in response to a question in a limited amount of time) on a particularly problematic theologian, Hans Urs von Balthasar. During the oral portion of the exam, one of my examiners asked if Balthasar's views on women were pervasive or if they were "like a tumor, where you can remove them and the rest of his thought remains healthy or mostly intact." It's a difficult question, and one that we struggle to answer about a lot of thinkers, artists, and institutions in an age of pervasive misogyny. I think it's an important question to ask not only of individual theologians but of the tradition as a whole.

Is the marginalization of women a localized, removable part of church history, or is it so much a part of Christian thought and practice that to remove it would fundamentally change what we understand as our tradition—and what would that result look like? In the previous chapter, we explored how, for some women, the kyriarchy and misogyny seem so ingrained in Christianity that the only way they see to survive is to leave the church behind. But must we all become renouncers in order to be good feminists? Or, if we choose to stay and resist and revise, what sort of work are we looking at? In this chapter we will look squarely at the subjugation of women that has existed in Christian thought and practice. We will highlight three major Christian thinkers—Tertullian, Augustine, and Aquinas—and then fast-forward to the present and see how these thinkers' views on women continue to shape the church today.

Symptoms, Diagnoses, Treatments

One way to think about our work as examiners of women's roles in the church is to pretend we are doctors. The work of a physician is to attend to a patient's symptoms, make a diagnosis, and suggest a course of action or treatment that would lead to better health. This is not a bad methodology for examining the misogyny that runs through the Christian tradition. We have to ask pertinent questions: Where do we see the misogyny? When did it start? How is it still present today? What environmental factors should we take into account?

A first step in figuring out the symptoms of sexism in the tradition is to specify where to look. After all, a doctor checks your vital signs to monitor your overall health. So let's ask: What are the vital signs of Christianity? Where do we get our information about this tradition? How do we know what we know? Where is the data? Some important sources are scripture (the Hebrew and Christian scriptures, or the Bible), the writings of theologians, and the liturgy and/or prayers. For each of these sources, we should consider when they were written, who they were written by and for, and their historical and social context at the time of writing. We should also think about the afterlife of these writings. The important thing is not just the writing itself but also how these texts have been interpreted and used in the history of the church. Who has been allowed to interpret scripture? Who has written and shaped the liturgy? Who has been elevated as an important theological voice, and who makes those decisions? All of these factors play a role in shaping the vital signs of Christian tradition.

While we don't know exactly who wrote the Christian scriptures (aka the "New Testament"), scholars have been able to estimate that the oldest literature in this group is the epistles and that the Gospels were written one to two generations after Jesus's death. Though we will go more in-depth with our examination of scripture in part 2 of this book, it's worth reviewing some basics about biblical literacy in Roman Catholicism.

The Bible is not a play-by-play of God's action in the world as it happened. As Vatican II teaches in *Dei Verbum*, the scriptures are the word of God, shaped by human hands and human intellect. That is, for Roman Catholics, the Bible is a divinely inspired collaboration between the Holy Spirit and the authors of the books.

For example, if you look at the Gospels, you'll note that each of them begins their story of Jesus's life in a different way. If the authors were reporters at the scene of Jesus's birth, wouldn't they narrate it with overlapping details? The fact that they don't, and that there are four canonical versions of Jesus's life story, tells us that these narratives reflect the faith of the early church, not a news story about Jesus's life. Remember, the earliest Christians were expecting Jesus to return imminently, without delay. They didn't write down the story of Jesus's life because they didn't expect the world to continue for very long. It was only after several years, when they realized that the Second Coming was not happening next week, that Christians saw value in writing down the narrative of Jesus's life.

We don't know who wrote every book of the Bible, and that is okay. Scripture scholars have been able to make inferences and confirmations about, for example, the documented letters of Paul versus those attributed to Paul (such as Hebrews) that were written by someone else. In many cases, we simply do not know the names of the persons who wrote the books of the Bible. To some people, this seems crazy. Contemporary scholars get very hung up on intellectual property and correct citation. Surely you've heard your fair share of warnings about the legal and moral dangers of plagiarism! But our understandings of authorship and attribution differ from those of the early Christians.

Our notions of authority and expertise have changed as well. But this doesn't mean that the Bible is by "unknown" and therefore can be discounted. Quite the opposite. The unknown pens that wrote the books, along with the unknown pens that copied the books by hand for centuries (and surely added or deleted a word here and there) and contributed to the many, many interpreters, mean that the Bible is, was, and remains a central source of faith for Christians of all denominations. The Bible is a work of community. It is a communal work not only in its production but also in its interpretation.

While we do not know if any women were authors of the books in scripture, we can say that women were not primary interpreters of scripture at first. This does not mean that women weren't an integral part of the earliest Christian communities. It does mean that because women lacked access to education, it would be rare for a woman to be able to read or write about scripture. Nevertheless, those women who were part of the earliest Christian communities shared their experiences of Jesus with others. They were able to reflect on who he was and what he meant to them, and they were empowered by their friendship with Jesus to share the good news of the resurrection with others as well. While scripture preserves the names of some of these women, like Mary Magdalene, many others are known only by descriptors like "the Syrophoenician woman" or "the woman with a hemorrhage." So while we can't say for certain that any women authored scriptural texts, we can confidently assert that women were important in Jesus's ministry and in the community he left behind when he died.

To sum up, we Catholics understand the scriptures as communally produced and reproduced, with the guidance of the Holy Spirit. Women participated in Jesus's ministry and in the continuation of Christianity's earliest communities in a variety of ways that we will discuss later in this book. In terms of the "vital sign" of scriptural production, that is where we stand with women. We can then turn to the aftermath of scriptural production: what happens after the New Testament is written down, codified, and put to use? Then the work of interpretation takes over.

Scriptural interpretation is a different matter from production because we know more about who is allowed and authorized to speak and write about the Bible. As Christianity migrates from being an oral tradition to a written one, a lot is happening in Christian history as well. Christianity moves from being an illegal religion practiced in secret, punishable by death in the Roman Empire, to a mainstream and then exclusive religion in four hundred years. That means that in its first four centuries, the church went from huddling in catacombs to becoming the official faith of the Roman Empire that once persecuted it. In the beginnings of the church, if you were accused of being a follower of Jesus, you could be prosecuted and martyred unless you denied that you were a Christian. This is the time when Christians were "thrown to the lions," also known as the age of martyrs. It was, we can definitely say, a very stressful era.

In the time of such persecution, though, many Christian thinkers wrote letters and treatises that formed a kind of backbone of the Christian tradition. After all, these early centuries were a time for Jesus's followers to take an initial stab at figuring out what exactly had occurred in Jesus's ministry. Many vital questions that we take for granted today, such as Jesus's salvific action, his human and divine natures, his incarnation and resurrection, were subjects of great debate in these early centuries. While we cannot cover all of these debates in this chapter, which focuses on women, it is important to remember that the thinkers we are looking at as examples of misogynistic thinking are also examples of how these early Christians were trying to navigate following Jesus in a hostile world. Let's look at the tradition, our second vital sign, through three exemplary thinkers: Tertullian, Augustine, and Thomas Aquinas.

Tertullian

Tertullian, whose full name was Quintus Septimus Florens Tertullianus (a mouthful!), lived from the middle of the second century into the third. He was not a priest or a monk, but a layman living in Carthage (in modern-day Tunisia). Although he was not a member of the clergy, he wrote and preached sermons to encourage early Christians to live their faith properly and enthusiastically. Though few of his writings survive, he is viewed by scholars as one of the major theological voices in Western Christianity before Augustine in the fourth century. Tertullian's writings on women are located in his treatises on wives (*Ad Uxores*) and on women's dress (*De cultu feminarum*). Here is one of his most notorious statements:

> Are you not aware that you are each an Eve? The sentence of God on this sex of yours lives on in our own time; the guilt must then, of necessity, live on also. You [women] are the devil's gateway; you are the unsealer of that [forbidden] tree; you are the first deserter of the divine law; you are she who persuaded him whom the devil was not valiant enough to attack. You destroyed so easily God's image, man. On account of your desert—that is, death—even the Son of God had to die. (*De cultu feminarum*)

From Simone de Beauvoir to Elisabeth Schüssler Fiorenza, feminists have rightly seized on this quote to point to the horrific misogyny inherent in the early thinkers we call the church fathers. Tertullian both reflects his cultural context, a Roman world that was very patriarchal, and helps shape the Christian tradition in that same patriarchal mold. While we cannot say he invented these hateful views of women (he was in all likelihood reflecting the culture in which he lived), neither can we absolve him of misogyny simply because we cannot know for sure that he hated all women.

In the passage above, we see Tertullian laying the blame for all sin on Eve, the first woman depicted in Genesis 2. The well-known story of Adam and Eve is foundational for Christian theological anthropology, which is the study of what it means to be a human being in light of revelation. The second chapter of Genesis contains a creation story that depicts Adam and Eve, the suitable partner made by God from Adam's rib, living in the garden of Eden until they disobey God's rule forbidding them to eat from the tree of knowledge. Tempted by the serpent, Eve and then Adam eat the fruit, God finds out, and they are banished from the garden and punished in other ways. They "fall" from grace but it is unclear what they fall into: humanity? the human condition? sinfulness? The story of the fall, of humanity's first act of disobedience, shapes Christian understandings of human goodness, of grace, of sin, and of redemption.

In Tertullian's commentary on the text, humanity does not share equally in this first disobedience of God's law; rather, women (through Eve) are the main cause of sin. For Tertullian, this is because the devil was "not valiant enough to attack" Adam, so he chose Eve for her weakness. This is ironic, in that he blames Eve for being "weak" and at the same time claims that because of her action Jesus had to die—a huge consequence that doesn't sound like it could be caused merely by someone being "weak." There's a lot going on in this passage, but blaming Jesus's death on Eve is a theme in scripture that a great many interpreters will repeat throughout Christian history to the great detriment of women. The combination of women's supposed weakness and their outsized responsibility for all that is wrong in the world will justify patriarchal and kyriarchal structures for centuries.

Is the blame for all of humanity's sinfulness to be directed at the first woman and, as a consequence, to all women forever? Or might there be alternative understandings to why human beings fail and do wrong? One might speculate that there could be a variety of reasons why evil exists in the world. Indeed, human beings have always wondered about the origins of evil and speculated as to its persistence. In societies dominated by sexist systems, women have often been identified as the sources of evil and bore the consequences of evil more than men.

Tertullian was merely the first major Christian thinker to elaborate a theory blaming women for sin and death. Many others throughout the Christian tradition echoed this idea. Particularly appealing was the parallel that some found between Eve's disobedience and blame and the Virgin Mary's obedience to God's plan in the Annunciation. Eve became a universal symbol of disobedience, temptation, and sin; her foil, Mary, has come to symbolize obedience, fidelity, and holiness. Women, then, are forced into one of these two categories. When we fail to read the story of Genesis or the infancy narratives with nuance or compassion for the women characters, we wind up with stereotypical figures who are then held up as "models" for women. Given the impossibility of Mary's life—a virgin and a mother at once—Christian women are all regarded as disobedient temptresses. As Tertullian put it: "you are each an Eve."

Augustine

In fourth-century North Africa, Augustine of Hippo emerged as a leading voice in the Christian church. He remains one of the most influential church fathers to this day. He is a major figure with which anyone must contend if they want to take Christianity seriously. Among the reasons for his importance, Augustine is the first and most prominent thinker to bring together Greco-Roman philosophy (especially Platonism) and Christian thought. Much of what we normally associate with "traditional Christianity" comes from this fusion of the philosophies popular in Rome with the gospel. The best example I have of this is how you answer the following question:

When you die, what goes to heaven?

Did you think, "Your soul, obviously"? If you did, thank the Greek philosophers, Augustine, and many who came after him. The notion that we are divided into bodies and souls, wills and intellects, passions and reason, is a dualistic view of the world that finds its origins in Hellenistic thought. Today, we think of it as unmistakably Christian. This makes sense because we don't have access to much material that could reconstruct for us what a "pre-Hellenistic Christianity" or purely Jewish Christianity might have looked like. Nevertheless, it's important to remember that what many of us consider signature Christian ideals are imported from a particular culture and a particular way of thinking. (This is true of all knowledge and systems of thought: they are all born from a culture and are culturally bound.) Not all cultures throughout time share the same ways of thinking about bodies or about reason. Christianity adopts Greco-Roman philosophical ideas and is shaped by them.

A convert to Christianity after a life of pleasure, Augustine puts forth some of the most misogynistic rhetoric in the tradition. To understand his thought, however, we should know a little about his life first. He lived after the legalization of Christianity and saw the end of the Roman Empire with the fall of Rome in 410. Augustine was a classic bad boy. He didn't smoke pot and ride a motorcycle, but nevertheless his youth was consumed with all manner of fun—like a college student, but a lot more partying. Partying in the fourth century consisted of enjoying gladiator contests, a variety of philosophical schools, orgies, and other forms of pleasure for pleasure's sake. Augustine had sexual relationships with women, and one of those resulted in a child born out of wedlock, named Adeodatus. He had affairs and was about to enter into a marriage when he left this all behind, converted to Christianity, and decided to become a priest. And he wrote about it. A lot.

Have you ever had a friend who found a neat new diet or gave up a bad habit? They can't stop talking about it or can't stop getting you to try it. They become evangelists, preaching the good news of their conversion, denouncing their old ways, and inviting you to join them on this new path to wholeness. Sometimes you wonder if this has more to do with their guilt about their previous choices and less about wanting you to join them on their wellness journey. Well, Augustine is like that with sex and particularly with lust.

Because he was one of the most prolific writers of the early church, we still have access to a lot of what Augustine wrote. Many of the themes in his writing reflect, like a mirror, his previous sin-filled life. Augustine's writing is very concerned with sin and how sin enters the world. The concept of "original sin" that Christians trace back to Adam and Eve is not in the Bible but is developed by Augustine. Basically we can say that this fourth-century thinker spent a lot of time and ink wondering why humans commit sins, possibly as a way to repent for, or at least understand the reasons for, the sins he had committed.

Augustine is probably the definitive interpreter of the story of Adam and Eve. That is, much of the way we imagine the story comes from Augustine's sexualized interpretation of it. The biblical story, while dramatic, is pretty barebones: Adam and Eve are put in the garden, the snake and Eve have a conversation (she asks the snake a question!), she eats the fruit (not an apple, per se), she gives it to Adam, and he eats it. Think of the images you have in mind for this story. Do they involve a voluptuous Eve, with her hair cascading over her breasts, an apple dangling from her fingers as she seduces Adam? What was the sin that was committed? Was it sex? For Augustine, it certainly was. In contrast to Tertullian, who believed the serpent had chosen Eve because she was rationally inferior, Augustine affirms that women and men are spiritually equal. But the sin of the garden, for Augustine, was pride—love of something that can elevate the human over love of God. That was, at its root, a sin of disobedience, and that disobedience ruined *everything*.

For Augustine, we are all born with original sin. It is passed down to us from our parents, and its origin is lust. Because humans reproduce through sexual intercourse, which depends on arousal (for men), this was how humans passed on sin. As uncomfortable as it is to think about, Augustine located original sin in your parents' sex act. Why does everything come back to lust for him? Lust, unrestrained sexual desire, is a perfect test case for how everything goes wrong in the fall from Eden. Perhaps because of his previous lifestyle, Augustine was concerned with how sexual desire can overwhelm reason and cause us to act in ways contradictory to it. In the dualistic setup where humans are eternal souls trapped in earthbound bodies, the way it is "supposed to be" is that the body should be regulated by the soul/spirit/mind. The intellect should be the boss of things, so we should act in accordance with reason. Reason, spirit, soul, and mind are all greater than passion, matter, body, and desire. But in lust, particularly in sexual arousal in males, reason cannot prevail. To be blunt, Augustine is profoundly disturbed that he cannot will away his erections. It is a part of his biology that is not subject to reason, that is controlled, it seems, entirely by passion. It's all upside down! It must be a consequence of sin.

If we had to isolate the two biggest contributions of Augustine's thought to misogyny in the Christian tradition, they would be the notions of hierarchical dualism and original sin. Hierarchical dualism refers to the division of the world into two kinds of things—the spiritual and the material, the soul and the body, the rational and the natural—and then elevating one kind over the other. Like this:

Eternal	Temporal
Soul	Body
Spirit	Matter
Intellect	Will
Rational thought	Natural world
Thought	Emotion
Reason	Passion
God	Creation

You might look at the chart above and wonder how we get from this to misogynistic thinking. But recall that for Augustine, and many thinkers, women's bodies bring them closer to nature. After all, women menstruate, give birth, and lactate. Moreover, in many societies, women bear the majority of the responsibility for care work, like childrearing and homemaking. To Augustine, this indicated that women's reason was more suited to the temporal realm—the everyday, the mundane. Men's rationality, however, was more focused on the eternal realm. Women are thus more tied to materiality, less able to escape or transcend their bodies and to contemplate the eternal God. For this reason, women tend to be on the "temporal" side of the dualistic worldview, not the eternal side. Because of their bodily contributions to human life (children, breastmilk, cooking, clothing), they are associated with materiality and bodiliness.

This dualistic worldview endures today, whenever we hear that women are "too emotional" to be world leaders or are "strident" instead of forceful. Women are stereotyped as overly passionate, irrational, and ruled by their feelings, whereas men are seen as more rational, more capable of overcoming their feelings and acting according to their intellects. And, if you look at the chart above, one side is clearly preferable to the other: who wouldn't want to be eternal or intelligent or rational? That winning side, coincidentally, is also the side associated with maleness. To divide the world into two realms like this and rank one realm as better or more godlike than the other is called hierarchical dualism.

Augustine's second contribution, original sin, locates sinfulness in the body, in lust or concupiscence. As mentioned above, lust is an exemplary sin for Augustine because it allows the passions to overrule the intellect. The body overrules the brain. That lust becomes the means through which the human race is continued means we are all born from, and with, the stain of that original sin in the Garden of Eden. Of course, because of women's association with bodiliness, emotionality, and passion, women are closer to sinfulness and, indeed, are an occasion of sin. Men, who are in this notion supposedly not associated as closely with their bodies and are able to engage in contemplation of the eternal God, are therefore closer to divinity than women. Augustine eventually concludes that because of women's focus on temporal reason (the reality of everyday life), they cannot be fully in the image of God on their own. Women are in God's image only when one considers them as part of a unit with her husband. Men, on the other hand, are capable of imaging God fully without a partner. This inability of women to reflect the *imago Dei* continues to serve as a main reason why the Catholic Church will not admit women to the priesthood. Ultimately, because of his dualistic view of the world and his understanding of sin, Augustine forges the tie between human bodiliness and sinfulness. This will cast a negative light on most sexual relationships.

Aquinas

Our third major figure is a medieval saint, a doctor of the church, and the patron saint of academics and theologians. Thomas Aquinas lived in the thirteenth century. He was the most influential thinker when it came to putting theological knowledge into a system, and in doing this, he codified systematic theology for everyone who followed. He envisioned all truth, including and especially all Christian doctrine, as interrelated, and he set out this synthesis in a text called the *Summa Theologiae*. It is a masterwork that all students of theology should explore. That text is magisterial in every sense: it brings, or attempts to bring, all knowledge into one system.

After Aquinas, students of theology know they cannot think about who Christ is (Christology) without thinking about the implications for salvation (soteriology) or sacraments. The *Summa* makes plain that all of these are interconnected. It's important philosophically and theologically. It ushers in a new way to think about the relationship between reason and faith. He also thought that women were "misbegotten males." But more on that later.

In short, Aquinas's work, especially the *Summa*, is foundational to the Christian tradition, especially in the West. He was a towering figure in Scholasticism, a way of doing theology that was based in universities. This movement in theology sought to bring together Christian faith and human reason. Housed in the great European universities (Aquinas was based at the University of Paris), the insights of Scholasticism dominated Catholic theology until the 1960s. Many students still learn Aquinas's "five proofs for God's existence" in high school.

Perhaps the most important legacy of Aquinas, and one I stress with students every year, is that he sought the truth in the contemporary knowledge of his day. That is, he read all the best thinkers, whether they were Christian or not. His thought is indebted not only to scripture and the church fathers that came before him, but notably to the Jewish philosopher Moses Maimonides, the Muslim philosopher Ibn Sina, and Aristotle. This got him into a lot of trouble with his bishop, who eventually silenced Aquinas. The lesson here is that theology has nothing to fear from genuine learning and inquiry. Aquinas was confident enough in the truth to look for it everywhere.

Theology is filled with studies on Aquinas's thought and writings. There is, in fact, an entire school of thought called Thomism that draws thinkers from every part of the ideological spectrum. Clearly, we don't need to explore every corner of the Thomistic world for the purposes of this text. We couldn't, even if we tried. When I was in graduate school, my cohort had a running joke wondering how many more dissertations could possibly be written about the work of a man who died in the thirteenth century. Well, students are still at it! So let's stick to our specific question in this chapter: what does Aquinas bring to the legacy of misogyny in the Christian tradition?

It begins with one of Aquinas's main strengths: his tendency to use the best of contemporary thought to explain and understand Christian doctrine. One of Aquinas's most important, relied-upon conversation partners is Aristotle. What Augustine did for Christianity in bringing Christian thought into dialogue with Plato, Aquinas does with Aristotle. On the one hand, this is a huge win for Christianity because it provides Christian thought with a robust rational scaffolding. On the other, it brings along any deficiencies in Aristotelian thought and pretty much establishes them as foundational in Christianity. Aquinas's reliance on the best of contemporary thought, and his foundational place in Christian theology, means that any errors in Aristotelian understandings of, for example, biology might be deeply embedded in Christian theology.

For Aquinas (and Aristotle before him), knowledge starts from experience. That is, we learn about higher, spiritual, invisible things through our experience of visible things. We know about God the creator through our experience of creation. One way to think about this is to think of how an art history student might know that a piece is by Picasso even before they see the signature: the creation bears the mark of the creator. When you want to learn to identify Picasso's style, you don't start by reading about his life; you start by looking at his paintings. So it is with God: we can know things about God by observing the natural world. This is where things start to go wrong for women.

What can we observe about reproduction from the natural world? Well, if we look at farming, or at a forest in the springtime, we see that seeds get planted in the ground, and if the ground is properly prepared, a new plant will grow. For centuries, this is what we believed about human reproduction as well. The homunculus theory of reproduction, which Aristotle held and Aquinas imported into Christian thought, held that human beings develop from miniature human beings contained, like seeds, in human sperm. (This makes sense in a world where we cannot know that women contribute an ovum to reproduction, because we cannot see inside the human body.) Sperm is the only visible "product" in the reproductive act, and, logically, people thought that it contained the seed that was planted in a woman's womb. This seed then grew into a child to which the woman gives birth. In fact, "seed" is still sometimes used as a euphemism for sperm.

As logical as this theory seems, we know it is not in fact how human (or mammalian) reproduction occurs. We now know that the female parent contributes an ovum or egg containing one half of the chromosomes that are necessary for a new being to exist, and the male partner contributes the other half of the necessary chromosomes through sperm. The female then gestates for a period of time (approximately thirty-eight to forty weeks, for most humans) and then gives birth. Arguably, the woman's body contributes more to human reproduction: not only does it give over genetic material in the egg, but the woman also grows a placenta, an entire organ devoted to nurturing and protecting the fetus. Women also produce two times the amount of blood during pregnancy, and that excess is filtered and shared with the fetus. Labor and childbirth are also difficult, potentially fatal contributions to the continuation of the species. Contemporary science has given us a more complete picture of how human reproduction occurs, and it completely debunks the Aristotelian theory in favor of one where both parties contribute equally, from a genetic standpoint, to the creation of a new person.

The legacy of the absolutely incorrect Aristotelian theory of reproduction is, however, immense. Immense. It persists in theological tracts and in offhand comments. It persists in how parents tell children about "the birds and the bees" and in how we think about egg and sperm coming together in reproduction as its currently understood. What persists about this erroneous theory of reproduction is the notion of the male as the active force in generating offspring and women as the passive ground in which generation takes place. Even the words I use in that sentence reflect the Aristotelian legacy. Men generate; women provide space. One is an action, while the other is an affect or a position; one is active, while the other passive.

Perhaps your parents or the parents of someone you know answered the question "where do babies come from" with some version of "the dad plants a seed in the mom and it grows into a baby." Or perhaps you have heard of someone calling a woman who cannot have children "barren," like a field. These are both callbacks to the agricultural understandings of reproduction that are the foundation of the Aristotelian theory. When I was in high school, we learned that sperm swam upstream, in an arduous journey, to fertilize an egg that was merely hanging out, waiting just outside the Fallopian tube. This maps neatly into a vision of humanity where men are adventurers and women are homemakers, where men do hard, dangerous work and women stay safe at home. The legacy of Aristotelian reproduction, coded into the stereotypes we have about masculinity and femininity, even influence our fairy tales. Maybe you've seen or read *Sleeping Beauty*, where the main character is asleep until the prince kisses her into life. In subtle and obvious ways, in public and private spheres, our cultures communicate the message that men are active and responsible, and women are passive and nurturing. Male activity and female passivity are everywhere. And we can trace it back to a theory of reproduction that we know is biologically incorrect.

Our language and our images of what is feminine and what is masculine are rooted in a theory of reproduction that is scientifically obsolete. While this is problematic because it perpetuates stereotypes, it becomes especially tragic when it infects our theology. And for centuries, including the present one, this theory of male activity and female passivity have undergirded Catholic understandings of what it means to be male and female and has therefore affected doctrine on marriage, ordination, sin, and grace, among other things.

Conclusion

In our quest to diagnose the origins of sexism in the church, we have found several sources that contribute to Christianity's "woman problem." First, the scriptures have been largely studied and interpreted by men and from a perspective that benefits men. Second, several key figures in the history of the church held misogynistic beliefs—at times reflections of the patriarchal setup of their cultural contexts, and other times intensified by their own interpretations of philosophical and theological truth. Third, the legacy of thinkers like Tertullian, Augustine, and Aquinas continues into the present. While we should not say that they are solely responsible for the church's misogynistic views and actions, we can say with certainty that their writings, which are studied and revered to this day, view women as inferior to men, as less capable of being in the image of God, as more closely associated with sin, and as passive reactors to male activity in the world. Their understanding of the relationship between men and women believed that men, who were more rational, were closer to God than women. The dualistic worldview and problematic assumptions about sexuality and reproduction continue to influence theologians, bishops, and the official magisterium of the Catholic Church. We turn to those more contemporary realities in the next chapter.

DISCUSSION QUESTIONS

1. Which of the understandings of sin introduced in this chapter is most compelling to you: Tertullian's, Augustine's, or Aquinas's? They can be compelling because they are convincing or just because they pique your interest. What makes them interesting to you? How might you formulate a theory of sin for the present day?
2. Recent scientific and social-scientific research has revealed gender identity, and even sexual differentiation, to occur along more of a spectrum than a strict binary. How would Augustine and Aquinas react to this development? Can you think of a Thomistic or Augustinian understanding of gender as a spectrum?
3. How do presuppositions about the strengths and weaknesses of men and women survive in the present day? Can you provide examples from media, law, or religion?

DELVE DEEPER

When it comes to theology, where do you stand on the renounce/reform/remain spectrum? How do you reconcile patriarchal writings that seem foundational to the faith? How have other theologians done it? Examine the work of Elizabeth Johnson, who retrieves the work of Aquinas throughout her writings. How does she approach this retrieval? Do you agree with her methods?

READ FURTHER

Johnson, Elizabeth. *The Quest for the Living God: Mapping Frontiers in the Theology of God*. New York: Bloomsbury, 2007.

———. *She Who Is: The Mystery of God in Feminist Theological Discourse*. New York: Crossroad, 1992.

LaCugna, Catherine Mowry, ed. *Freeing Theology: The Essentials of Theology in Feminist Perspective*. San Francisco: HarperOne, 1993.

Schüssler Fiorenza, Elisabeth. *Bread Not Stone: The Challenge of Feminist Biblical Interpretation*. Boston: Beacon Press, 1985.

———. *In Memory of Her: A Feminist Theological Reconstruction of Christian Origins*. New York: Herder & Herder, 1994.

5

THE PROBLEM OF FEMINISM

In the previous chapter, we explored some of the roots of misogynistic thinking in the church's tradition. While Tertullian, Augustine, and Aquinas are not the only contributors to women's subordinate status in the church, their writing offers us important hints about where the disdain for women's bodies, sexuality, and spirituality comes from. But the history of the church is long, and within it women's influence has waxed and waned. In the late medieval and early modern centuries, the church executed many women, burning them alive for being "witches." Yet that same church celebrates many women as saints, figures who can intercede before God, like spiritual lawyers, if you pray to them. While the church has not ordained women in the modern era, in the medieval era abbesses functioned as quasi-bishops, demanding sacraments for their cloistered communities and disagreeing publicly with the hierarchy while rarely facing consequences. Women were not allowed to study theology until the twentieth century, but there are women doctors of the church, and Catherine of Siena (a saint) even reprimanded the pope. The image of God is relentlessly male, yes. But the church also had to invent a category of praise (hyperdulia) to talk about how we should revere Mary—higher than any saint, the mother of God! So a simple "the church is misogynistic" doesn't do justice to the complex history of Christian attitudes toward women.

This ambiguity exists not only regarding the church's relationship to women but also in terms of feminism's relationship to

Christianity. Both feminism and Christianity are global realities that exert influence on cultures, and the relationship between them is marked by tension, change, and mutual effects. The feminist movement, which has taken place at different times and with different emphases throughout the world, has clashed with the church, collaborated with it, and been ignored by it. Women have thrived in semi-independent roles in the church and have also been victimized by it. At times, feminism's goals and the church's goals have seemed to align. At other times, even into the present, more conservative parts of the church view feminism as an ultimate enemy of the gospel. Many in the church propose alternatives to feminist theory and theology, including popes.

This chapter explores the fraught relationship between feminism and the church. Together we will look at some parts of the legacy of the three thinkers from chapter 4, as well as the challenges posed by the emergence of the women's movement beginning around the time of the industrial revolution in the nineteenth century. As women began to leave the home for work in cities and factories and discovered a new role in society that was independent from their fathers and/or husbands, the church was forced to confront this reality. The last two centuries have forced the church's magisterium to elaborate in great detail its thoughts on the nature of women, the roles women can and should occupy in the home and outside of it, and the relationship of these natures/roles to society. In all, the past two hundred years have revealed a church that has thought a lot about what a woman is and what she can or should do. So have feminists. This chapter tells that story.

Before we delve into the controversies about women's roles that emerge in the nineteenth and twentieth centuries, we should note that in the church's long history women have been influential in many ways. From the deaconess Phoebe who appears in Acts, to the medieval abbesses like Radegund who wielded spiritual and political power, to spiritual and scientific guides like Hildegard of Bingen, to important prefeminist writers like Sor Juana Inés, Catholic history is filled with women who influenced the church and the world with their intellect, leadership, and bravery (such as Joan of Arc). Nor has the entirety of the church always embraced the scholastic dualism that separated the world into nature versus intellect, female versus male. Indeed, popular piety has always seemed to make its own cultural rules about how God should be imagined and engaged. Popular piety has always been how most of the church relates to God. So when we analyze theological treatises and papal documents, we must always remember that most Catholics in every age prayed locally, in local dialects, to local saints, in local churches. The average Catholic did not even know the pope's name for much of church history—only the advent of communication technology like television helped bridge the gap between the global church and Rome. It's understandable that people's prayer (popular piety) did not necessarily follow scholastic rules set out by Thomas Aquinas. Many medieval saints, like Hildegard, refer to Jesus's mothering of Christians, to God's maternity as well as paternity. As the era of colonization absorbed indigenous and African prayer styles into the church, many Catholics retained local images of God with a veneer of Catholicism. All of this is to say that even if the church's teaching arm, or magisterium, claims that all Catholics believe a certain thing about the nature of women and men, or about God, you can probably find a Catholic somewhere in the world who prays to God in a way that doesn't quite conform to those rules.

The Question Behind the Questions

Feminist concerns came to the fore of historical consciousness during the industrial revolution, when rural life and farming gave way to urban living and factory work as the primary way in which humans made a living. Along with the migration from country to city came the emergence of women in a growing workforce. This raises important questions. Should women be working outside the home or are they more valuable to families by taking care of domestic duties? Should childless women be working outside the home? If women learned to sew for their families when they were little girls, why shouldn't they put these skills to use for pay in an industry? If a woman works outside of her home, what should those working conditions be like—should there be limits on hours or minimum wages? Who should make decisions about childcare? In fact, when women are employed outside the home, aren't they actually working two jobs, while their husbands come home from work but don't continue to work once at home?

Ultimately, these point to a political question: if women are going participate in life outside the home, should women have the right to vote in democratic countries? The women's movement emerges from people grappling with these important issues of parity and equality, particularly when it comes to privileges and rights. Nevertheless, as the intertwining of work, poverty, and access in the above questions shows, issues of rights and responsibilities must be viewed intersectionally: we cannot talk about whether women and men are equal without looking at their working conditions, their responsibilities in the home, the skills their educations give them, and their access to the ballot box.

A few years ago, the feminist theologian Elisabeth Schüssler Fiorenza spoke at my institution and began her lecture with a simple question: "Are women people?" Many in the audience (myself included) laughed. She just watched us, waiting. She wanted us to know it was a genuine question. In fact, it's a genuine question asked by feminists: Who gets to be a person? What does that mean, and what does it require? Feminism, for her and many others, begins with that simple assertion: women are people. That's it. Are women people the way that men are people? Or are women a special class of people, with particular gifts and handicaps that require policing by people who are superior to or in charge of them (that is, men)? These questions are similar to those asked in the colonial era, for example, about subjugated and enslaved indigenous and Afro-descendant people: to what extent is the category "human" applicable, and what rights and responsibilities correspond if we answer "yes, of course we are all human beings"?

If women are people in their own right, we should assume of them what we assume of all people, namely, that they can and should be educated, that they can and should determine the course of their lives, that they can and should make decisions about their own futures. In short: if they are people, then they should have the same fundamental human rights as all people. But for centuries, women weren't viewed as people. They were viewed, as I frequently say, as "people*." People-with-an-asterisk means that women were almost people, not-quite-people, or, most likely of all, "special" people, which meant that many of the rights and privileges that apply to actual people (men) are slightly different in their case. Women can be classified as "people*" in a variety of ways—they can be thought of as mentally inferior, as frivolous or immature, or as too precious and pure to delve into the messy world outside the sanctuary of the home. I should clarify that here I am referring almost exclusively to white, European, and Euro-descendant women. Indigenous, Afro-descendant, and other nonwhite women were classified by dominant Euro-American culture as subhuman and were treated as such.

For centuries, societies in Europe and the colonized Americas classified white women as "people*" by denying them access to education. The logic went like this: women did not need to be educated in philosophy and other intellectual pursuits because they would grow up to be mothers and housewives, so it made sense to educate them in homemaking skills like cooking, sewing, and embroidery. As a corollary, women's biology (which destined them to being wives and mothers) meant they could not be taught academically. Therefore they were viewed as less intelligent, more immature, and more concerned with "frivolous" things like clothing and decor. Refusing to educate women and girls and then faulting them for not being intelligent is circular logic. Giving them access only to homemaking skills and then classifying these skills as frivolous or unimportant (when, as anyone who has lived alone knows, they are vitally important) is similarly a no-win situation.

Another way in which women were classified as "people*" was through the assertion that they were morally and spiritually superior, in possession of greater patience and a more sure moral compass, and therefore had to be protected from the messiness of the world outside the home. Politics, business, commerce: all of these were dirty, messy affairs that would sully a woman's pure soul. It was better for women to remain safe inside the sanctuary of their homes, where they could practice their moral purity and impart it to their children. In all these ways, women were deemed to be people, but subordinate people. People, but not the kind of people who deserve to choose their educational paths or determine their futures. People, but not the kind who are free to leave their homes without permission. People, but not the kind who can vote for their leaders. Of course, we can also call this subordination. Women are not the only group subordinated to men. Poor women, Black men and women, indigenous men and women, and all nonwhite persons were also relegated to this subordinate status. Interestingly, many scholars term the subordination of nonwhite men and colonized men either an "emasculation" or a "feminization" of men. That is, when men are treated as subordinates, they are being feminized, treated like women. This is how you know that to be a woman and to be subordinate to men were identical.

Anthropology: Secular and Theological

At the heart of the question "are women people?" is the subject of anthropology. As an academic subject, anthropology has historically observed humanity, sometimes in different cultures, to discover what, if anything, is central to being a human being. Are there qualities, abilities, connections that make us human and distinguish us from other animals while at the same time binding us to other humans in different cultures? This is what anthropologists seek to explain. Different branches of this discipline approach the question from different angles. So, for example, a linguistic anthropologist studies language, while a cultural anthropologist makes cross-cultural comparisons to see what different cultures might have in common and what that tells us about humanity's essence. Archaeology is a branch of anthropology that contributes to our understanding of humanity by studying artifacts from long ago.

Theology also studies what it means to be a human being, in a subfield aptly named *theological anthropology*. This differs from secular anthropology in its starting point. Theological anthropology sets out to explain what it means to be human in light of what we know from revelation: faith, scripture, and tradition. Secular anthropologists might study religion as a common thread in humanity, but theological anthropology, as a subfield of theology, fundamentally defines what humans are in relation to God. For theologians like Karl Rahner, who saw grace as God's presence everywhere, our sense of self is deeply tied to our sense of who God is. Christians can know what they think about God by exploring how they understand themselves. Both anthropological fields inquire about human nature, which brings us to our next set of questions: What does it mean to be a human being created by God? Are humans basically good or evil? And is there one human nature, or are there a variety of natures—gender, economic status, race, and so forth? To answer these questions, theological anthropology relies on the creation stories in Genesis, on philosophical understandings of what a human being is, and, more recently, on human experience.

Models of Engagement

In the previous chapter, we explored a bit about what Augustine and Aquinas understood about humanity from their readings of the Bible and their understanding of Greco-Roman philosophy. For Augustine, the story of the fall is very important. We see this reflected in his theology of sin and grace, especially in his emphasis on original sin. Augustine viewed women as subordinate to men after the fall, and he thought all humans were dominated by their sinful impulses. Women were closer to nature, which was aligned with passion and emotion, as well as unpredictability. Men, on the other hand, had the capacity to control their wills and appetites. Aquinas relied a bit more on the philosophical angle, arguing with Aristotle's support that women were subordinate to men. He claimed they were misbegotten males—that something had gone wrong in the act of conception that led to the conception of a girl child instead of a boy. At the same time, for Aquinas, women's capacity to reproduce, their bodies' ability to give birth and nurse, revealed, according to the natural law, that this was their main purpose in the divine plan. Neither of these great Christian thinkers encountered a women's movement as we know it. But their thoughts on women's inferiority and the ties between women's biology and their social roles influenced how Christianity met the challenge of the women's movement.

Feminist theologian Rosemary Radford Ruether outlines three models of male-female relationship in theological anthropology. The first is domination. In this model, the human race is divided into two kinds, men and women. Nature (or God, or God's punishment for sin) dictates that men be the dominant kind of humanity and rule over all other creatures, including women. The domination model can be enhanced through intersectional analysis. If we look at, for example, the history of colonization, we can see that religious reasons played a role in the violent domination of indigenous cultures. The idea that European culture (and males within that culture) was better or closer to God and therefore destined to dominate the world informed the "conquest" of the Americas and the Global South. Views of indigenous and African peoples and cultures as primitive, backward, or in need of civilization exemplify this paradigm of domination. For many European explorers, it seemed obvious that the persons they encountered in their travels were inferior in their customs, language, dress, and religion, and that therefore the Europeans had a responsibility (even a moral, religious responsibility) to civilize these barbarians, as reflected in Rudyard Kipling's poem "The White Man's Burden." This effort included civilizing them through violence. The repercussions of this model continue into the present, not only racially and ethnically, but also in terms of gender. Some used this thinking to justify slavery, as we noted earlier.

Ruether's second model of theological anthropology is complementarity. The complementarity model currently dominates official church documents about ordination, the sacrament of marriage, and the vocations of women and men. It's worthwhile to spend some time on this model, which is based on the idea that men and women complement each other, in the sense of completing. Think of complementary angles, which add up to 180 degrees, or a yin-yang symbol, or the line from a romantic comedy: "You complete me." The idea of complementarity begins, like the domination model, by separating humanity into two kinds: men and women. Then, instead of declaring that God or nature has decided that one must dominate the other, complementarity takes a more deductive approach, similar to what Aquinas would do.

We begin by noticing that women and men complement/complete each other biologically: men have penises and women have vaginas. Penetrative vaginal sex is how the human species is continued. This kind of sexual activity is crucial and not something we can biologically discount. From this biological complementarity, the model makes an extrapolation into society. Just as men's bodies and women's bodies are different but work together to do something important, so too men's roles and women's roles differ and work best together when they do not overlap or try to do the same thing. From biology to society, from what men and women are to what men and women do, from physical bodies to social roles, these are the moves that the complementarity model makes.

The strength of the complementarity model is that it seems to make good sense. After all, who could deny that men's bodies and women's bodies are different? It's one of the first things we learn as children. Moreover, a lot of conventional wisdom centers on this idea. Have you ever heard that "opposites attract" when it comes to romantic relationships? Or that "men are from Mars and women are from Venus"? These are popular ways of talking about a complementarity model, where men and women are fundamentally different, and those differences have consequences not only biologically but also psychologically, intellectually, and socially. Every pot has a lid.

This doesn't stop with reproduction. No, the complementarity model relies heavily on the notion that bodily difference makes a huge difference. So, biological difference (penises vs. vaginas) mean psychological differences (aggression vs. receptivity), which mean intellectual differences (the hard sciences vs. the social sciences and humanities and creative work; right brain vs. left brain) and also social differences (decision-making vs. care work). If this sounds familiar to you, you are probably thinking of the hierarchical dualism we covered in earlier chapters.

Complementarity grounds its thinking in the natural law tradition. By observing something we can see in nature—for example, that women can get pregnant and give birth to and nurse babies—we can draw conclusions about the divine plan. Because women *can* give birth, this means women's purpose can be found in mothering. Motherhood then shifts not from a potential use of a woman's body but instead to her fundamental purpose, her *telos*, or the end she was created for. The natural law tradition holds that God's creation doesn't make mistakes. If women have wombs, then they are meant to be used. The womb is therefore integral to what womanhood means. Women are designed to have children, and therefore motherhood is the destiny of all women, their highest calling, and the best use of their gifts.

For Ruether, a third and most preferable model of male-female relationality is the equality model. In this model, men and women are equal and relate to each other in mutuality. It is important to note that, for Ruether and for most feminists, equality does not mean sameness. Equality does not negate that men and women are different; it merely claims that the differences between men and women do not determine the arc of their lives. Moreover, as Elizabeth Johnson has noted, all humans have similarities and differences. For Johnson, we live in a matrix of qualities that include sex and gender, race and ethnicity, class and opportunity, among many others. Within this matrix, we share qualities with some people and don't share them with others. Those differences affect our lives in various ways (e.g., race and class affect access to educational opportunity). But those differences do not necessarily determine the course of our lives, or at least they shouldn't. In the equality model, humans relate to one another in a model of mutuality, where each works according to their unique gifts for the good of all. In this model, biology alone does not determine our gifts to the world.

Gender and the Magisterium: From Domination to Complementarity

The church has elaborated theories of gender and anthropology at different points in history. Usually, these pronouncements have come in response to a wave of the women's movement or the labor movement. When women first began to work outside the home during the industrial revolution, the papacy viewed this as harmful to women and to families but did not blame women for this failure. Rather, it was a social failure—low wages—that forced women into the workforce. Therefore, around the turn of the twentieth century, Popes Leo XIII and Pius XI advocated for higher pay for men, which would allow women to stay home. This remedy made sense since the natural law assigned men the role of breadwinning and women the role of caregiving. Women working in factories or in cities in any capacity violated the created order. It could only be happening because women were forced to work out of poverty and desperation. Initial responses to women's work outside the home centered on improving wages for men so that women could stay home.

These early forays into gendered understandings of anthropology were focused not so much on the nature of women and men but on social justice issues in the new labor force. A second challenge from the women's movement came in the 1960s with the advent of birth control and the sexual revolution. The church's response to second-wave feminism came from popes and the

Second Vatican Council. In 1963, Pope John XXIII demanded that women's working conditions not conflict with their roles as wives and mothers. A few years later, the bishops at Vatican II declared that discrimination should not be allowed and that women should be allowed to pursue education and cultural benefits equal to those recognized for men. By 1965, Pope Paul VI ushered in the shift from a domination model to a complementarian one. In his address to women at the end of Vatican II he affirmed, as many popes would after him, that even though women's roles in society had changed, they had a unique nature, different from men. A few years later, Paul VI relied heavily on the spousal metaphor in his controversial encyclical prohibiting artificial birth control, *Humanae Vitae.* One reason for this prohibition, according to the pope, was that contraception would lead men to view their wives as objects for pleasure and not as partners. As with most encyclicals, he omits women's perspective entirely. As Susan Ross points out, the implied reader of *Humanae Vitae* is male.

Perhaps the greatest proponent of the complementarity model in the modern era is Pope John Paul II. This pope's legacy of teaching on gender rests almost exclusively on it. His papal and theological writings both reflect a mind indebted to the notion of male/female dichotomy. We can see this in his encyclicals and his theological work, especially on the theology of the body. In these writings, John Paul II sought to respond to second-wave feminism and the rise of a self-defining feminist theological consciousness, which included calls for women's ordination, with what he termed "the new feminism." This new feminism is in fact a complementarian gender ideology.

John Paul II's *Mulieris Dignitatem*

In 1988, John Paul II published an apostolic letter in which he aimed to define women's special, unique nature. Titled, in English, "On the Dignity and Vocation of Women," this text lays out his case for the complementarity of men and women and what this means for women's lives. Interestingly, neither this document nor any other written during John Paul II's thirty-eight-year pontificate outlines what complementarity means for the lives of men.

Because *Mulieris Dignitatem* is a centerpiece of the church's gendered anthropology, it's worth reading closely. The pope wrote it to mark the beginning of a Marian year, so Mary figures heavily in the text. As you might recall from our discussion of Tertullian, Augustine, and Aquinas, the symbolic pairing of Mary with Eve is in the background of this letter. The first sixteen paragraphs outline women's roles in salvation history. The text emphasizes Eve's importance in Christian history and spends several paragraphs discussing the fall, sin, and its consequences. This is how we know that John Paul II was talking about theological anthropology. In paragraph 10, the pope addresses women's liberation movements specifically, noting that the push for women's rights should not lead to women's masculinization. In other words, women's demands for equality with men in terms of rights endanger their "uniqueness" and their "originality," which is rooted in their difference from men. The text expresses dismay that women's liberation might "deform and lose what constitutes [women's] essential richness." What is that richness? The goal of the letter is to make that clear.

After concentrating on Eve, *Mulieris Dignitatem* turns its attention to Mary, the new Eve, the mother of a New Creation, and Eve's foil. Paragraphs 12 through 16 highlight Jesus's ministry to women, women as witnesses to the gospel and the resurrection, and their fundamental equality in dignity before God and before Christ. Then the letter turns its attention to women in the present, with prescriptive sections on women's vocation.

Given the Marian focus of *Mulieris Dignitatem*, it's no surprise that the letter identifies, in paragraph 17, the two dimensions of women's vocation as motherhood and virginity. The text identifies these two life situations to be the fulfillment of female personality and as the two dimensions of the vocation of women. Because Mary figures so greatly in this letter, it makes sense that these two realities come together in her. We should note, however, that virginity and motherhood coexist only in Mary. For all other women (until the advent of scientific interventions like in vitro fertilization), biological motherhood and sexual virginity are mutually exclusive. This is why so many women have objected to elevating Mary as a model for all women: she represents an impossible ideal from the outset. None of us can be both virgins and mothers at the same time.

In that same paragraph, Mary is described as "firm in her resolve to preserve her virginity." This understanding of Mary's virginity is not found in the Bible. Instead, for many years the church has relied on a text called the Protoevangelium of James as a basis for much of its Marian devotion and information about Mary's life. This noncanonical text, meaning it is not included in sacred scripture, nevertheless has had profound influence in Catholicism especially. It's where we get the teaching on Mary's perpetual virginity (the idea that she was a virgin before, during, and after the birth of Jesus). Though there's much we could say about the value that has been attached to women's virginity and whether this is truly verifiable or biologically possible, I want us to note that it's a bit strange to hear that Mary was firmly against living a married life with Joseph that included sexual intercourse. The Gospels of Luke, Matthew, and John claim that Mary is a virgin at the time of Jesus's conception, but they are silent on her married life with Joseph and most other details of Mary's life. Why, then, insist that Mary decided to remain a virgin for her whole life? What sort of message does "firm in her resolve" send about women, even married ones, who do engage in sex? And why might sexual intercourse be so important?

One answer comes from remembering that when we talk about complementarity, we are engaging in reasoning that is based on natural law theory. The notion that human biological difference accounts for all manner of different social roles and psychological dispositions is especially important if we are to understand this text. Where are men's and women's biological differences most evident? In their sex organs. Let's look at the next paragraph in *Mulieris Dignitatem*. Here motherhood is explained as an openness to new life within the woman herself. "Scientific analysis fully confirms that the very physical constitution of women is naturally disposed to motherhood—conception, pregnancy, and giving birth....At the same time this also corresponds to the psycho-physical structure of women." Here John Paul II makes a key move from women's biology to women's social and psychological destiny. Because women are physically capable of motherhood in that they have a uterus, which is a space where a fetus grows, we can therefore conclude that women are psychologically disposed to make room for others, to serve, to sacrifice themselves for the greater good.

From the "space" of the womb, and the uniqueness of this space (in that a life can grow there, unlike lungs, nasal cavities, stomachs, intestines, or other spaces in the human body), *Mulieris Dignitatem* determines that women are people-who-make-space-for-the-Other. This is echoed in the following paragraphs where the text speaks of motherhood as something a woman is ready and indeed pays for: later in paragraph 18 it says that fathers owe women a debt because of pregnancy and childbirth. Motherhood affects how women relate to everyone. From the presence of a womb, *Mulieris Dignitatem* declares that women are *more* capable of paying attention to another person physically, psychologically, and socially. Because women are more capable of paying attention to other people, then they should take positions in society where their job is to listen and pay attention to others, not to glorify themselves. Women, claims paragraph 20, have a naturally spousal predisposition.

This glorification of biological motherhood leaves many women out of the equation of essential, natural femininity. Many women are infertile. Many women choose not to have children or to marry. Some women are lesbians. Some women are transgender. For many women, motherhood is not a key that unlocks their truest self but one part of many parts that make up a fulfilling life.

If a woman is unmarried, how can she participate in motherhood, which is the centerpiece of women's uniqueness? *Mulieris Dignitatem* has the answer to this problem in paragraph 21: spiritual motherhood. This is defined as concern for others. In the end, then, a woman is married either to a man or to Christ. At the end of paragraph 22, *Mulieris Dignitatem* states that a woman is a virgin, a mother, and a spouse. All these titles, you will note, are relational, and none are determined by a woman alone. All depend on the intervention (or resistance to intervention) of a man. Throughout this text, including its robust defense in paragraphs 23–27 of the spousal metaphor that we mentioned here in chapter 2, we see that women are defined over against men. Femininity is a responsive, receptive reality. It is not initiatory because that is masculine and therefore cannot overlap with women's nature.

When the text arrives at the spousal metaphor, we do get a bit of gender-bending. Paragraph 25 asserts that the Bride of Christ is the whole church, made up of women and men, but paragraph 26 asserts that because Jesus called only men to be among the twelve apostles, priestly service is only for men and therefore masculine. Mary is a figure of the whole church (men and women) in paragraph 27, but in the previous paragraph to be "*in persona Christi*" as a sacramental priest is reserved only to men. Complementarity applies selectively to the church and apparently only flows in one direction: men can be in the feminine role of the bride, but women can never cross into the role of the bridegroom.

Mulieris Dignitatem defines women's nature in its last few paragraphs. Women are brides who first receive love: "The bridegroom is the one who loves, the bride is loved" (29). While many proponents of the complementarian view claim that women are equal to men, just different, the construction of this sentence gives away the truth: the bridegroom's action is in the active tense, and the bride's verb is passive, "is loved." Women are self-sacrificing humans who can find themselves only by giving themselves to others. Paragraph 30 makes it plain: the perfect woman is a support or source of strength *for others.*

Complementarity and the New Feminism

It is important to read a text like *Mulieris Dignitatem* closely because it outlines many of the claims that complementarity theology makes about the nature of women (and, if we assume that women are men's complements, about men too). Among the assertions that women are equal in dignity to men are parallel assumptions about women's essence. This essence is usually tied to someone else. The identity of motherhood situates women in relation to children. The identity of virginity situates women in relation to potential sexual partners. The identity of spiritual motherhood also places women in relationship to those they care for.

Are opponents of complementarian theology saying that relationships aren't important? No. Instead, these opponents note that relationality seems to define only part of the human race, not the entirety of it. The burden and sacrifice of being in relationship falls to women, who are always supposed to be "for others" if they are to be truly happy and fulfilled. By configuring human beings as a kind of ledger, where one side balances out the other, we must ask ourselves:

Who gets the credits and who is forced to handle the debts? The supportive benefits of being in relationship go where? To the other side of the balance sheet. All too often, women are expected to be self-sacrificial for the benefit of others. It's no wonder Valerie Saiving claimed in the 1970s that for women pride is not the manifestation of original sin. For her, women's fundamental flaw is that they fail to assert themselves enough, are always sacrificing and forgetting themselves, suffering because of too little self-regard.

Critics of John Paul II's new feminism have also recognized the similarities between this so-called new philosophy and the old sexism. By emphasizing the biological difference between men and women and making this difference the cornerstone of their theological anthropology, "new" or "difference feminists," as they are sometimes called, engage in biological determinism. This means that one's biology decides or determines one's fate in life. To conclude from the presence of a womb that women's entire nature can be boiled down to motherhood is essentialist; it overlooks the variations not only in women's preferences and life experiences but also biological variations such as intersex persons. It completely erases history—the circumstances that have meant that women of color, for example, have frequently been exploited sexually and in the world of labor. Painting all women with this broad brush erases key factors that affect women's lives all over the world: racism, colonialism, economic exploitation by Euro-American corporations, and so on. What's more, complementarity enshrines the gender binary as divinely ordained, claiming women's association with receptivity and passivity as God's design. Any woman who doesn't fit that mold, or who fights against passivity and receptivity as their true nature, is therefore going against God's will.

The rise of complementarian theology seems like a step back from the earlier assertions of the Second Vatican Council that women should be allowed to pursue education and other benefits equal to those enjoyed by men. We can hear echoes of Augustine's claim that women are in the image of God only when taken together with their husbands (inherent relationality, ordained by God). The desire to define women's essence and true nature hearkens back to Thomas Aquinas's desire to define women's essence (misbegotten males). Further, the centrality of women's interior sex organs to their essence as "receptive" and "open to the other" relies on the deductive reasoning of natural law theory. Why did complementarity, which relies on and reiterates the problematic theological anthropologies of old, make a comeback in the 1980s and 1990s?

One answer is contextual. Many mainline Christian churches, such as the Lutherans and Anglicans, began ordaining women to official ministerial roles in the 1970s and 1980s. At the same time, the liturgical reforms ushered in by the Second Vatican Council had more women participating in public roles at Mass, as lectors and eucharistic ministers. Catholic women, claiming their baptismal dignity, began arguing strongly for ordination as well. Many of these women supported their case using theological expertise they had gained when graduate programs in theology and ministry were opened to them after the council. So one could say that second-wave feminism was gaining ground within the church globally.

Theological trends provide a second answer. The decades after the council included some significant backlash to the progressive theology that had been embraced by Vatican II. Certain theologians who sought to diminish or reframe the council's reforms as less revolutionary gained prominence. Out of concern that theology had become too sociological or too focused on humans and not enough on God, theologians who proposed taking a divine perspective as a starting point for reflection on God became popular. One of these, Hans Urs von Balthasar, was influential in John Paul II's promotion of complementarity as the correct form of feminism. For Balthasar, sexual difference is the fundamental feature of humanity that explains salvation history. He casts Christianity as the drama between a masculine, initiatory God and a feminine, receptive church. Jesus's maleness affirms God's maleness, and maleness means action and heroism on behalf of salvation. The church, Christ's bride (the spousal metaphor is key for Balthasar, unsurprisingly), is receptive, the place that nurtures salvation like a child in her womb. Balthasar defines woman as fundamentally receptive and open, as "man's answer" and as the "vessel of man's fulfillment." He holds up Mary, Jesus's mother as the quintessential exemplar of this femininity. What do we know about vessels? They are useful because they are empty, waiting to be filled by someone else. They have no meaning or function unless acted upon. This is how Balthasar views the essence of femininity. As with the spousal metaphor, the inequality is essential. This inequality makes good theological sense when talking about the church and God. It is misogynistic when you use it to talk about any divinely ordained relationship between women and men.

Conclusion

The church has had to confront the reality of the women's movement, including its various waves, in particular ways in the last two centuries. Ultimately, the challenges posed to Christianity by women's liberation are questions of theological anthropology. What does it mean to be human? Is there one human nature or two? What difference does difference make? Do some differences, like biological sexual differences, matter more than other differences, like racial or economic ones? Feminism has also challenged the church to examine its stance on labor and economic justice, on whether women should enjoy education and self-determination like men do. Throughout, the church's magisterium has responded with models of domination, complementarity, and, in some cases, equality. Most recently, the complementarity model has held sway in official church teachings. With its focus on defining women's special nature and its insistence on receptivity and passivity as hallmarks of God's intent in creating women, complementarity stands at odds with many feminist goals. Can you imagine a way forward from this apparent impasse?

DISCUSSION QUESTIONS

1. The struggle for women's rights has not ended in the United States. Where do you see pressure for women's equality in politics, in the church, in the media, or elsewhere in the public sphere? Where does the Catholic Church put its efforts institutionally, and do most Catholics' views align with those efforts? Use research from CARA or Pew to investigate.
2. Are women and men fundamentally different or fundamentally the same? What are other factors that you consider when thinking about how to understand human beings?

3. In the earliest days of modern feminist theology, Valerie Saiving suggested that men and women do not tend to sin in the same ways: men's overestimation of self causes them to sin, whereas women's underestimation of self is what causes them to sin. Does this make sense in our contemporary world? Why or why not?
4. Is sex the fundamental difference between humans? Many thinkers argue that the Western, colonialist construction of race has been far more fundamental to the way our society is structured than sexual difference. What is your take?

DELVE DEEPER

Theological anthropology has a long way to go to incorporate contemporary understandings of sexual identity as a spectrum and gender identity as performative. Explore how queer theologians enter into discussions of the *imago Dei*, sin, grace, and redemption.

READ FURTHER

Carr, Anne. *Transforming Grace: Christian Tradition and Women's Experience*. New York: Continuum, 1996.

Hinsdale, Mary Ann, and Stephen Okey, eds. *T & T Clark Handbook of Theological Anthropology*. New York: Bloomsbury, 2021.

Loades, Anne. *Feminist Theology: A Reader*. Louisville: Westminster John Knox Press, 1990.

Ross, Susan. *Extravagant Affections: A Feminist Sacramental Theology*. New York: Continuum, 1998.

Ruether, Rosemary Radford. *Sexism and God-Talk: Toward a Feminist Theology*. Boston: Beacon Press, 1983.

Saracino, Michele. *Christian Anthropology: An Introduction to the Human Person*. Mahwah, NJ: Paulist Press, 2015.

PART 2

WOMEN, SCRIPTURE, TRADITION

This section builds on the history we learned in part 1. We explore feminist hermeneutics, which applies feminist theological method to the analysis of scripture, and important female figures in the Hebrew and Christian scriptures. We take a special look at the figure of Mary, the mother of Jesus, and her role in Catholic theology and piety. Then we turn to different women in the earliest Christian communities to investigate the roles they played in their historical context and what that might mean for ours.

6

WOMEN READING SCRIPTURE

The introductory course I teach in my religious studies department focuses on storytelling as a way to understand religion. This makes sense because so much of our sacred imagination builds from stories. Young children receive illustrated Bibles or books of Bible stories about creation, about David and Goliath, about Jesus letting the little children come to him. I remember that when my first child was born we received at least four different Noah's ark play sets: a felt one, one with puppets, a plastic one with a very fancy boat, and an add-on package for more animals. That one was a popular toy for a long while. I'm not sure what people meant by giving us so many Bible-story toys, but the kids enjoyed the animals, and I'd like to think they learned a bit of this important ancient story through play.

We learn about ourselves, our communities, our origins, and how we fit in with all of these through storytelling. Stories are vitally important in communicating heritage and identity, values and morals. What's more, we interact with stories in a variety of ways: we hear them, sometimes we read them, we share them, we embellish them. Each of these ways to engage with narratives produces different results. When parents read to babies, they want to encourage a love of books and language acquisition. When we read a short story or text for a college class, we want to extract and retain accurate information. When we tell stories around a campfire, we create and solidify communal bonds. When a grandparent tells stories about their youth, they want to preserve and pass on important memories and values. Even though so much of our worldview is comprised of stories, we come to know these stories in different ways and for different purposes.

Christian life is also based on stories, especially the story of Jesus's life, death, and resurrection. But the stories we hear at Mass are not the entirety of scripture. Sometimes students will encounter a biblical text that is unfamiliar to them. "I have gone to Mass every Sunday of my life and have never heard this! How is that possible?" One reason for this is that the readings in the liturgy aren't a march through every verse of scripture. The readings come from the lectionary, a selection of biblical texts for worship compiled by church officials, in this case the Congregation for Divine Worship in the Vatican, with the bishops' conferences having some authority when it comes to translations. So regular Mass-goers hear much of scripture, but not all of it. Even daily Mass-goers don't hear every word.

The lectionary is not, however, the only reason some biblical stories sound unfamiliar. In my years of teaching, I've learned that there is a big difference between stories we know and stories we read. The Bible is the most glaring example of the gap that exists between stories we know and stories we read. Our familiarity with biblical stories can lead us to make assumptions about scripture, its contents, its coherence, and its internal agreement that simply aren't warranted. In fact, scripture is way more complex than the average churchgoing Catholic might think. There are still biblical texts that must be read and discovered. And so now we will turn our attention to some of these discoveries as well as to learning how feminist, womanist, and mujerista scholars have read a biblical text that has been largely written, edited, compiled, and interpreted by men.

Every year, at least one student in an introductory course will mention, as a way of showcasing their religious studies knowledge, that they have "read the Bible cover to cover." Usually this happens when I mention some literary fact about scripture, such as the presence of more than one creation story in Genesis, or a story that mentions that the punishment for rape is to marry your rapist, or some such thing. A student will interject, surprised and horrified, saying, "That's not possible! I have never heard that story and I've read the Bible cover to cover!" While it might sound like an impressive feat, this statement reveals the very first mistake that students of religion make about the text we know as "the Bible." It is not one book! The Bible is more like a library, or at least like one shelf in a library. I am not impressed when a student tells me they read the Bible cover to cover, because it is like telling me you read all the books on a shelf, from one end to the other. All I can discern from this is that you like to read. Without an appreciation for the Bible as a collection of texts that were written by different people in different places at different times for different audiences and purposes, we cannot approach the Bible in a scholarly way. Of course, there are many ways to read the Bible; we don't all have to read it from a scholarly perspective. We might read it liturgically or poetically. Nevertheless, to read or understand the Bible as one large text erases the very important differences and contradictions that exist within scripture. It makes assumptions about the authorship and genres of wildly differing texts. More important, it sets us up for disappointment when someone points to the glaring contradictions contained in the words of scripture.

Luckily for all of us, we are not the first to notice the two creation stories in Genesis or any of the other contradictions in the Bible. Many readers have long recognized that the Bible is not self-evident, that it is a text that demands—needs—interpretation. What that does not mean is that any interpretation is as good as the next, or that anything goes when it comes to the meanings of scripture. Roman Catholics in particular rely on a long tradition of biblical interpretation to shape and inform present understanding. We must make clear, however, that this tradition, like the texts themselves, is a product of kyriarchal, misogynist contexts and therefore reflects anti-woman sentiments. Similarly, readers' own contexts and unacknowledged biases shape their understandings of the texts and what the texts mean. So, when we are dealing with scripture, we have two mountains to climb: the text itself, which is a product of a multilayered process of writing, collecting, editing, and handing down, and our relationship to the text, which is a product of our contexts, histories, linguistic proficiency, and acknowledged or unacknowledged biases.

To illustrate our complex relationship to scripture, let's return to a distinction mentioned early in this chapter between knowing a story and reading a story. We can do a kind of meditative or contemplative exercise where we imagine ourselves in a Bible story

(Ignatian spirituality refers to this as "composition of place"). Think of a Bible story with which you are very familiar. Who are the main characters? Who is responsible for the action in the story, the doing? What happens in the story, and who does it benefit or hurt? Who does most of the speaking in scriptural stories? Here is another important question: What do the characters in this story look like? If there is a crowd, what does the crowd look like? Are they mostly European looking? What about famous biblical characters like Adam, Eve, Noah, Mary, Jesus, Isaiah, John the Baptist? Are they also light-skinned, Euro-American looking?

For many of us who were brought up and educated in the United States, most biblical characters are imagined to be white and male. Furthermore, the scriptures as written, preached, and interpreted foreground men's voices, men's perspectives, men's interpretations. Children's Bibles frequently illustrate all or most biblical characters as European-looking people. While there are some women in scripture, they are the products of men's imaginations and interpretations, since in all likelihood most of the writers and editors of scriptural texts were men. How can women, people of color, the LGBTQ+ community find solace, liberation, or salvation in a series of texts that systematically excludes them? Is there a way to interpret scripture from a feminist, intersectional lens?

Feminist scholars have worked on this question for quite some time, and we can take comfort in this. Similar to the classifications we used to describe feminists' relationship to the church, we can look at how different feminists frame their approach to scripture. Some discard it, some sift through it looking for stories that promote liberation, and most combine these methods with other strategies for reading, in a discipline scholars refer to, broadly, as hermeneutics, which is the science of interpretation. Religion scholars use this term to refer to strategies, frames, and principles people use in order to interpret important texts, like scripture.

There are many hermeneutical approaches one might take when reading scripture. For example, some medieval scholars had a system they called the *quadriga*, which they used to reveal a "fourfold meaning" of scripture. Thinkers who used the quadriga approached scripture with an understanding that any text in there might have up to four levels of meaning. The first is the literal sense, which is merely what the words say. Second is the metaphorical or typological sense, which reveals what the text is saying about Christianity, even if it was part of the Hebrew scriptures. Third is the eschatological or anagogic sense, which discovers what the text means about the future of Christian history: heaven, hell, the last judgement. Here we can pause to note something about hermeneutics: readers using this type of interpretation assumed that all symbolism in scripture was somehow pointing to Jesus's incarnation, passion, and resurrection, or to Christian interpretations of the end of history. So they looked for that meaning in the text. Why was this an assumption? Because they lived in a cultural context where Christianity was dominant, and so it was assumed that all other faiths, including and especially Judaism, were just laying the foundation for Christianity, the ultimate revelation of God. The final sense of the quadriga was the moral sense, which seeks to uncover the ethical lesson that the passage is meant to teach. This tells us that the interpreters also assumed that all of scripture was useful for ethical learning, that all of it could teach us something about how to live well.

So, even very early readers of the Bible (to say nothing of the rich talmudic and rabbinic traditions in Judaism) knew that there was more to the Bible than just the words on the page. When they stumbled on a problematic, contradictory, or seemingly nonsensical text, the readers assumed there was a deeper meaning. This deeper meaning was always something related to Christianity's view of the world because their entirely Christian context wouldn't really allow for anything else. For example, the sacrifice of Isaac in Genesis 22. The story is a bit absurd on its face. Why would God demand that Abraham murder his son Isaac, the only avenue by which God has lived up to the promise to give Abraham descendants? Recall that the initial covenant with Abraham promised him many children, which seemed silly to Abraham since his wife was barren and old. So when this same God demands that Abraham take Isaac up to a mountain and kill him, well, at the very least it seems odd, or contrary to God's own promise. But to the medieval reader, nothing in the Bible is nonsensical—the seemingly contradictory nature of this passage is there to prompt us to deeper reflection. Instead of reading on a surface level a story about a child sacrifice averted, the medieval interpreter sees instead a preview of Jesus's sacrifice on the cross. There, God does sacrifice God's only son to redeem the world. The story of the binding of Isaac, then, is really a foretelling of the story of Jesus's passion.

That's how they read the Bible. Centuries later, after the Renaissance, when scientific reasoning held Europe's attention, biblical scholars focused on discovering the "truth" of scripture through scientific means: archaeological, linguistic, and historical-critical analysis of the text. By reconstructing the biblical worlds through scientific research and removing the so-called mythical parts of scripture, scholars felt they could demythologize the text to get at the kernel of reality in it. So you could overlook the claims that Adam was 930 years old when he died and keep the important lessons of the origins of humanity in God's creative activity, because everyone knew, scientifically, that humans don't live that long. This interpretive move was a product of their context—an emphasis on truth exclusively as that which is able to be proven through science and research leads to scientific, research-based approaches to scripture.

In fact, we all read the Bible from a particular historical, social, and communal context. We can't help it. It is why we must work to ensure that we are reading from the broadest, most inclusive context possible when we approach scripture. The contexts from which feminist, womanist, and Latinx or mujerista scholars approach biblical hermeneutics share some important presuppositions and characteristics. Let's explore some features of these hermeneutical strategies.

Feminist, womanist, and mujerista scholars all share a fundamental presupposition that women are fully human, made in God's image, and deserving of the right to self-determination. This presupposition leads them to see the kyriarchal, androcentric context of the text and interpretive traditions of the Bible and find them insufficient. The stories in scripture center the experience of men, so the interpretations we have of these stories also center male experience and understanding. For example, in the Gospels we hear that Jesus fed the five thousand. That story concludes in the gospel narratives with some variation on the phrase "not including the women and children that were present." This means that women and children were not counted in the "five thousand" of the title. So the "five thousand" were actually only the men who were there. If all the people had been counted, there would have been many more. In some cases, like this obvious one, women are literally not counted among those present in Jesus's life and ministry. In other cases, such as some sections of Jewish law (halakhah), crimes and punishments treat women like property and rape like theft, where reparation was due to a woman's husband or father. One punishment for the crime of rape was that the rapist must marry the victim. The victim's perspective was irrelevant. The central concern of the text is that the male in the woman's life not lose status or wealth on account of the crime. Feminist hermeneutics presupposes the idea that because scripture was composed, compiled, and largely interpreted in patriarchal contexts, we must work to look beyond these shortcomings and remedy them when possible.

These are just two obvious examples, but the kyriarchal and androcentric focus of biblical texts is pervasive, and feminists therefore approach the Bible with a hermeneutic of suspicion. Though it's a weird phrase, it needn't be read as aggressive toward scripture. Rather, the fundamental insight of a hermeneutics of suspicion is a questioning insight. We suspect that the texts are not telling the whole story. How many people did Jesus feed? How often did women have to marry their rapists? Were women free to reject the advances of a man, or were they often forced into sexual relationships that were then classified as "adultery"? One consequence of this hermeneutic of suspicion is that many feminists approach scripture with what scholars call an "advocacy stance." Advocacy means to work on someone's behalf, and feminist hermeneutics work to tell women's stories. They ask, from an advocacy stance, are there other ways of interpreting these stories so that women's lives are given the weight and import that men's lives are?

Womanist, mujerista, Asian, and other nondominant feminist scholars come to scripture with a hermeneutic of suspicion and a stance that promotes advocacy, as mentioned above. In addition, these scholars question not only the patriarchal ways in which the text has come down to us but the racist and classist strains in scripture and interpretation. What, they ask, are the forces that exclude nonwhite voices, faces, and bodies from our understanding of the biblical world? Access to the Bible and to the education required to be able to read it has always been limited by the powerful elite. Scripture has been misused by the church in aiding colonial expansion and by legitimating the slave trade all over the world. To assert the humanity of nonwhite, nondominant, nonmale persons amid this legacy of limiting the Bible to the elite is a task that we must undertake. Womanist and mujerista theologians remind us that we are all capable of narrating our own experiences. Further, they emphasize the importance of including nonprofessional, marginalized voices of women and the poor in the work of biblical interpretation. For mujerista scholars like Ada María Isasi-Díaz, this means paying particular attention to the everyday lived reality of marginalized Latinas and trusting their interpretations of what scripture means for their lives. For womanist scholars like Nyasha Junior, it means including nonprofessional women's voices in our biblical interpretations, in recognition of both the systematic exclusion of Black women from higher education and their persistence in reading and interpreting scripture in ways relevant to their lives.

Methods and Tactics

Feminists reading scripture employ a variety of tactics to understand and interpret scripture. The goal of these is to be faithful to the text while at the same time avoiding the further marginalization and silencing of women. Scholars like Clarice Martin, Jacqueline Hidalgo, Elisabeth Schüssler Fiorenza, and Phyllis Trible have outlined different approaches to scripture, to its liberative stories and its problematic stories, to its skewed portrayal of exemplary women like Mary and its disregard of other women like Hagar. Let's explore some of these tactics.

In almost all feminist theological schools of thought, scholars use some variation of a three-part method. This methodology involves the three steps of deconstruction, looking for alternatives, and reconstruction. Feminist scholars deconstruct symbols, stories, and doctrines that have been used to justify the subjugation of women. In biblical hermeneutics, this means that in order to understand how the Bible is used to uphold kyriarchy, you must first document the stories used to portray women as less than human, whether by maligning them, by excluding them, or by failing to account for their perspectives, their hopes, their justice. Take the story of David and Bathsheba, which is told entirely from David's perspective and never from the perspective of the woman who was merely bathing when the king took note of her, lusted after her, summoned her to his castle, and had sex with her. Could she really say no to the king? Then he has her husband killed, leaving her completely at his mercy. We hear this story interpreted as something about the beauty of women and the weakness of David. But if you look from her point of view, the story is different indeed.

We cannot account for the misogynistic use of scripture without accounting for these stories: Where are women portrayed? Where are they left out? How are they portrayed? Are women valued as much as men, daughters as much as sons? In the Hebrew scriptures, much of this comes through in legal writings: Were women allowed to own property? Was rape a crime, and how was it punished?

Deconstructing scripture by noting all the places where women are treated violently and unjustly can take a negative toll on readers. Phyllis Trible remarks that it would be easy to conclude that all biblical faith is hopelessly misogynistic, that the best thing to do would be to dismiss it. In many of the stories of violence and injustice, marginalized women see reflections of their own lives. Thus, when thinkers like Ada María Isasi-Díaz suggest that we look at the everyday experience of marginalized women for their insights into scripture, I think it's important to understand that for many women, violence is an actual part of their everyday lives. While some might think that seeing violence and injustice in scripture would justify it, in some cases it lends credibility to women's experience of their own lives. To see injustice replicated in scripture doesn't necessarily sanctify it. Instead, this can be an entry point for someone. A point where they feel seen by the scriptures. Even deconstruction does not have to be hopeless. It is, rather, an important invitation to deeper engagement with the Bible.

Scouring the Tradition

The second step in feminist theological method is to search for alternatives. In biblical hermeneutics, this is the task of recovery. Scholars sift through scripture for overlooked or forgotten stories, try to uncover women's roles that have been erased or silenced, and recover traditions that go against the cultural context of whatever text is being analyzed. This task might involve highlighting neglected text or recovering texts that are obscured by translation. For example, many references to God use feminine nouns and images in the original languages of the Bible: Hebrew and Greek. Words like *rechem*, meaning mercy, share a root with the word for womb—which is unmistakably feminine! Similarly, the words for wisdom and spirit—*Sophia* and *ruah*—are both feminine. So, while we may rarely hear God referred to in the feminine in English (because our nouns aren't all gendered like Spanish or Italian), there are nevertheless ways to name God that are not exclusively male. God is a mother hen and a woman in labor in the Hebrew scriptures. God is like a woman who has lost a coin and finds it and rejoices. God is even like the excitement and attraction between two lovers in the Song of Songs. Many students are floored by the revelation that God is not always spoken of using male language and imagery, but it's biblical! Even (especially) if the texts are neglected because of the language used in translation, we are invited to dig more deeply, to see what is really there. And what do we find? Not an exclusively male God, as it turns out.

A second aspect of recovery is the unearthing of previously neglected women in the Bible. Do you know the names Shiphrah and Puah? What about Phoebe? Some neglected women are presented as nameless: the daughter of Pharaoh, for example. Trible notes that one thread that unites the women who are overlooked or silenced in scripture is that they tend to be the ones who counter patriarchal culture or disobey patriarchal orders. Shiphrah and Puah are the original heroes of the exodus: they are the midwives who ignore Pharaoh's decree to kill all newborn Hebrew boys. They spare Moses's life, and he goes on to free the Israelites from slavery. Why aren't they household names? Phoebe is a deacon, as Paul says plainly in the sixteenth chapter of his letter to the Romans. Those are some women who have been neglected, even though the authors of scripture felt the women were important enough to record their names.

Other neglected women in scripture are unnamed. You've probably heard the parable of the mustard seed. But did you know that immediately following that story Jesus tells the story of a woman who adds yeast to flour? Many of Jesus's most well-known parables have a "twin" parable that follows it, usually featuring a woman protagonist. The good shepherd is twinned with the woman who has lost a coin. But there are so many depictions in art, music, and stained glass of the good shepherd. Where is the woman with the coin? Where is the faith-as-leavening song? And why don't many of these women have names?

A third kind of recovery involves reinterpreting familiar women characters from scripture. Once again, the difference between knowing and reading becomes apparent. What do you know about, for example, Mary Magdalene? Is she a repentant prostitute who became one of Jesus's closest followers? Some popular literature has asserted that she was secretly married to Jesus. Sometimes we imagine her dumping a jar of scented oil on Jesus's feet and drying it with her hair. And yet, none of these things are true of Mary Magdalene. We can look through the Christian scriptures and find absolutely no evidence that Mary Magdalene was a prostitute. She is identified in Luke 8:2 as a woman from whom Jesus had cast out seven demons. That is all we know of her life before she knew Jesus. In no way does cure of demons imply or necessitate prostitution. So why does so much Christian art, so much lore, turn Mary Magdalene into a whore? Was it discomfort with a woman so close to the center of the Christian movement that made interpreters decide that she must be discredited? More likely, Mary Magdalene is confused or fused together with other, unnamed women in the Gospels. A leading theory states that she was conflated with the unnamed woman in Luke 7 who washed Jesus's feet with her tears and dried it with her hair. This unnamed woman is said to have sinned greatly, but nowhere is her sin identified as prostitution. It is possible that readers merely assumed that any great sin by a woman must be of a sexual nature and therefore that the combined figure of Mary Magdalene/unnamed tears-and-hair woman had to have sinned sexually in a great and significant way, like prostitution.

Eve, the woman created out of Adam in Genesis 2, suffers a similar fate. She is often used as a foil (a character displaying opposite qualities) to Mary, Jesus's mother, in the writings of early church thinkers. Since the Virgin Mary was, quite literally, how Jesus came into the world to save it, Eve was deemed the reason why the world needed saving at all. She was the portal of sin, the "devil's gateway" that Tertullian railed against. Perhaps it is because of women's association with the body, and the body with sin, that the original transgression of eating the forbidden fruit was sexualized. Many believe that Eve seduced Adam with sin, that she used her "womanly wiles" to convince him to fall from grace with her. The biblical text gives no such embellishment. In Genesis 3, we see that the serpent convinces Eve to try the fruit because it will give her wisdom, and Eve considers this, eats the fruit, and "gives some to her husband, who also ate it." That's it. No elaborate ploy or deception. Very little interaction at all. Here, eat this, says Eve. Okay. And yet when we see artists' depictions of Eve, or even in some commercials meant to refer to something "forbidden," the image of Eve is one of a sexual temptress, with her long hair covering her breasts, staring seductively at Adam or the viewer. She alone is responsible for all the evil in the world. As Tertullian said, because of her the Son of Man had to die!

Neither Eve nor Mary Magdalene deserve to be maligned as sexual deviants or as prostitutes or sex workers. These assertions, while popular, are not supported by the biblical text. There are other instances of people who sinned greatly and were forgiven by Jesus, and there is a scene where Jesus forgives a (yet another unnamed) woman who is about to be stoned for adultery (though we can argue whether men were ever punished for adultery, or if the woman was about to be stoned after being raped). But neither Eve nor Mary Magdalene are those women. Part of searching the biblical tradition for alternatives to misogyny is unearthing the true pictures we have of the women in scripture, not the caricatures that have emerged from years of male-centered interpretation.

A fourth and final aspect of recovering women's voices in scripture (and these are not listed in order of importance, but are equally important and interconnected) has to do with recovering the reality of nonwhite characters in the Bible. Euro-Americans, and through colonization and modernity the whole world, have been taught to imagine the characters in scripture as people who resemble them, that is, as light-skinned Europeans. But the books of the Bible contain characters from areas we now know as the Middle East and North and Central Africa. It is not realistic to assume that every character in scripture looks Nordic. And yet, many Christians see exactly this in the portrayals of Jesus and Mary that populate our churches and religious art here in the United States. Black and Latinx scholars invite us to re-race (or de-race) the Bible by analyzing our presuppositions about what biblical characters looked like. Some would likely have semitic features or dark olive skin; others would look African since they are from Africa. As an example, let's take Zipporah, the wife of Moses. As Latinx biblical scholar Maricel Mena Lopez points out, many biblical scholars have dismissed the possibility that Zipporah was from modern-day Ethiopia. For Mena Lopez, the racialization and sexism of the biblical world derives from the context of the interpreter. That is, we tend to read into scripture the biases that form our worldview. If, for an interpreter, Black people cannot be as civilized or as close to the divine as white people, then naturally they will interpret the majority of actors in scripture to be white or as close to white as feasible. Thus, even though Zipporah is identified as being from Midian (where Moses meets her), and though there is evidence that she is a "Cushite," which makes her Ethiopian, many scholars nevertheless believe her to be light-skinned. This imposition of race into scripture happens in more subtle ways as well. For example, the drama of the exodus occurs in Egypt. Egypt is located in Africa, not the Middle East. And yet, in the Christian imagination, Egypt is de-Africanized and understood instead to be part of the Semitic universe of scripture. But this flattening out of racial difference serves a racist purpose: to keep blackness far from divinity, to ensure that holiness and divinity are more closely associated with light skin. Womanist scholars in particular see it as a crucial task to critique feminist hermeneutics when this approach excludes race or when its focus is too narrow.

It is important, then, for feminist biblical scholars to reclaim race in scripture. Not because race as a category has always been understood in the ways it is now, but because to make assumptions about what Bible characters looked like reveals our own biases about how God works in the world. Moreover, if we are taking intersectionality seriously, we know that limiting ourselves to unearthing women's characters or roles in scripture without paying attention to race and class merely re-creates the inequalities we are trying to upend. To reclaim women in scripture means that we must reclaim them in their specificity, not as general avatars for our dreams or desires. When we reclaim race in scripture, we also analyze how racist understandings of the Bible have had negative effects on Black and Afro-descendant persons throughout the world.

So, let's review feminist biblical methodology so far. First, we deconstruct problematic aspects of the biblical text and its interpretation by documenting how women are mistreated, sidelined, abused, and forgotten in scripture and in our reception of it. Next, we scour the tradition to reclaim what we can of women's lives that are documented there. This means recovering feminine images for the divine, female characters who have been silenced and ignored, known women who have been misremembered, and racial identity in scripture.

Some biblical stories are so horrible that they cannot be rehabilitated or reimagined, such as the rape of Tamar in 2 Samuel 13. Here, a daughter of King David (Tamar) is raped by her half-brother, Amnon. Though the text represents Tamar's firm rejection of Amnon's plan, nevertheless the motive is described as Amnon's romantic love for Tamar. Tamar never gets justice. The text merely tells us that after being sent away, crying and screaming, she lives out her life as a desolate woman in her brother Absalom's house. Another example is the murder of Benjamin's concubine in Judges 19, where a woman is offered to an angry mob, gang raped, and killed. Later Benjamin himself dismembers her. The story is horrific and traumatizing. It cannot be reframed as anything other than a terrorizing abuse of a human being. What can be done with awful texts like these? If they are irredeemable, should feminists just disregard them or discard them? Phyllis Trible suggests another option: these stories should be told in memory of the wronged women, as a kind of litany of lament. To forget these women would be to heap more violence upon their memories. Instead, the retelling of these stories becomes a living memorial to the trauma of the women and to the continuing violence against women, especially Black women and trans women.

Reconstruction

To reconstruct biblical narratives that lack female agency and meaningful participation, we have to be creative interpreters. Some feminists opt to add creatively to scriptural stories, to fill out the silences of women we know were present. Judith Plaskow, for instance, fleshed out the story of Lilith, Adam's first wife according to some Jewish midrash (interpretive texts). Others, like Elizabeth Johnson, use the tools of historical-critical methods to reconstruct the biblical contexts of the women in scripture and thereby fill out what we know of their lives. Johnson's magisterial book *Truly Our Sister* does exactly this with the biblical passages about Mary the mother of Jesus. There, Johnson analyzes what the life of a first-century woman in Palestine would have looked like: her daily tasks, her living arrangement, her religious observance. Though it does not tell us for certain the details of Mary's life, it helps give Mary a more robust personality, almost a reality, that is not present in the brief sketches of her life we get from scripture. This method is not new. The Protoevangelium of James, a second-century (around 145 CE) text where Catholics get much of their devotional information about Mary (for instance, that she was a virgin before, during, and after giving birth to Jesus), is a similar work attempting to fill in the blanks of Mary's life that the Gospels don't address. So it's not just feminists that take up the task of creating new narratives as a form of interpretation. As long as Christians have been curious about what the Gospels leave out there have been writers seeking to imagine what details might fill the gaps.

Reconstructing biblical texts and biblical criticism will never result in a completely balanced, liberating view of women and marginalized persons. It's a bummer but it's true. The fact is that scriptural texts are compilations that have passed through many misogynistic contexts before they arrive on our bookshelves. So the most effective way to reconstruct scripture into a more just model is for women, people of color, and all the marginalized to continue to read and write biblical interpretation as a counterbalance to this kyriarchal legacy. Further, scholars must continue to critically analyze how the Bible serves as a legitimating tool for all manner of social and personal evils that have caused women, Afro-descendent people, indigenous people, and others to suffer. From slavery to colonial violence to domestic violence to white supremacy, scripture has been used as an endorsement from God for humanity's most vile impulses. We must examine how and why this happens—and then seek to dismantle these abuses of scripture. That, too, is a task of reconstruction.

Why should we bother with the task of reconstruction? After all, if the Bible is so thoroughly misogynistic in its creation, editing, compilation, and history of interpretation, why don't women just move on? This is a choice that many women make. After deciding that it is simply too exhausting and too much work to try to rehabilitate a series of texts that are so far gone, many women simply stop believing that scripture has an authoritative place in their lives and their worship. But for others, reconstructing the texts, reinterpreting the figures, and retelling even the texts of terror are necessary steps if women are ever to feel at home in the church. Reconstructing is about building that home, about reclaiming our place in the sacred, and about forcefully restating that women and all those who live on the margins are made in God's image. I find particularly compelling this insight by Judith Plaskow about Judaism. In her book, *Standing Again at Sinai*, she states, "To commit oneself to recovering women's experiences within Judaism is to say that women as well as men define Jewish humanity, and that *there is no Judaism*—there is only male Judaism without the insights of both" (12).

To reconstruct scripture with an intersectional feminist lens is to claim that white men are not the preeminent shapers of the Christian tradition, even if that has until now been the case. It is not enough to allow women a seat at the table, to confer the privileges of discipleship on women equally with men. We must instead go beyond this "seat at the table" feminist vision and push further, to a place where women and all the marginalized are seen as co-heirs of Jesus's promises and as co-shapers of the Christian tradition, not merely the recipients of that tradition. We must come to understand that women are central to the Christian story, both as protagonists and as storytellers in their own right.

The next two chapters will examine female figures in the Hebrew and Christian scriptures as well as what different interpreters have understood about these figures. Through our exploration, we will see how scriptural narratives must move women from the sidelines to the center of the church's story. Moreover, we will explore how centering these forgotten, overlooked, and maligned women in scripture opens our eyes to how sacred texts are used as tools of misogyny, of classism, and of white supremacy. Feminist biblical interpretation invites us as scholars to move between the worlds of scholarship and activism and to think creatively about how these worlds intersect and inform one another. The way we read and understand scripture helps us think about God's visions of justice and therefore informs our ethics and our work on behalf of justice. This is good news for our work. Intersectional feminism is at home in these in-between spaces, where the possibility of change is at its greatest.

DISCUSSION QUESTIONS

1. What images of God were prevalent in your religious education, if you had one? If not, what images of God are popular in media and art? Can you think of art and media that portray God in different ways? How is it received?
2. With a partner or a small group, make an artistic depiction of the divine. It can be in any medium: paint/draw/sketch or write a song, a poem, anything. Whatever kind of art seems appropriate to the group. How did you come to an agreement on what to do, what to depict, and how to depict it? What values or goals guided your process?
3. In your view, what should be done about texts of terror embedded in scripture? Should they be read at liturgies, even if they cause harm to members of the congregation? Should they be discarded, even if they are part of the canon of scripture? Is there some other way to handle them that you can think of?

DELVE DEEPER

Explore the tradition of Black Madonnas throughout Catholic piety. Where are they situated geographically, historically, socially? How does devotion to these Madonnas function today? What conclusions can you draw about divine imagery from these traditions?

READ FURTHER

Hidalgo, Jackie. *Revelation in Aztlán: Scriptures, Utopias, and the Chicano Movement*. London: Palgrave Macmillan, 2016.

Junior, Nyasha. *An Introduction to Womanist Biblical Interpretation*. Louisville: Westminster John Knox Press, 2015.

Mena Lopez, Maricel. "Because of an Ethiopian Woman." In *Feminist Intercultural Theology: Latina Explorations for a Just World*, edited by Maria Pilar-Aquino and Maria Jose Rosado-Nunes, 145–65. Maryknoll, NY: Orbis Books, 2007.

Trible, Phyllis. *God and the Rhetoric of Sexuality*. Philadelphia: Fortress Press, 1978.

———. *Rhetorical Criticism: Context, Method, and the Book of Jonah*. Philadelphia: Fortress Press, 1994.

———. *Texts of Terror: Literary-Feminist Readings of Biblical Narratives*. Philadelphia: Fortress Press, 1984.

7

WOMEN IN THE HEBREW BIBLE

Whenever we study the Bible, any part of it, we should recognize that we approach the text as readers and interpreters, but we are not alone in this endeavor. It is helpful to think of undertaking biblical study as stepping into a river: a lot happens upstream before we encounter the river, and there's a lot happening downstream, beyond what we can see. When we step into this river as Catholics, we go in with company: biblical interpretation done by popes, bishops, and theologians, scripture scholars, and the text itself. In this way, we can account for more of what is going on in the river—after all, more people cover more area. But let's not kid ourselves: we cannot contain all the flowing water. Meaning and interpretation overflow around us, upstream and downstream, and even around our feet. Our goals when studying scripture, then, should be to see as clearly as possible, to look at the water, to be able to take a life-giving drink.

What makes for a life-giving drink, particularly for those of us with feminist commitments? We must keep in mind the feminist strategies for biblical interpretation that we discussed earlier: reading against the grain, adopting a hermeneutic of suspicion, elevating and celebrating underappreciated women characters, and retelling texts of terror in memory of women who are wronged.

Our study of the Hebrew Bible invites us to wade into a particularly ancient, wide, winding river. The Hebrew Bible, or Old Testament, consists of forty-seven texts from a variety of authors, comprising a great many different genres and styles, and (at least for Catholics) in two languages: Hebrew and Greek. We enter this part of the scriptures as guests—we recognize that the Hebrew Bible is the sacred scripture of our siblings in faith who practice Judaism. For a long time, Christians read the Hebrew Bible through what we call a *supercessionist* lens. This means that interpreters read everything in the "Old" Testament as a prelude to the life of Jesus. Any event that was described, any person, place, or thing either predicted or pointed to the life, death, and resurrection of Jesus. More recently, as a result of Vatican II and some earlier movements in biblical studies, Catholics have been invited to engage the texts as sacred in themselves, not merely sacred to the extent that they prefigure Christian ideas. As Catholics, we can affirm the close relationship between the Hebrew and Christian scriptures without reducing everything in the Hebrew Bible to a preview of what's to come. We can think of the traditions as siblings. Because of this close sibling relationship, we must explore the topic of women in the Hebrew scriptures in dialogue not only with Christian interpreters but also with Jewish theologians who also wrestle with these texts. Our goal in feminist interpretation is threefold: to chronicle how women have been portrayed throughout the Hebrew Bible, to lift up exemplary or overlooked women in salvation history, and to memorialize women who were terrorized in and through these texts. It's an enormous task before us, and we should be clear that we will not traverse the whole of this river. We won't even see most of it. We're here to get our feet wet. This process begins with getting a map of the territory. So, what is in the Hebrew Bible?

Practitioners of Judaism know the Hebrew scriptures as the TaNaKh. This is an acronym, where each capitalized letter stands for a part of the whole. The acronym is as follows:

T is for Torah, or the Law. Included in this are the first five books: Genesis through Deuteronomy. The Torah introduces us to major figures in Judaism and Christianity, such as Eve, the first woman; Miriam, the sister of Moses; Sarah and Hagar, the mothers of Abraham's children; and Bathsheba, whom David desired. We meet the patriarchs, their spouses, and their concubines in the books of the Torah. We also begin to glimpse how the writers and editors of scripture regarded women, particularly through the laws to which men and women of Israel were bound.

N is for Nevi'im, or the Prophets. Here we see the big names like Isaiah and Jeremiah and the minor prophets like Amos. None of the prophetic books is named for or attributed to a woman. Does this mean that there were no women prophets?

K is for Ketuvim, or Other Writings. This encompasses a great deal of texts and genres, including the Psalms; apocalyptic books like Daniel; wisdom literature like the Song of Songs; and theological history like Judges, the Books of Kings, and so on. The Ketuvim includes texts that personify God's wisdom. We note that most of that language uses feminine nouns and pronouns: Sophia, or the indwelling presence of God, Shekinah. These texts include Hebrew, Greek, and even Aramaic writing.

Knowing the parts of the TaNaKh is one useful way to classify the books in the Hebrew Bible. Another way is to approach the texts according to their genres. The Hebrew scriptures contain a wide variety of genres: poetry, history, myth, law, apocalypse, prophecy, aphorisms. The way we read biblical books should not differ very much from how we approach books that are not considered sacred scripture. One would not read a medical textbook the same way one would read a graphic novel. Similarly, when we read the texts in the Hebrew scriptures, we must be attentive to genre: we cannot read Song of Songs, which is erotic poetry, in the same way we would read Deuteronomy, which is a book of law. Appreciating the genre of the individual books prevents us from flattening out the rich diversity of viewpoints the Hebrew Bible includes but also allows us to enter the world of a text prepared for what we might encounter. In a book of poetry like Song of Songs or the Book of Psalms, we inhabit a world described by rich metaphor and symbolism. A theological history, like Judges, invites us to view political and military victories and defeats through a prism of Israel's rocky relationship with God. An apocalyptic text like Daniel critiques the present by depicting a richly imaginative, sometimes frightening future. When we incorporate an appreciation of genre into our biblical understanding, we comprehend in a deeper way that the Hebrew Bible isn't one seamless story, but rather more like a patchwork quilt or a complex garment that includes different fibers and different fasteners (stitches, zippers, buttons, sequins) that fulfill different goals (structure, stability, beauty). Or, to return to our river metaphor, appreciating the genres of different texts allows us to see the topography of the river: from the different elevations of the riverbed to the texture of the rocks that make the water seem more calm in some places and more agitated in others.

As we read and examine these texts, we must keep in mind the predominantly patriarchal nature of both their composition and their interpretation. That is, as far as we know these books were written by and for men, and interpreted by and for men throughout their history. We know this in large and small ways. For example, the story of the exodus is familiar to many Catholics because of its depictions in film. Perhaps you've seen the Disney adaptation (*The Prince of Egypt*) or the older, more melodramatic 1956 version, *The Ten Commandments.* In each of these retellings, the hero of the tale is Moses, and his brother Aaron is a crucial supporting character. But how many of us know the names Shiphrah and Puah? Have you ever heard of these women being referred to as heroes in the exodus? Probably not.

Shiphrah and Puah appear early in the Book of Exodus, just after Pharaoh has decreed that all infant males born to Israelite women should be killed. These brave women are midwives who dare to disobey Pharaoh's orders, so when Moses's mother gives birth to him, Shiphrah and Puah spare the baby's life. Without their actions, Moses would not have lived to grow up in Pharaoh's household, kill an Egyptian slave driver, be cast into exile in Midian, and return as the liberator of the Israelites. But Shiphrah and Puah's identities remain obscure, their actions an overlooked detail despite being of great consequence. Similarly, we know Moses's brother Aaron worked alongside him in the confrontation with Pharaoh, but his sister Miriam did too. The patriarchal bias of both the texts and the interpretive history ensure that we don't regard these women as crucial to the exodus story, though they are.

The act of diminishing women's roles is not limited to figures who act in heroic ways but also to women's everyday presence. Jewish theologian Judith Plaskow notes this in her magisterial text, *Standing Again at Sinai*. She says that the Torah claims the mantle of being Jewish teaching, but because it centers on male experience, on covenants with patriarchs that marginalize the contributions of the matriarchs, and on laws that treat women as objects not subjects, it in fact "speaks in the voice of only half the Jewish people" (5). If the Torah, as we receive it in the present, accounts for the experiences of God had by only one-half of the population, then the teaching is incomplete, missing the other half. One key task of feminist theology, for Plaskow, is to do justice to women's experience of God (that crucial other half) and, in this way, to complete the Torah.

Doing justice to women's experience of God, particularly Jewish women's experience, as Plaskow suggests above, is far beyond the purview of this text. What we can do, however, is highlight several places where women are featured in the Hebrew scriptures and how these women are portrayed. These include as named characters, as unnamed but important characters, as persons/objects bound by laws or involved in law, and as symbols for the relationship between God and God's people.

Eve: The First Name

Women characters in the narratives of the Hebrew scriptures can be broadly classified into those whose names we know and those who are unnamed. Some of the named women are quite consequential for Christian history and theology, like Eve, Sarah, and Miriam. Others are vitally important to Jewish history, like Esther. Bearing in mind that these women's stories are products of men's imaginations and interpretation, we can nevertheless use feminist hermeneutics to read their stories against the grain, to reveal women's creativity and agency in the biblical text. Along the way, I hope we will see that what we understand to be "traditional womanhood" or "biblical understandings of womanhood" are quite unrelated to the portraits of women we encounter in scripture.

Let's begin with Eve, the first woman we meet in scripture. Eve's story begins in Genesis 2, when she is created by God out of

Adam's body to be his helpmate and companion. In this dramatic second story of creation (the first is the poetic seven-days version of Genesis 1, where man and woman are created simultaneously in verse 27), after she is created by God, we see Eve be tempted by the snake (3:1–4) and make a determination about whether to obey God's command or not (3:6). Then, she gives the fruit to Adam who eats it without hesitation. God finds out and we have what Christians commonly call "the fall" from grace. Because of her role in the story, Eve has borne the blame for sin entering the world, and while this may sound like a harsh and awful judgement, for Christians she also represents the beginning of salvation, so that she and Mary the mother of Jesus are portrayed as bookends in salvation history. Eve's story begins the drama of salvation, and Mary's story begins the end of the drama in the Christian tradition.

From a literary standpoint, the history of interpretation has tended to view Eve and Mary as foils of one another. This means that the characters are opposites and their qualities mirror each other: Eve is responsible for sin, so Mary is responsible for salvation. Eve is bad; Mary is good. Eve is consistently portrayed as seductive and sleazy; Mary is pure and virginal. But this interpretation has no basis in the text of Genesis, where sex doesn't even come up. In fact, we can assume from the text that sex was part of creation before the fall and remained so afterward. The only sex-adjacent thing mentioned in Genesis 2 happens after they eat the forbidden fruit. Both Adam and Eve notice that they are naked and feel shame. We might even say that shame is the first consequence of the fall, though not the only one.

Next in the story, God condemns Adam, Eve, and the serpent, offering each a specific list of consequences for their disobedience. For example, the serpent must crawl on its belly, and Adam must work for his food. Eve will experience labor pains, and her husband will "rule over her" (3:16). What might the authors of this part of Genesis have intended to convey with these consequences? Were they meant to describe reality as we know it or to be a cautionary tale about disobeying God and the wrath that follows?

It's helpful, I think, to do a thought experiment here. Let's ask ourselves: What was God's plan before the fall and its consequences for how humans would eat and give birth? How was the snake to move around? If it isn't slithering on its belly, isn't it a lizard of some sort? What I am really asking here is: Are the "consequences" of the fall just descriptions of the realities of being human (or snake)? Birth is painful. We do have to toil for our food (or, more likely these days, pay someone to toil on our behalf). And if "consequences of the fall" means "an explanation of things as they are," we must turn our attention to one of the consequences given to Eve. Labor pain makes sense from an anatomical perspective, but what about "your husband shall rule over you"? Is it possible that the author is describing patriarchy as part of being human, as an inherent, almost required aspect of the status quo? Some feminist theologians have read this verse as indicating that patriarchy is a consequence of sin and therefore not intended by God. This is surely an interpretation that is valid and helpful, as oppression is never part of God's plan for humanity. But given the situation of this consequence in a list that includes something as inevitable as labor pain, perhaps the author is telling us something about what he sees as "the way things simply are." It's possible, then, that the author(s) of this passage viewed the subjugation of women to men as something quite natural, like a snake slithering around or a person having to work for their food.

Women We Know: Prophets, Poets, Warriors

After Eve, we encounter a number of significant women in the Book of Genesis. What makes them significant is their role in the covenant relationship God establishes with Abraham. So Hagar, Sarah, Rebecca, Leah, Rachel, Bilhah, and Zilpah are mothers of Israel in that they are the wives and concubines of the three patriarchs: Abraham, Isaac, and Jacob. We get glimpses of these women's lives in scripture. For example, the story of Sarah and Hagar highlights the jealousy and bitterness of Sarah at not being able to give Abraham a child. After Sarah encourages Abraham to have a child with Hagar, a servant, Sarah is consumed with jealousy. Later when Sarah discovers she is pregnant, she banishes Hagar and her son Ishmael into the desert to die. A similar dynamic is at work in the story of Leah and Rachel, two sisters who are married to Jacob. Jacob prefers the beautiful Rachel over the plain, tired Leah but is forced to marry the older sister and only subsequently gets access to Rachel. Both women bear Jacob's children.

In these stories of the patriarchs and matriarchs of Judaism, the women are instrumentalized and caricatured. That is, the primary purpose of the women in these stories is to bear children, the descendants God promised Abraham in exchange for Abraham's faith when they enter into a covenant. Without the women the covenant would not exist, but the women themselves aren't much more than simplistic figures. We hear of their jealousy, their physical appearance, but not much about their hopes or aspirations. We know little of how they related to God and much more about how the men in their lives (fathers, husbands, masters) relate to them.

Just as these matriarchs whose names we know are important in the success of the covenant, other women whose names are preserved for us also play key roles. Prophecy is one example. Miriam, Moses's sister, and Hulga, who appears in Judges, are two examples of women we can describe as prophets: they speak for God on behalf of justice to the whole community. In Miriam's case, she is explicitly called a prophet in the Book of Exodus (15:20), right before she breaks out a tambourine and leads the community in a song celebrating the triumph of God over the Egyptians. Scholars have noted that this moment is important, as it allows the women in the community to have their own moment of celebration (Miriam is said to have led the women out in singing). At other points, Miriam's work is crucial. For example, early in the story of the exodus, it is Miriam who makes sure that Moses is safe in the Nile, and when he is found by Pharaoh's daughter, Miriam ensures that her mother nurses Moses. Like Shiphrah and Puah, Miriam's actions ensure Moses's survival and, thereby, the survival and liberation of the Israelites. It's no wonder that Miriam later attests that God has spoken through her (Num 12), not only through Moses. This proclamation, however, leads her to be punished by God, with a skin ailment that lasts a week. Interestingly, and in a move we can interpret as a sign of her importance to the community, the Israelites do not leave Miriam behind while she heals. They wait for her before continuing their journey to the promised land.

A second example of a woman known to be a prophet is the little-known (in Christian circles) Huldah, who appears in the Second Book of Kings (chapter 22). Josiah, the king of Judah, is presented with an unknown book that foretells the destruction of Judah. When the king sends his servants to ask the Lord if this is true, the servants consult Huldah, the prophetess. She confirms the truth of the predictions in the book, using the phrase "thus says the LORD" multiple times, as one hears the major prophets like Isaiah and Jeremiah proclaim. Huldah declares that there will be destruction in the land and names the sins of the community, including abandoning God and worshiping idols. She also tells the servants that God has seen Josiah's contrition (he tore his garments, a sign of repentance, in v. 11) and that therefore Josiah will be spared. The servants take her message back to Josiah without hesitation.

It is precisely this lack of hesitation, explanation, or justification of the women's roles as prophets that merits our attention. Nowhere in either of these stories do the authors go out of their way to explain why they are calling a woman a prophet. It seems to require no special reasons, no ceremony, no clarification. They are simply prophets. Everyone recognizes them as prophets.

For the authors of these texts, God speaks to God's people through human intermediaries, regardless of their sex. Moreover, God speaks equally reliably through women and men. There seem to be no special ceremonies or markers, only the act of being chosen by God. It seems that grace does not discriminate on the basis of sex. Nor does it seem odd to the people of Israel and Judah that a woman would convey God's message. They don't discount it in any way or qualify it—she merely delivers God's message in a very regular way. Even though the Hebrew scriptures rarely profess the equality of men and women in regard to the law, to their standing in the community, to their ritual purity and other religious roles, it would seem that prophecy has no such sex divisions. How would our understanding of ministries be different today if we accepted that God speaks regularly through people of all genders, regardless of how they are regarded by the wider society?

Women and Sexual Violence: Bathsheba

So far we have looked at heroic women like Shiphrah and Puah and prophets like Miriam and Huldah. But not all the women with recognizable names in the Hebrew scriptures are known for heroism.

Indeed, some are known to us as victims of sexual violence, such as rape victims like Dinah. The clearest example of this is the woman after whom King David lusts, Bathsheba. The story of Bathsheba is well known and, for feminist biblical scholars, provides an example of how, by excluding women's perspectives and telling biblical stories solely from men's points of view, we might not notice instances of misogyny and sexual violence. King David, hailed as one of the greatest figures in Israel for his wisdom and political savvy, sees a woman bathing and is consumed with lust. That woman, Bathsheba, is married to Uriah, a general in David's army. Presumably because of her great beauty, the king decides he must have her and orders her to his palace where, in the words of the text, "he took her" (2 Sam 11:4). David also orders that her husband be sent to the front lines of battle, ensuring that he will be killed. The drama of this story plays out when the prophet Nathan confronts David for his misdeeds, namely, adultery and murder. But the charge of adultery instead of rape is an interesting one. Though we will get into women's relationship to the law later in this chapter, we must take note that David's crimes are stealing another man's wife and having that man killed. Nathan assures David that he has incurred God's wrath and must repent. David does and God forgives him. Nathan in this exchange becomes one of the few prophets to challenge political authority and live to tell about it.

Feminist biblical scholar Cheryl Exum invites us to look more closely at the story of David and Bathsheba, told to children basically as a romantic tale of love at first sight. Exum invites readers to note that this episode occurs in the context of a war (Uriah is away at battle) and to remember how rape and sexual violence are used as weapons of war. We must also ask ourselves whether Bathsheba is free to turn down a summons from the king of Israel. If she had not wanted to go to David, if she had known full well what his intentions were and been terrified or repulsed, it would have changed nothing. The power differential between the king and his subject Bathsheba ensures that she cannot make a free choice in this scenario. But beyond all this, says Exum, since we cannot know the motivations or inner workings of these characters as presented in the Second Book of Samuel, we must instead examine the text itself. There, Bathsheba is treated as an object. Says Exum, "The point is not what Bathsheba might have done or felt; the point is we are not allowed access to her point of view."[1] By erasing her subjectivity, by robbing the reader of Bathsheba's thoughts, motivations, and experience, the narrator objectifies her, making her merely a pawn in the story of David's lust, power, and possibly violence. It becomes a story of a king's repentance, not of the violation of a woman.

When we assume that the sight of a woman bathing makes men's lust uncontrollable and therefore a sexual encounter inevitable, we are perpetuating a culture of rape. David could have felt many different things when he looked out from his rooftop and saw a naked woman. He may have felt sheepish, intrusive, or ashamed. Instead, he wanted to take possession of her. David is the aggressor, and Bathsheba has, as far as the reader knows, no say. By repeating this story, and indeed casting it as a romantic one—"she was so beautiful he had to have her"—readers, catechists, preachers, and teachers perpetuate the falsehood that women's beauty is their primary source of value and that this beauty is also a liability. If she's seen by a powerful man, she can expect that he will "have to have her." Some interpreters focus on Bathsheba's beauty or her brazenness in being visible while bathing. Perhaps these thinkers do not realize how their emphasis on Bathsheba's action (or inaction), on her physical attributes, makes her at least partly responsible for David's transgression. This is rape culture: the assumption that unless women take precautions against it, the way of the world dictates that men will sexually violate them. The charge is made that her rape is her fault. But it doesn't have to be this way. We can read Bathsheba's story against the grain: look at David as a flawed man who sins greatly. We can strive to have empathy for how her subjectivity has been erased (like so many victims of sexual violence), and we can commit to seeing how the Bible and its interpreters have served to endorse a culture where rape is inevitable.

Sadly, Bathsheba's story, though perhaps the most well-known, is far from the only instance of sexual violence recorded in scripture. Feminist interpreters have pointed out that Esther, who is hailed as a queen who helped deliver the Jews from destruction at the hands of Haman, is a victim of sexual violation and even of human trafficking. Perhaps the most horrifically abused of these victims are the unnamed women (a virgin daughter and the concubine of a Levite traveler) in Judges 19. Faced with an angry mob asking to rape the traveler, the old man who has sheltered him delivers his virgin daughter and his guest's concubine out of the house in order to appease them. The old man encourages the mob to "use them and do to them whatever you wish" (v. 24) as long as the male traveler is spared. When the concubine is returned, gang raped and dumped half-dead on the threshold, the Levite continues to his home, where he dismembers her. There is, as Phyllis Trible points out, nothing redeeming in this story. We nevertheless must look at it in order to remember the story as a memorial of the terror visited upon women in every age.

Women as Warriors

We have seen women as prophets and women as victims of sexual violence. Women in the Hebrew scriptures are also warriors for justice, like Judith or Jael. Judith, a beautiful widow, famously beheads Holofernes in the thirteenth chapter of the book that bears her name, delivering the Israelites from the Assyrians. Jael kills Sisera, a general, by driving a tent peg through his temple (nobody said the Bible wasn't explicit!) in Judges 4. The following chapter (Judg 5) hails Jael as a warrior—certainly not a beautiful maiden and mother, the roles associated at present with so-called biblical womanhood. Both women defy the stereotypical roles assigned to holy women as meek and subservient. They are brave warriors who plan and execute these plans to fulfill an objective: the protection and liberation of their community. Their actions are violent, even gory. God is understood to be working through them.

The Book of Ruth is a tale of female friendship and loyalty. Ruth, the heroine of the tale, is recently widowed and childless. She and her mother-in-law, Naomi, form a bond and work together to ensure their survival in a world where a woman who was widowed without children had zero in the way of a social safety net. What's more, their community is in the midst of a famine, forcing them to leave in search of food. Destitute and without protectors, Ruth and Naomi experience precarity and hunger. They are forced, as Juliana Claassens points out, into degrading and dangerous work like gleaning in the fields, where men harassed women working alone. Naomi, like Job in the Hebrew scriptures, names her anger at God and declares herself a bitter woman. Her husband and sons have died! But rather than remain in this bitterness or fall into despair, Naomi is instrumental in identifying a means of liberation for herself and her daughter-in-law, Ruth. In a foreign land, Naomi finds Obed, a man willing to marry Ruth and eventually give her a son, ensuring that both Ruth and Naomi will be cared for and protected. The story of the unbreakable bond between Naomi and Ruth, the daughter-in-law who refuses to abandon her to her misery by saying, "Your people will be my people and your god my god" (Ruth 1:15), depicts a different sort of warrior. Naomi and Ruth are both warriors against despair. It requires no less courage than that of Jael and of Judith to stare starvation and violence in the face and refuse to give up. Indeed, our world is riddled with stories of women who are forced to migrate, who are taken advantage of, who are left for dead. Naomi and Ruth model courage in the face of social injustice.

In short, women's stories are portrayed in the Hebrew scriptures with more variety and more fidelity to women's lived reality than we often appreciate. Whether as violent warriors willing to do whatever it takes to save their communities, or as women discarded by society after tragedy, biblical womanhood encompasses far more than obedience to a husband or a father. Women in the Hebrew scriptures are persistent, inventive, and brave.

Women in the Law

What accounts for the difference between how we think biblical women behave and how they are portrayed in the stories above? While part of the answer is certainly the male-focused writing and history of interpretation, we must also look at the difference between descriptive and prescriptive language in the texts. In short, not all language accomplishes the same thing. Some language (descriptive) tells a story, gives details, paints a picture of how things are/were. Many of the stories of the women named above are descriptive: they tell specific stories of women, how they act in certain situations, what happens to them. Other parts of the Bible are prescriptive, especially commandments and laws. Prescriptive language tells us how things *ought* to be, not necessarily how they are. Women's lives figure in important ways in prescriptive languages as the law (Torah) discusses specific rules for women's lives. Some of these (the more infamous ones) relate to women's sexuality. One particularly stark example is Exodus 22:16, which decrees that a man who seduces a virgin who is not betrothed to any man (an act feminist interpreters have pointed out is rape, since her consent is nowhere mentioned) should pay a fine and marry her. The only consent mentioned is that of the virgin's father, in the next verse. If her father refuses to give her to her rapist, the fine increases. Other laws, known as the laws of niddah, have to do with menstruation and impurity. Leviticus 15:19–32 declares that women who are menstruating are unclean and outlines the process for cleansing a woman after she has menstruated. Similarly, Leviticus 18:19 prohibits a man from having sex with a woman while she is having her period because the act renders him unclean or defiled. While it is not unique to Judaism to consider menstrual blood as something that is impure and that therefore should be avoided, like the issue of rape above, it treats women as a class and prescribes how the community is to treat them. Jewish law also delineates liturgical responsibilities or ritual obligations based on sex, rooted in the gendered language found at various points in the Torah, such as Exodus 23:17, which asks that all of Israel's males take part in the harvest festival. By excluding women from this obligation, legal scholars surmised that women were not obligated to take part in many religious festivals that happened at specific times during the year. Judith Plaskow points out that throughout the law, women are viewed collectively as a class, largely through prescriptive language: there aren't laws pertaining to individual women so much as to women in general. This class is viewed as marginal to the major players in Jewish law, all of whom are men.

It is the realm of women's sexuality where the prescriptive law is most attentive to women's lives. Recall that part of the feminist approach to scripture involves acknowledging that these texts are written and interpreted from a male perspective. Thus, women's most intimate lives, and indeed the laws that determine their fate in many cases, are written and interpreted without their input. The most salient of these laws pertain to virginity. A woman's sexuality was the property of her family—first her father and then her spouse. In the Hebrew Bible, sex is allowed only within marriage. Extramarital sex is permitted with an unmarried woman, otherwise it is considered adultery. Women, on the other hand, may not have sex outside marriage. The sin of adultery, however, is not primarily a sin of lust but rather of theft. How do we know this? Because the punishments involve financial restitution or some other restitution that prioritizes the owner's property. For example, the punishment for rape of an unmarried (virgin) woman is that the woman must marry her rapist and he must pay a fine. Evidently no women were consulted about this arrangement. Laws controlling women's sexuality remind us that women's lives have historically been determined by marriages in which they have had little or no input. This is reflected in scripture, in the story of Rachel and Leah we mentioned earlier, to cite just one example.

Women's bodies are also a locus of sin and grace. For this reason, many laws in the Hebrew scriptures pertain to women's menstrual cycles, the avoidance of sex during this time, and the rites of purification that make a woman available for sex to her husband once again. Women's bodies are also bound by modesty laws that dictate how and when a woman should cover her hair and skin so as not to arouse men or tempt them. Throughout the Hebrew scriptures, Plaskow points out, female sexuality is viewed as powerful and therefore in need of control. Often that control is exerted by rules made by men and imposed on women.

Women's Resistance

Some feminist scholars believe it is important to read the Hebrew scriptures against the grain, emphasizing different aspects of women's lives, such as in the ways they resist social norms and work against violence and injustice. One such thinker, Juliana Claassens, reminds us that reading against the grain, with an emphasis on women's agency (however subtle it might seem), allows readers to grasp the fullness of women's experience in the Hebrew scriptures. Claassens identifies various forms of resistance used by women facing dehumanizing circumstances. Some of these include lament, hospitality, legal appeals, and trickery. So, for example, in the story of the rape of Tamar in 2 Samuel 13, where her brother Amnon rapes and then discards Tamar like a filthy object, Claassens focuses on Tamar's shaming speech in verses 12–13 begging her brother to reconsider his violence in light of what it means to her, to his family, and to the broader community. Though in the end this resistance does not convince her rapist, and Tamar is still victimized, that the resistance is included in the text is significant for those of us reading with an eye toward women's agency. Even in the face of total dehumanization, Tamar has the courage to stand up to the man who will do violence to her.

There are many stories like Tamar's in the Old Testament that document the dehumanization of women. In Genesis 34, Dinah, the daughter of Leah and Jacob, is raped by Shechem. The text adds, by way of explanation, that his "soul was drawn" to her and that he loved her, even though the previous verse says plainly that he forced her to have sex. The thirteenth chapter of the Book of Daniel recounts the planned rape of Susanna by two elders of Israel, who were "overwhelmed with passion" for her. Her rapists lie and have her condemned to death, and she is saved only by the intervention of the prophet Daniel. Women endure all manner of violence including rape, murder, dismemberment (see the Levite's concubine in Judg 19), famine, barrenness, and exile (Ruth and Naomi as well). For scholars like Phyllis Trible, we must remember these stories as texts of terror because to forget these women victims is to victimize them anew. And indeed, as Claassens points out, much of the work of resistance to dehumanization throughout history is done by women whose names are never known. Countless actions of hospitality, trickery, bravery, active and passive resistance, and lamentation have occurred in history and are very likely to be forgotten since women's work has existed at the margins of society. But in lifting up these stories and looking intently at the resistance strategies embedded within them, we memorialize not only the scriptural characters but also the women in the past and the present whose lives are acts of resistance to violence and death-dealing social systems.

It is impossible to do justice to the varied ways in which women are portrayed in texts as complex as the Hebrew scriptures. What this chapter has tried to show is that if we pay attention to genre and characterization, what we see in the Old Testament about women's lives is far more intricate than the notions of "good biblical womanhood" that are passed down to us in prescriptive religious language. Indeed, the Hebrew scriptures include many examples of prophetic women, warrior women, brave, defiant women. These texts also include examples of women who are killed, raped, and violated, treated as objects and disregarded. Some women are symbols, like Eve. Others are inspirations, like Miriam. There are tales of female friendship, like that between Ruth and Naomi, and tales of erotic love, as the one found in Song of Songs. While many of the laws and commandments in the Hebrew scriptures treat women as objects and as others, there are many ways that we can trace women's resistance to objectification and dehumanization in these same texts. As we look toward the portrayal of women in the Christian scriptures in the next chapter, we would do well to remember the context set forth in the Hebrew scriptures of women's complex relationships to the law, to the covenant, and to prophecy.

DISCUSSION QUESTIONS

1. Many students are shocked that women weren't considered reliable witnesses at trials in the ancient world. Can you think of contemporary examples where women's testimony was discounted or ignored, or does this phenomenon not happen anymore?
2. Reflect on how menstruation is introduced and taught to adolescents in your experience. What prevailing feelings are associated with this biological reality? How are girls taught to think about and deal with menstruation in your community? What about boys?
3. Does your institution have a handbook for students? Go through it and identify examples of descriptive and prescriptive language. Do these modes of discourse tend to apply to different groups? Why is this?

DELVE DEEPER

Recently, feminist authors outside Catholicism, such as Beth Allison Barr, have begun reflecting on how notions of "biblical womanhood" have been used to uphold patriarchy. What do you think of when you think of the phrase "biblical womanhood"? Design an ad campaign for a product or service of your choice that features some women in this chapter like Ruth, Judith, or Jael.

READ FURTHER

Claassens, Juliana. *Claiming Her Dignity: Female Resistance in the Old Testament*. Collegeville, MN: Liturgical Press, 2016.

Exum, Cheryl. *Fragmented Women: Feminist (Sub)versions of Biblical Narratives*. New York: Bloomsbury, 1993.

Junior, Nyasha. *An Introduction to Womanist Biblical Interpretation*. Louisville: Westminster John Knox Press, 2015.

Plaskow, Judith. *Standing Again at Sinai: Judaism from a Feminist Perspective*. San Francisco: HarperOne, 1991.

Scholz, Susanne. *Sacred Witness: Rape in the Hebrew Bible*. Philadelphia: Fortress Press, 2010.

Trible, Phyllis. *Texts of Terror: Literary-Feminist Readings of Biblical Narratives*. Philadelphia: Fortress Press, 1984.

8

WOMEN IN THE CHRISTIAN SCRIPTURES AND THE EARLY CHRISTIAN COMMUNITIES

The New Testament, or Christian scriptures, provides Catholics and other Christians with the foundational narratives of our faith. Like the Hebrew scriptures, the Christian scriptures were composed over many years and by different authors in different historical, social, and religious contexts. Inevitably, there are differences between and among the texts we find in the New Testament, and these differences add richness to the tapestry that forms the foundation of our faith.

Reading the Christian Scriptures: Genres and Blind Spots

Like the Hebrew scriptures, the Christian scriptures contain a variety of genres, though because there are only twenty-seven books, the number of genres is also smaller. The texts of the New Testament are gospels, epistles, theological history (the Acts of the

Apostles), and apocalyptic literature. While all Christians are surely familiar with the stories of Jesus's life retold in the Gospels, it is important to remember that gospel, as a genre, is not the same as a biography. So, while the Gospels narrate Jesus's life, they are written in order to inspire belief and not as an eyewitness account of Jesus's life story. This is why there are several versions of the same stories and sayings in the four Gospels.

One way to think about this is to imagine yourself writing a biography of a famous person. Let's say you are tasked with writing a biography of Kobe Bryant. A student athlete might begin the story with Kobe's early success in pee-wee basketball and trace his career, his training tactics, his nutrition and diet, his pregame and postgame rituals. A business or international marketing major might begin the Kobe biography with his days in the European basketball leagues as a precursor to his success securing sponsorships in the United States and abroad. A student interested in gender studies might probe the sex assault allegations against the player, while other students might not even mention those. All biographies, then, are perspectival—the details and stories an author selects for inclusion depend on what the author wants to emphasize in a person's life, who the audience is, and what sources are available to draw from (personal interviews, news reports, government records, etc.).

In some ways, the Gospels are like this. There are four accounts, each written at least one generation after the death of Jesus, when it had become apparent to his followers that his promise to come again wasn't to be fulfilled next week or even next year. Keep in mind, the earliest followers of Jesus believed the second coming was imminent—due next week or next month, so it seemed impractical to write down the story of his life. Eventually, when the apocalypse never came, the written accounts followed an oral tradition. But the Gospels are more than just written accounts of Jesus's life. They are "written so that you may believe." They are meant to inspire the reader to believe that Jesus is the Messiah. In this way, they differ even from traditional, perspectival biographies. The four Gospels that are in the New Testament take different perspectives and have different audiences in mind, but all of them seek to move the reader in a spiritual way.

Perhaps the most misunderstood genre in the New Testament is the apocalyptic literature we find in the Book of Revelation. Long the source of speculation about the end of the world, the content in Revelation has spawned many a History Channel show about how humanity will meet its demise. The "secrets" contained in the Book of Revelation lead people to look at the text as if it were something from Nostradamus or a psychic. But apocalyptic literature is more like contemporary science fiction. It's a reflection on the present, a type of literature that says, "If things continue as they are, this is what the future will be like." Think of *The Handmaid's Tale*, not the Psychic Friends Network. Adding to the difficulty in deciphering Revelation is that because it was written when Christianity was still illegal, it uses coded language to deliver a message of consolation to persecuted Christians. If persecution continued as it was, Christians should be prepared for a battle, but God would emerge triumphant over the heavens and the earth. That is certainly a consoling message for a persecuted community. And that is what we have in the Book of Revelation (please, notice it does not have an *S* at the end!): not a play-by-play of the end of time, but a promise of victory over unjust suffering.

Apocalyptic literature might be the most obscure or difficult to decipher. The Gospels constitute the core of the New Testament, where we learn about Jesus's life, his words, and his actions. But neither of these are the oldest literature in the Christian scriptures: that title goes to the letters traditionally attributed to Paul, sometimes called epistles. Maybe you have read an epistolary novel like *The Perks of Being a Wallflower*, which is a story told through an exchange of letters. The epistles of Paul are like *half* of an epistolary novel. In other words, what we have as the letters is one-half of an exchange, usually Paul's response to specific questions from or issues that arose in communities of Christians that he had founded throughout the Roman Empire. We don't have any of the letters that came from the community. So, in this genre, we frequently see Paul contradicting himself—he says in a letter to the Galatians (3:28) that in Christ there is no male or female (a sign of fundamental equality), but to the Ephesians, he says that women should submit to their husbands. Did he have no integrity in his views? More likely, each community was dealing with different realities. After all, you wouldn't have to caution women to be quiet in church if they weren't speaking to begin with!

While the situations that prompted Paul's written responses are lost to history for the most part, we do know that the earliest Christian communities had different geographic and social contexts, different needs and organizational structures. Men and women worked together in these communities, in different ways, to live out the message of Jesus and prepare for the coming reign of God. We know that the Middle East in the first century was marked by patriarchal social structures, where women were viewed as property and men were the decision-makers. We also know that the first-century matrix out of which Christianity emerged also brought about Rabbinic Judaism and that these two faith traditions are like siblings in many ways. The familial relationships between early Judaism (where worship was based in the temple) and the emerging group of Christians might be likened to a divorcing couple.

At first, all Christians were Jewish. When it became clear that this group was asserting that Jesus's spirit was still with them, and as characterizations of Jesus made clear that this community saw Jesus as divine, the relationship between Judaism and the Christians became strained. Judaism is strictly monotheistic, and any talk of an enduring Spirit sounds like a second God. If you factor in the political and social difficulties that the Jewish community was experiencing under Roman occupation, including the destruction of the second temple, then the expulsion of Christians from the Jewish community makes more sense. It just wasn't a tenable relationship anymore.

Why do we need to know this? Because along with a patriarchal backdrop, the New Testament contains many passages that disparage the Jewish community. These passages have fueled anti-Semitism by Christians, often including physical violence. When we view the New Testament as literature written in the midst of a nasty divorce, we contextualize the disparaging portraits of "the Jews." Contextualization and historical consciousness are vital if we are to understand the Christian scriptures or indeed any text at all.

A further issue that complicates Catholics' understanding of the New Testament is that for many years, Catholics didn't really read the Bible. Most Catholics are exposed to the scriptures through liturgy, in other words, at Mass. The Mass readings are from the lectionary, which is a selection of biblical passages that moves in cycles (two-year cycles for weekday Masses, three-year cycles for Sundays) in order to cover the majority of scripture in the liturgy. The Roman Catholic lectionary is determined by a panel of experts under the auspices of the Vatican, and it is periodically revised. There are historical reasons for this, of course. As Latino theologian Orlando Espín has pointed out, the vast majority of Roman Catholics for the vast majority of the church's history have been, and continue to be, the lay poor. This overwhelming majority was, for the better part of history, illiterate and therefore could not read the Bible. But that was okay, the church claimed, because the Bible is not easy to understand. Thus, the way to ensure that people learned what was in the scriptures was to have them hear it and explained to them at Mass.

Times have changed, and more people can and do read the Bible on their own (thank you, printing press and Martin Luther!). But still, many Catholics hear and learn the scriptures primarily at Mass. The problem is that the text we read from at Mass is the lectionary, which consists of reading from the scriptures. The lectionary is not, however, the whole Bible. Pieces are left out, especially problematic ones (sometimes this is good, as in the case of the texts of terror mentioned in the previous chapter). The lectionary also adds phrases to make the narratives flow better. For example, at Mass we often hear “Brothers and sisters” before any reading from the epistles (usually the second reading). Paul doesn’t say it that often! It’s there to let the listener know that this is from a letter. The lectionary is one reason why some stories feel familiar and others do not. When feminist theologians point out, for example, the many places in scripture where God is represented by a feminine image (a mother hen in Matt 23:37 and Ps 91:4), many Christians react in shock. “I didn’t know that was in the Bible!” they say. One reason is the lectionary. Christian understandings of the New Testament are mediated through the lectionary, and the lectionary doesn’t contain every single passage in the New Testament! This is why some stories seem familiar and others not.

Here’s another example. How often do you hear Jesus or God referred to as “the good shepherd”? A good shepherd who leaves the ninety-nine sheep in order to seek out the one who is lost is the central image in a parable in Luke 15:4–7. That chapter also features the parable of the prodigal son (vv. 11–42). These are two well-known stories told by Jesus to explain the reign of God and the kind of mercy God shows to people. Tucked between those two famous stories is the parable of the lost coin (v. 8–10). In that one, God is like a woman who has lost a coin, who turns her house inside out to find it. When the coin is found she has a party with her neighbors. All three parables (the sheep, the coin, the prodigal son) are about the joy God feels when someone lost is returned to God's embrace. But the woman rejoicing in the coin is as obscure as the prodigal son and lost sheep are well-known. The lectionary is one reason because we rarely hear this one at Mass. Patriarchy is another, not-unrelated reason. After all, who compiled the lectionary? Not women.

Jesus and Women

Just because women were likely not the writers or compilers of scripture or the lectionary doesn't mean that women aren't all over the New Testament. They are. All four Gospels contain stories that feature Jesus's mother, Jesus's women disciples like Mary and Martha of Bethany, or Mary Magdalene. The Gospels also show Jesus interacting with women: he heals them, speaks to them, teaches them, and learns from them. It seems ridiculous to even mention it, but at no point do the gospel writers isolate Jesus from women. Their presence is unremarkable because women are part of Jesus's context and because there was no shame in that fact. Similarly, the letters of Paul and the other epistles in the New Testament demonstrate clearly that women were part of the earliest Christian communities, even though their roles in these communities are varied and somewhat difficult to map onto contemporary church structures. Even the Book of Revelation contains women characters. At no point is the New Testament a set of narratives about men only. Neither can we characterize early Christian communities as exclusive boys' clubs.

It would be impossible for us to explore every single woman mentioned in the New Testament. Our work gets even more daunting if we take a look at Jesus's interactions with women, his attitudes toward women. We might also ask how Jesus's actions relate to the prevailing attitudes about women. In approaching any kind of study of the Bible, for our purposes, it's also very important to examine how feminist interpreters have gone about their work. Whew. That is a lot for one course, let alone one textbook. The most we can do is highlight important persons, themes, and methods in this chapter. Future chapters will look at Mary, Jesus's mother, and at the roles of women in ministry in the early church and beyond, so we can bracket both of these topics for now. We will proceed as follows: first, a close look at Mary Magdalene, who is a towering figure in Christianity. Then we will examine how Jesus interacts with women in the gospel narratives: in friendship with women, in defense of women, as a healer of women, and as a student of women. We will then look at the resurrection narratives to see how feminist scripture scholars understand the testimony of women in the Gospels. Finally, we will take a brief glance at women's roles in the earliest Christian communities as those are presented in the Pauline and Catholic epistles.

Mary Magdalene: Her Reputation and Her Reality

Perhaps the most important thing to communicate in this chapter—and maybe the most important fact about a woman in the New Testament—is that what you may have heard about Mary Magdalene is all wrong. In fact, it's difficult to imagine a more effective smear campaign than the one that has been waged against Mary Magdalene in the history of Christianity. Poets, painters, sculptors, authors have all participated in the effort to portray Mary Magdalene as a reformed prostitute, a woman of ill repute, and a whore—but a whore who saw the light, whose friendship with Jesus brought her out of a life of sin and into one of virtue. You have to admit it's a great redemption story. Unfortunately, it's false. Not the part where a friendship with Jesus changes someone's life—we see that happen many times in the Gospels. The whore part. Despite centuries of theologians and authors and priests and poets clamoring about Mary Magdalene's sordid past, despite the many artistic masterpieces that depict her as a seductress, and even despite *The Da Vinci*

Code, which made this fabrication into a Hollywood legend, Mary Magdalene is not a prostitute. At no point does any gospel narrative say that Mary Magdalene was caught in adultery. Look for yourself in the Gospels. So how did she get such an awful reputation?

Mary Magdalene's origin story in the Gospels appears in Mark 16:9 and Luke 8:2. Mark is the older text, and there the author mentions that after the resurrection, Jesus appeared to Mary Magdalene "from whom he had cast out seven demons." Luke gives us Mary Magdalene's story well before Jesus's death and resurrection, during his ministry. In Luke 8:1–3, we see Jesus journeying through the countryside with the "twelve apostles, some women who had been cured of evil spirits and infirmities: Mary, called Magdalene, from whom he had cast out seven demons." Nevertheless, the scripture makes no mention of Mary Magdalene being an adulteress, a woman who had had several husbands (that's an unnamed Samaritan woman in John 4), or a repentant sinner. Instead, we have a woman who had been cured of many demons. Are we accustomed to equating husbands with demonic possession? Not exactly. We do learn from the author of Luke that Mary Magdalene and some other women provided for Jesus out of their own resources. So she was a woman of means, not a woman with a past. She was one of the women who bankrolled Jesus's ministry, not his secret wife. (Sorry, Dan Brown. Though I wish I had thought of that story!)

How did she get cast as a prostitute, and in such a convincing way that she is painted as a wanton woman in nearly every depiction of her in the Western canon? There are many explanations for this. The first is that readers, like nature, abhor a vacuum. Most of the women in the New Testament (and, indeed, in the entire Bible) are unnamed. The woman with the five husbands? Not Mary Magdalene. The one who is caught in adultery? Also no. The one who breaks the alabaster jar of perfume over Jesus's feet and dries them with her hair? Dramatic, amazing, memorable, but not Mary Magdalene. In fact, we know none of these women's names. They all had names and lives and unique identities. They were all drawn to Jesus for a variety of reasons: for healing, for praise, or just because they were in the right place at the right time. But importantly, they were not all the same woman. And most certainly, none of these women were Mary Magdalene. How do I know this? Because Mary Magdalene is named. She is important to the gospel writers. Whenever she appears as part of a group, her name appears first in the list of women, and this is a testament to how important she was to the early Christian communities. They knew her, they remembered her, and they thought she should be remembered by name. If any of those unnamed women had been the Magdalene, the gospel writers would've said so. They didn't!

A second reason for Mary Magdalene's bad reputation is that it provides an important contrast to the image Christians have of Mary, the mother of Jesus. Like Eve, Mary Magdalene provides a good foil for Jesus's mother. Since the Gospels have little to say about either woman, readers, interpreters, and preachers filled in the tradition with contrasting lives and personalities to highlight Mary's virginal purity and God's boundless mercy (in Mary Magdalene's case). This also speaks to how patriarchal cultures reduce women to caricatures. Because women are excluded from meaning-making and public discourse in patriarchal societies, the full range of their humanity remains hidden away. In the twenty-first century, we know that women are more complicated than the sexual expression that takes place in their lives. But, in a culture where women were viewed as property and valued based on their virginity or lack thereof, we were limited to two views of women: good/virginal and bad/impure. Because Mary Magdalene is nowhere referred to as a shy, retiring virgin, she must be the "other kind of woman." She wasn't, of course. She was a woman of means, who had been healed by Jesus. Ultimately, this good woman/bad woman binary says more about patriarchal culture than it does about biblical women, who are portrayed in a variety of ways: as mothers, as independent women, as friends of Jesus, as workers and ministers in the earliest Christian communities. Many women in the New Testament are married, and many are not. We do not know the marital status of many others. So, while a woman's sexual status (married, unmarried, virginal or not) might be the measure of her value in societies marked by sexist values, the writers of the New Testament did not necessarily see women this way.

Some of you may be wondering if the Hollywood versions of Mary Magdalene's life have some truth to them. Was she married to Jesus? Is it possible that they had a family that was hidden by the gospel writers to preserve the idea of Jesus's godliness? The answer is simple: no. Scholars are certain that the answer is no because the question, like the question of whether women must fall into the "virgin or whore" categories, says more about our culture than it does about Jesus's. If Jesus and Mary Magdalene had been family, or betrothed, the gospel writers would have mentioned it. Our desire to believe that Jesus was "secretly married" says a lot about how we feel about genuine friendship between men and women (that it's not really possible without sexual attraction, which is silly), and, more important for our work here, it says a great deal about what we think about the relationship between sexuality and the divine. Put simply, it is our own puritanical understanding of sex as dirty or wrong that leads us to think that someone would hide their marriage if they were "really" the messiah. Jesus could have married but did not.

Let's look at Peter, who Catholic tradition reveres as the first pope, the man upon whom Jesus built the church. Obviously, modern-day popes are not married. But Peter was. Many Catholics are surprised to learn this and assume there is a record of Peter's marriage in some obscure historical text. The answer is plain in scripture: Jesus heals Peter's mother-in-law. Three of the Gospels narrate this (Mark 1:29–31; Luke 4:38–39; Matt 8:14–15) in a matter-of-fact way. Only married people have mothers-in-law. The straightforward way in which the narratives present Peter's wife's mother tells the reader that there is nothing unusual or untoward about Peter having a wife. It's not a surrender to his baser instincts, as marriage would come to be viewed later in Christian history. The story of her healing is merely another sign of Jesus's power and his service to his friends.

So if Mary Magdalene wasn't a prostitute, and she wasn't Jesus's wife, and she wasn't a repentant, shamed sinner, then who was she? And who might she be for us today?

First and foremost, Mary Magdalene was an apostle of Jesus. While she was not a member of the symbolic Twelve (meant to mirror the twelve tribes of Israel), she was an important follower of Jesus, a witness to his many miracles and his ministry, a patron of that ministry, and among his most loyal friends. All four Gospels name her as a witness to the crucifixion and the resurrection. She never abandoned Jesus, even when all of his male friends did. She was also one of the first people to see the risen Jesus, to know that God's promises had been fulfilled in him in a way none of his followers had imagined.

Mary Magdalene's presence in all four resurrection narratives demands our attention. Rarely are all four Gospels in agreement about witnesses to a particular event. Moreover, the writers of the Gospels came from cultures (first-century Judaism, as discussed in the previous chapter) where women's testimony was essentially worthless. And yet, all the narratives of Jesus's resurrection portray that central fact of the faith through the testimony of a woman. Mary Magdalene sees the Lord (or the angel in the garden, or the empty tomb, depending on the gospel), and then she runs to tell the other apostles. In Greek (the original language of the New Testament), apostle means "one who is sent." Surely, Mary Magdalene fulfills this role, as she runs from the empty tomb to tell the disciples who were in hiding that Jesus is alive. For this reason, she is known in the tradition as the "Apostle to the Apostles." But she is also the first to preach the gospel—the good news of Jesus's resurrection—when she says, "I have seen the Lord." As Fr. James Martin has pointed out, in the time between leaving the empty tomb and reaching the room where the other disciples were gathered, only Mary Magdalene bore the truth of the paschal mystery. Only she knew the key to the story, the resurrection of Jesus that the church still proclaims. For this reason, in those minutes between her realization and her proclamation, says Fr. Martin, Mary Magdalene was the whole church.

One biblical scholar, Dr. Joan Taylor, has advanced a fascinating theory about Mary Magdalene's name. While this theory isn't official church teaching, it's an interesting scholarly theory and one that might be fun to consider. Normally, scripture characters are identified by their places of origin (Jesus the Nazarene, Joseph of Arimathea) or by their familial relationships (the sons of Zebedee, the wife of Pilate). Mary Magdalene presents a peculiar case because she is not named for any male relation (a father or husband). Further, Professor Taylor notes that there is no specific town named "Magdala" in first-century Judea and no such town mentioned in the earliest New Testament writings.[1] There were, however, towers, called *migdala*, scattered throughout the region. While many people assume that Magdalene is a reference to her place of origin, like Jesus the Nazarene, Taylor suggests the possibility Magdalene might be a particular nickname given to her by Jesus. Something like calling Simon "Peter" or "the Rock." Drawing on the ambiguity of the word and the lack of evidence of a specific town of origin,

Taylor thinks that perhaps Jesus called this Mary "the Tower" as a sign of her closeness to him, or her prominence among his followers, or something like that. As a thought experiment, let us imagine that Taylor is correct and that, just as Peter was somehow the rock of the church, Magdalene is its tower. How does that change our perception of Mary Magdalene? What sort of art might depict this new image? How might the tradition surrounding her change?

Jesus and Other Women: His Friends, His Confidants, His Teachers

Mary Magdalene is the most prominent and well-known of the women in the New Testament (with the exception of Jesus's mother), but there are many other women with whom Jesus interacted throughout his ministry. For example, Mary and Martha of Bethany were some of Jesus's closest friends, along with their brother Lazarus. The Gospels show us Jesus staying at their house, dining and talking with them, as friends do. When Lazarus dies, Jesus goes to his friends and shares in their grief ("Jesus wept" is the shortest sentence in the New Testament). He absorbs Martha's anger at his delayed arrival, he mourns with them, accompanies them, and revives Lazarus, restoring the family to wholeness. These moments of genuine humanity and friendship from Jesus help us to see him as a caring person, someone who formed lasting, significant relationships.

Jesus healed many women too. He heals the woman with the hemorrhage who touches his cloak, Jairus's daughter, and Peter's mother-in-law, as mentioned above. In a countercultural moment of bravery, Jesus defends a woman who is caught in adultery and about to be stoned to death. By coming to her defense, he questions the justice that would punish a woman for a sin that two people commit together. Knowing what we know about the prevalence of sexual assault, how many women must have been punished by death after being raped and "caught in adultery"? Jesus steps in to spare this woman, pointing instead to the sin of those who would condemn her. While we couldn't exactly call this a feminist move on Jesus's part, it is a move toward justice, toward solidarity with the victims of injustice.

A final interesting relationship between a woman and Jesus happens when he meets a Syrophoenician (or in some accounts, Canaanite) woman whose daughter is ill. The Gospels of Mark and Matthew both narrate an encounter that takes place in Tyre, which is a region in Lebanon. As a Syrophoenician/Canaanite, she was a Samaritan, a member of a group hated by Jews of Jesus's time because they were viewed as traitors. Jesus's disciples urge him to shoo the woman away as she begs him to save her daughter from demons. Several things are fascinating about this scene. First, Jesus is kind of a jerk. He sees a person in need, and we know he's not against helping Samaritans or seeing them as good people (remember the parable of the Good Samaritan!). But Jesus compares her to a dog (a dog!) in saying that it is not fair to take the children's food and throw it to the dogs (Mark 7:27). It is strange for us to see Jesus refusing to help someone. Perhaps that's why this was a memorable moment that made it into the Markan account of Jesus's life. Further, it's weird for Jesus to refuse on the basis of her being an outsider. After all, wasn't Jesus's whole ministry about reaching out to outsiders and undesirables? Sinners, tax collectors, prostitutes, women caught in adultery all find a home in Jesus's circle.

A second remarkable thing is that the woman is not dissuaded by this insult. She has, in fact, a quick reply, the kind we all wish we could think of on the spot when someone surprises us with rudeness. Immediately she notes that even the dogs get the crumbs that children drop from the table (v. 28). What is amazing about this retort is that she responds to Jesus using his own imagery and his own method of using imagery to teach. So she runs with the idea of the dogs and the kids and the table, and she turns it around. In doing this, she challenges Jesus to reconsider his attitude, to go beyond what he thought was possible.

The most remarkable thing about this passage is that we see Jesus learning from a woman in real time, as it were. How do we know that Jesus learned something? Because he changes! He changes his mind, and he changes his attitude. The very next verse tells us that he reconsidered, telling the woman that her words have saved her daughter. In Matthew's account, Jesus effusively praises this woman for her faith (Matt 15:28). This encounter with the Syrophoenician woman teaches Jesus a new way to become who he is more fully. Her challenge prompts him to live deeper into his mission to be a feeder of multitudes.

Later in the Gospel of Mark, Jesus incorporates the image of the little child in his own preaching. She gave him an image that he then used to teach others. Like all good teachers, we see that Jesus is first and foremost an avid learner. This moment of encounter with a bold woman who challenges Jesus using his own words and images shows us something about Jesus's ministry to and with women. He was unafraid to learn, to grow and change, and to accept new information, deeper challenges, no matter where they came from. Even if those challenges came from a woman derided by his closest followers.

Women at the End and the Beginning: Earliest Christianity

We noted above that women were the witnesses to Jesus's last moments on the cross and also that all four gospel accounts have women as the first witnesses to the resurrection. As such, Jesus's female friends serve as the hinge in the pivotal moment of the paschal mystery: the suffering, death, and resurrection of Jesus. It is important that Mary Magdalene is in both groups, as biblical scholar Claudia Setzer notes,[2] because having Mary Magdalene as a witness to Jesus's death and his resurrection provided evidence against claims that Jesus had simply survived somehow or that the body had been stolen. Remarkably, this crucial part of the Christian message—that Jesus definitely died, was buried, and then rose from the dead—is attested to by a woman.

Women's testimony was essentially worthless in Jesus's time (and still is today in many parts of the world). And yet, the gospel writers kept this detail. What conclusions might we draw from this? Did they keep it to be countercultural? That is unlikely since it would not convince anyone to have the word of women asserting the resurrection instead of men. Perhaps they kept the women's witness as a sign of Jesus's egalitarian mission. But scholars note that having such an important fact rely on women's reports would be embarrassing to the earliest Christian communities. Despite this embarrassment, the details remain in the Gospels. We can infer, then, that the tradition tying Mary Magdalene and the other women to the crucifixion, burial, and empty tomb was powerful and pervasive, and the gospel writers couldn't help but include it. That makes the witness of these women indispensable.

There are many instances in the New Testament where the misogynistic shame of having women associated with important roles among Jesus's followers has obscured women's involvement. In other words, scribes, translators, copiers, or interpreters would spot a woman's name listed as an apostle (or a deacon, as we will see in a later chapter) and assume there was an error. The new scribe would then replace the woman's name with a masculine version, obscuring her role as it was written. How can this be? First, we should remember that Christianity was illegal for the first four decades of its existence. As such, there was not a great deal of coherence and consistency among the Christian communities because communication was difficult and had to be done secretly. Churches met in secret, often in households. Different local churches had different needs and different ministerial structures to meet those needs. There was, of course, no printing press, so any "copies" of scriptures were done by hand, which is not unlike a written game of telephone. Mistakes creep in, misspellings, skipped words from time to time. But some mistakes are actually judgement calls, where a scribe decides "that can't be right" and corrects the record. This happens consistently to women with important roles in the early church, according to feminist scholars. But by uncovering early manuscripts, comparing different scrolls and different scribes' work, scholars have been able to unearth the complicated reality of women in the early church communities.

Though chapter 10 will deal with this more specifically, we can look at the figure of Junia in the Pauline epistles. Junia, counted there among the apostles and a believer in Christ before Paul was, had also been incarcerated with Paul, which tells us she was well-known enough to be perceived as a threat by Roman authorities. The earliest Christian communities were marked by their variety of contexts, of demographics, of problems, and of ministries. The letters in the New Testament show us this with their varied uses of terms like *catechist*, *elder*, *apostle*, and *deacon*. While it's possible to draw some broad conclusions about what, for example, a catechist did, we are less sure about deacons and presbyters. In part because the earliest communities of Christians were focused on the imminent end of the world, it took a long time for ministries and worship to establish themselves in any kind of pattern that we might recognize. We know from very early Christian literature that the followers of Jesus and those whom they converted would meet regularly to share a meal in someone's home, to break bread and remember Jesus. His admonition of remembrance, "whenever you do this, remember me," seems to have been a central feature of the Christian community from very early on. Who "presided" at these house church gatherings, who said what and in what order, is not something we can ever know. But we do know that households were generally made up of men and women, that women had important roles to play in hosting dinners, and so the idea that a woman would have a prominent role in a church that met in her home is not outrageous.

We also have examples of specific women who held prominent positions in the earliest churches. In Paul's letter to the Romans, he mentions several prominent women by name. Chapter 16 of this letter begins with Paul commending Phoebe, a deacon (*diakonos*) into the care of the Roman church. There will be more about Phoebe in a later chapter. Paul also mentions Prisca as a fellow worker or partner in the church. Her name is mentioned before Aquila, a male disciple. Paul also mentions Andronicus and Junia as prominent among the apostles. While all the earliest versions of this epistle list her by her name, at some point an *s* was appended, making it into the male name Junias (which was not in use in the first century). Of course, this might be an error, but it might also be a choice to conceal the embarrassment of having women be important figures in the church. More troubling, the change may have been part of a deliberate campaign to exclude women from ministry by erasing evidence that they had ever filled these roles.

Paul's letters also include many instructions and warnings about how men and women are to act, how marriages should work, whether women are equal partners in the Christian community or whether they should be silent and submissive. In all these cases, readers of the New Testament should be aware of context—the issues in the Galatian church are different from those in the Corinthian church. Since we only have Paul's letters, we can only surmise what he may have been responding to. Many observers note that Paul seems antimarriage and antisexuality in his writings. We should remember the apocalyptic expectations of early Christians when evaluating Paul's views on institutions as permanent as marriage and family. If, like Paul and the early followers of Jesus, you were expecting the end of the world to be imminent, why would you encourage people to marry? Marriage is, after all, about a future together. If you thought the future was quite short, marriage might not seem like an important priority. The context of these letters matter to readers who are interested in the content of the letters and the broader issues they present.

Why would later Christians want to change something that was common in the early church? As Christianity was legalized and began to gain acceptance in the Roman Empire, Christians strived to make the religion look respectable. Like respectability campaigns today, what we mean by respectable is fitting in with the social mores of the dominant culture, including, if necessary, misogynistic ones. If Romans did not think women were capable of public roles and ministries, it would be a liability for the Christians to hold women in such high regard. It would be easier to make it seem as if Christians had always gone along with Roman social mores excluding women from public life.

It would be impossible to outline all the different roles women played in the early church or all the different women Jesus interacted with throughout his ministry. This chapter has, instead, focused on key moments in the Christian scriptures, on the person of Mary Magdalene, on the kinds of relationships Jesus had with women, and on the kinds of roles women like Prisca and Junia had in the earliest churches. Women's presence and prominence in Jesus's life, his ministry, and the lives and ministries of his followers cannot be disputed. What we make of that prominence, how it might affect the way the church is run today, remains to be seen.

DISCUSSION QUESTIONS

1. Given that the Pauline epistles are only one-half of a conversation, try to reconstruct the other part of the conversation with the Galatians, Ephesians, or Corinthians. What complaints might they have directed to Paul? What was

the situation of that church community that needed help or guidance?

2. What makes a witness more believable? How is women's testimony treated today? Are some witnesses inherently more credible? Reflect on criteria for believability and who receives the benefit of the doubt in our society.
3. Many people find the actions of Jesus in conversation with the Syrophoenician woman to be objectionable or offensive. Why might the gospel writers have included this story? How would you present this story to a class of teenagers, for example?

DELVE DEEPER

Mary Magdalene has consistently been an important figure in the church. Research ministries in your area that have Mary Magdalene in the name, both contemporary ones and historical ones, and explore how these reflect the actual and/or desired role of women in their respective contexts. Reflect on how these patterns of naming embody both descriptive and prescriptive understandings of women's roles and of Mary Magdalene's role.

Or watch the 2018 movie *Mary Magdalene* (dir. Garth Davis), and write a movie review that incorporates biblically accurate understandings of Mary Magdalene's role in Christianity.

READ FURTHER

Johnson, Elizabeth, ed. *The Strength of Her Witness: Jesus Christ in the Global Voices of Women*. Maryknoll, NY: Orbis Books, 2016.

Setzer, Claudia. "Excellent Women: Female Witness to the Resurrection." *Journal of Biblical Literature* 116, no. 2 (1997): 259–72.

Smith, Mitzi J., ed. *I Found God in Me: A Womanist Biblical Hermeneutics Reader*. Eugene, OR: Cascade Books, 2015.

Thurston, Bonnie Bowman. *The Widows: A Women's Ministry in the Early Church*. Philadelphia: Fortress Press, 1989.

Zagano, Phyllis. *Women: Icons of Christ*. Mahwah, NJ: Paulist Press, 2020.

9

THERE'S SOMETHING ABOUT MARY

The longest, most in-depth research I did in college, my senior thesis, was about Mary. I was fascinated by how prominent a position this woman held in Catholicism, even as she was lauded for being pure and virginal and quiet and complacent. My feminist commitments prompted me to understand Catholic fascination with Mary. Was it because God was thought of as so overwhelmingly male that we needed a feminine quasi-divine figure to balance out God? Was it because of some curiosity about Jesus as a young person or a child, or a desire to know who raised someone who turned out to be the Messiah?

Or was it something more sinister, a desire to have women imitate a figure who was defined by virginity and assent in order to make women's subjugation seem divinely ordained? After all, men were told to be like Jesus, but women were told to be like Mary. Jesus is God; Mary is human. There's already a fundamental inequality there. Moreover, though Jesus is also fully human, Mary remains an impossible ideal as a virgin who is also a mother. Is she just there to be used by men to lord over women who can never measure up? Is the pedestal we put Mary on also a tool with which to punish women? Or is it a prison for Mary and for those who imitate her? Why do some of the Catholics who are most loudly devoted to the Virgin Mary also hold deeply misogynist views? All of these questions animated the research of a twenty-year-old college student.

Eight years later, I was still writing about Mary in my doctoral dissertation. This time, I looked at how thinkers with a very exalted view of Mary (a "high" Mariology is what it's called) tended to have a low opinion of the laity's role in the church, assuming we were there to pay, pray, and obey. People with a more human, complex view of Mary (you guessed it, a "low" Mariology) tended to have more faith in the laity's ability to participate in the church's mission.

In both cases, how a person views Mary tends to reveal a lot more than their feelings about Jesus's mother. It's a window into their views of women, of laypeople, of bodies and sexuality, and of how the church should be organized. The proliferation of local devotions to Mary reveals what matters to particular populations and how non-Christian influences make their way into the fabric of Christianity. Ongoing Marian apparitions also show us how Christians turn to God in turbulent times. Because of her central place in the Catholic imagination, in doctrines about Jesus's nature, and in the devotional lives of Catholics, there can be no doubt that Mary deserves her own chapter.

Feminist theologians have a complicated relationship with Mary. On the one hand, a powerful, nearly divine female figure who is an object of devotion in Catholicism seems like an asset to people who work for women's equality and self-determination. On the other hand, the features of this powerful woman (virginity, submission to men, including and especially her son) would be considered antifeminist. What to make of her and of her prominence in Catholic life? It is impossible to dismiss Jesus's mother and foolish to think we could replace her with another Mary, like Magdalene, whose life seems better suited to contemporary feminist goals. Rather, we must reckon with Mary and the role she has played in the church.

Of all the women in Jesus's life, none figures more prominently in the imagination and devotional lives of Catholics than his mother, Mary. Though the scriptures do not provide us with much in the way of data about Mary's life, devotional practices and noncanonical traditions have filled in the blanks to suffuse Christianity, especially Catholicism, with images, prayers, processions, cathedrals, and more that prominently feature the Virgin Mary. Her name has adorned chapels, ships, queens, cathedrals, cities, and countless numbers of women (including this author, whose middle name is Maria). Nearly every region where you find Catholics also has its own "version" of Mary tied to the local cultures, an expression of the power of the Catholic imagination to make this faith tradition relevant in any context. She is called Guadalupe, Altagracia, Coromoto, Nieves, Caridad. We find specific devotions to her on every continent. Catholics venerate her as the Immaculate Conception, Immaculate Heart, Our Lady of Sorrows, Our Lady of Perpetual Help. Even the ability to undo knots is ascribed to her and praised. It makes sense to devote an entire chapter to the woman whose prominence in Christianity even rivals that of her son.

Why are Catholics so fascinated with Mary, and when did this fascination begin? The letters of Paul don't mention Mary, and Mark, the earliest Gospel, has no account of Jesus's birth. In fact, one way to trace the deepening understanding of early Christians is to look at where the Gospels begin. For Mark, Jesus was important (and therefore worth writing about) from the moment he began his public ministry. For Luke and Matthew, written around the same time and both after Mark, Jesus was important from the time he was conceived—this is where we find the infancy narratives, the annunciation story, and other scenes from Jesus's early life that feature Mary. John's Gospel, the last canonical gospel to be written, opens with words that echo the first lines of Genesis: "In the beginning." By the time the Gospel of John was written, Christians had begun to understand that Jesus was in fact God, that he existed as God "from the beginning," and that therefore he was important from the beginning of time. This deepening understanding of who Jesus was shows us that even though Christians affirm that revelation in Jesus is complete and that no further revelation is forthcoming, our understanding of the God revealed in Jesus is always capable of reaching new insights and new depths.

Mary and Hermeneutics

Our approach to this complex figure will be modeled on a kind of scriptural analysis that for simplicity's sake we can just refer to as a variety of postmodern hermeneutics. For postmodern thinkers like Paul Ricœur and Hans-Georg Gadamer and Catholic thinkers like David Tracy, texts have multiple places where we can find meaning. One can find meaning in a text, behind it, or in front of it. While this might sound strange, it's actually pretty intuitive. Think of yourself holding an open book in front of you, as if you are reading it. Now, let's start with the meaning in the text. As you read the words, you decode the letters and sounds and language. It makes sense to you, conveying a meaning. This is the meaning in the text.

Behind the text is where the author, the editor, and the compiler all live. What did the author intend? In what context did this book come to be written? What were her motivations and life experiences that prompted this particular work? How did it get into your hands? Is there a translator, and so on? These are all "behind the text" questions. For a long time in the modern era, biblical scholars sought to understand the scriptures and their meaning by re-creating the world behind the text. We've seen glimpses of this when, for example, we mention which of the Gospels was written first (Mark). Archaeology, linguistic analysis, and other disciplines can help scholars piece together the world behind the text. This world then helps us get new meanings from the book we are reading.

Take, for example, Arthur Miller's play *The Crucible* about the Salem witch trials. Many high school students are assigned this text and read it in English class. The play is about a chaotic time in American history, when women (and men) were killed because they were believed to be witches or involved with witchcraft. A reader can easily see the perils of mob rule, what mass hysteria looks like, and the power of rumors to ruin people's lives. All these meanings can be gleaned from a simple reading of the story of John Proctor's demise. If you know nothing at all about how the play came about, you are still getting some interesting and important meaning from it.

If, however, your teacher happens to contextualize the text a bit, they might let you know that Arthur Miller wrote this play in 1953 at the height of McCarthyism. This bit of "behind the text" information unlocks a new level of meanings for the reader. Now we can see that it's not just a play about morality but a contemporary social commentary. It's about the Salem witch trials and simultaneously about the witch hunt in the U.S. government, as people were denounced as "communists" by their political enemies. While you can understand the play without the behind-the-text information, once you have this bit of context, you understand it differently, maybe even more completely.

What about the meaning in front of the text? Let's return to our image of you holding an open book in your hands as if you're reading it. There is space between your eyes and the book. Imagine that hanging in this space is all your knowledge, your life experiences, your mood, your biases and prejudices, your way of understanding the world. This is your horizon of understanding. It includes the language(s) you know, your facility with it, as well as your comprehension of the world and ability to make sense of it. As you read, your horizon of understanding interacts with the horizon of the text—what it is saying about the world, the subject matter, and so on. When those two horizons meet, meaning is created.

Have you ever read a book, seen a movie, or heard a piece of music that changed your life? Maybe it was particularly profound or maybe it came along at the perfect time, but this near-universal human experience is an experience of meaning-making in front of a particular text (or movie or song, etc.). Some element of the art unlocks something in you, and you see things differently, more clearly, or more problematically than before. This is the meaning in front of the text—the text interacting with the reader/listener/viewer to create meaning that might go beyond what's in the text ("I should change my life!") and might even never have been intended by the author who lives behind the text. At the same time, the person sitting next to you may take something completely different from that same book, movie, or music. Both takeaways are valid, but one is more meaningful to you individually.

This excursus on hermeneutics is important to our work on Mary because in Catholicism the figure of Mary functions very much like a "text" that has a surplus of meaning. Behind the "text" of Mary we find the circumstances of her life, that of a first-century woman living in Palestine. The meaning "in" the text of Mary can be found in the little bits of biblical evidence we have of her life, as well as in some non-canonical sources like the Protoevangelium of James. Doctrines about Mary, such as the notion of her as *theotokos* and the Immaculate Conception, also provide "in" the text meaning for us to discover. Finally, the many faces of Mary in different cultures, the variety of practices that characterize Marian devotion, and the sheer number of cultural artifacts (art, architecture, music, cinema, etc.) about Mary give us a glimpse into the breadth of meanings "in front" of the Marian text throughout the church's history. We will use this behind/in/in front of frame for our study of Mary in this chapter.

The World Behind the Text: Mary's First-Century Life

We know, and can know, very little about Jesus's mother, her life, or her specific circumstances. Feminist theologian Elizabeth Johnson's masterful work about Mary, *Truly Our Sister*, does an excellent job of reconstructing the few clues we have about the woman who gave birth to Jesus. We know that Mary was from Galilee, from Nazareth. We can infer that she was poor from Luke 2:24, when she sacrifices pigeons after Jesus's birth, instead of a sheep, which is what people who had means were obligated to do. Armed with this information, Johnson engages archeological, historical, and social-scientific sources to reconstruct a vision of the first-century world Mary might have inhabited. She does this to shine a few beams of light into the world that produced Mary of Nazareth and in which she lived, had and raised Jesus, and died. Politically and economically, Mary was a peasant in a politically oppressed Jewish community, where Roman exploitation and public violence were commonplace. Religiously, Mary was and remained Jewish her whole life since she surely died before the destruction of the second temple, which marked the separation and emergence of Christianity and Rabbinic Judaism. Socially she took part in an arranged marriage, spent the majority of her days tending to food preparation and clothing her family. Mary likely lived in community with other peasant families in a compound that included a shared kitchen garden, hearth, and other common amenities. As Johnson states, "It is precisely in this economic, political, and cultural setting living out her Jewish faith as a peasant woman of the people, that she walked her journey of faith with enormous consequence."[1] To fill out the world behind the figure of Mary of Nazareth is to commit ourselves to remembering her context, which is the context in which God became incarnate.

We know that the authors of the New Testament show little interest in Mary except insofar as she is a character in Jesus's story. We don't know much about her background or about what happens to her after Jesus's death. The earliest mention of Mary comes in Paul's letter to the Galatians (4:4) where he says that Jesus was "born of a woman, born under the law." So we know Paul wanted to communicate that Jesus was born to a Jewish mother. Next come two small mentions in the Gospel of Mark. The first involves Jesus's family trying to curtail his ministry for fear that he is insane, and the second is a passing reference to Jesus as "the son of Mary" (6:3). So for the earliest Christian writers, Mary was only significant to the extent that she played a role in the life of Jesus. Thus, as mentioned earlier, the appearance of infancy narratives and the Prologue of the Gospel of John coincides with a deepening understanding of Jesus's divinity in the first few decades after Jesus's ministry. Mary's role is never about Mary—it's about what the gospel writers (or the epistle writers) are trying to convey to their audience about who Jesus is and how Jesus saves.

There's little evidence of veneration or worship of Mary until later in the development of Christianity. From this peek "behind" the text of Mary we can see that her role was somewhat limited and that we don't have too much access to what her life may have been like. But the meaning behind the text that is Mary might be the least interesting part of the phenomenon that is Mary in the church. It's what's in and in front of Mary that occupies the Christian imagination so compellingly.

The Meaning in the Text: Mary in the New Testament and Noncanonical Literature

The major scenes in the Gospels that feature Mary have to do with Jesus's birth, the beginning of his ministry, his death, and his resurrection. Mary is also mentioned as being in the room at Pentecost. While we won't cover each of these scenes in great detail, some of them deserve our close attention.

Both Luke and Matthew begin their stories of Jesus with accounts that let the reader know that a very important person will be born. Annunciation narratives are what biblical scholars call a "form," which is like a template that is used several times throughout the Bible. The parts of the story are set in a specific order to tell the reader that "a great figure in salvation history is about to be born." In the annunciation to Mary, an angel appears and announces to her that she will conceive and bear a son. Astonished, Mary asks a question: "How can this be since I am a virgin?" The angel reassures her, she gives her consent, and then she is promised a sign. Similar accounts occur in the birth of Isaac (Gen 17:15—18:15) and in the birth of John the Baptist (Luke 1:5–25). But both of those annunciations happen to men, the fathers of the children. In keeping with the ancient tradition of Jesus's unknown paternity attested to by non-Christian sources as well, the foretelling of Jesus's birth happens to Mary alone.

We should note several things about the annunciation story. Mary, though understandably caught off guard and afraid, nevertheless summons the courage to ask the angel a very logical question: how can I be pregnant if I am a virgin? Only when this question is answered does she give her free consent. While many interpreters and theologians have focused their attention on Mary's assent to the will of God, holding her up as a model of how women should submit their will to those more powerful than they (ahem, men), these same interpreters frequently gloss over her bravery in questioning the angel and demanding a satisfactory answer. Moreover, readers can draw from this text the implication that God, though all-powerful, nevertheless will not make the incarnation happen without Mary's consent and collaboration. God works with and through humanity, not over against our desires or our will.

After her encounter with the angel, Mary verifies the sign that was given to her: that her cousin Elizabeth, who was thought to be infertile, is pregnant as well. So Mary goes to visit her family, and while there we have the longest scene where only two women speak in the New Testament: the visitation. Mary's song, the Magnificat, details a vision for the reign of God that turns the order of the world on its head. The rich are sent away, the lowly are lifted up, the hungry are fed, and God does great things for those who have very little. Elizabeth Johnson has claimed that if we want to know where Jesus got some of his ideas about justice, we should look to his mother in the second chapter of Luke. Certainly, the Magnificat previews many of the themes of Jesus's preaching, his beatitudes, and his parables. This prefiguring occurs in a scene where the only characters are two pregnant women. We might theorize that the author of Luke's Gospel put these words in Mary's voice as a foreshadowing of the work of Jesus's life.

The New Testament gives us no tender moments between Mary and her child. We get a glimpse of her panic and anxiety after losing him in Jerusalem (Luke 2:41–52), and Mark's Gospel shows some antagonism between Jesus and his family when they try to take him home (Mark 3:31–35), fearing he is insane. Even the wedding at Cana in John's Gospel, where we have an extended interaction between Mary and Jesus before he officially begins his ministry isn't overly sentimental. In that story Mary is portrayed as a bit of a nagging mother, asking her son to do something in order to save their hosts from embarrassment, despite his reluctance to do so. No scenes of hugs or lullabies or cuddles. We do, however, see her anguish at the foot of the cross, and we know from the first chapter of Acts that she was welcomed into the Christian community because she is present when the Holy Spirit comes upon the believers at Pentecost.

If this is all the Bible has to say about Jesus's mother, where does so much of the "stuff" we know about Mary's life come from? Nowhere in canonical scripture does it say the names of Mary's parents or that she remained a virgin her whole life. These details come from a little-known text, the Protoevangelium of James. This text, like many others in the ancient world, existed alongside the ones that made it into the New Testament but was either not widely used or wasn't deemed reliable enough to include it in the canon. Nevertheless, despite the relative obscurity of the text, many Catholics know its contents well. Have you ever heard that Mary's parents were named Joachim and Anne? Revered as saints in Roman Catholicism, their names appear nowhere in scripture, but they do appear with those names in the Protoevangelium. Similarly, Catholics proclaim the perpetual virginity of Mary. That is, they claim that Mary never had sexual relations—neither before nor after the birth of Jesus. This detail is also nowhere to be found in the Bible. Where did we get this? The Protoevangelium of James.

This text dates from the late second century (which means at least 150 years after Jesus's death), and it focuses on Mary's life. It provides us with evidence that early Christians speculated about Jesus's mother, just as we do. Though the text reads much like a gospel, it is about Mary instead of Jesus, though it's clear the author has Jesus's humanity and divinity in mind throughout. There's a great deal of emphasis on Mary being "inviolate." This symbolism occurs throughout the story, as the author portrays Mary housed in the temple, in her childhood bedroom, and so on, that no one can enter. Most consequentially, the notion of being "inviolate" is symbolized through female biology, particularly through Mary's virginity, symbolized by her hymen remaining intact before, after, and even during the birth of Jesus. Though this belief, a doctrine in the Roman Catholic Church, emboldens people who support purity culture to elevate virginity as a marker of a woman's value, this is not the reason why the text was written. Rather, like all texts, it was prompted by its context. The second century, or the age of martyrs, was filled with persecution of Christians. Martyrdom, imprisonment, and malignant rumors we used by the authorities against the Christian community in an effort to discredit the faith. The emphasis on Mary's perpetual virginity counteracted claims that she was a prostitute or that she had been raped, which would have undermined Christian claims that Jesus was the son of God. So, like all authors, the author of the Protoevangelium was responding to the world around them.

Another source of information about Mary (and about meaning in her person as text) comes from church teaching. The earliest teaching to be proclaimed by the church about Mary isn't really about Mary, as you probably guessed. It's about Jesus. In 431, the Council of Ephesus convened to settle a nasty, dramatic dispute. Nestorius, the patriarch of Constantinople (remember, Christianity had been legalized in 313 and made the official religion of the Roman Empire in 380), taught that Jesus's human and divine natures were distinct. Jesus definitely was both human and divine, but these two natures could be separated. Therefore, it wasn't appropriate, thought Nestorius, to teach that Mary was the mother of God. God is eternal, and God therefore cannot have a mother. Makes sense, doesn't it?

But, countered the bishops at Ephesus, if you say that Mary was only the mother of Jesus's human nature, then there's a split, however small or momentary, between his divine and his human natures. There may be a moment when he is purely one or the other. This cannot be. In Jesus's two natures, there is a hypostatic union, which means that the natures are so closely fused that they cannot be separated. Nestorianism was defeated at Ephesus not merely, or even primarily, because of the many protestors who clamored that Mary was indeed God's mother. No, Nestorius was declared a heretic because his teaching endangered the reality of who Jesus was. As with many biblical scenes and church doctrines, it's not what they say about Mary but what this language about Mary implies about Jesus that matters. Jesus's humanity and divinity, the central claim for Christians, is weakened if we think Mary was the mother of only his "human side." The reality of Christ as the son of God is strengthened when we recognize that Mary was indeed the God-bearer, or Theotokos. This honorary title, the first given to Mary, inspired a great deal of devotion to her but was intended primarily to keep Christians on the same page about what happened in Jesus's incarnation.

The Good in Front of the Text: Mary Belongs to the People

Mary doesn't belong to the theologians or to the thinkers deemed heretical. She belongs to the people. We opened this chapter reflecting on the many faces and guises and cultures that Mary has taken on in the history of the church. In all these particular Marys, these different virgins who have appeared throughout the world and encouraged Christians to practice their faith fervently, we see the church becoming acclimated to different historical, cultural, and racial contexts.

Though the history of evangelization is characterized by violence, and we cannot overlook this fact, the emergence of so many different depictions and manifestations of Jesus's mother points to how the Christian message can travel and has traveled, has been translated, and in many cases has flourished globally. Moreover, this flourishing most often happens as a result of the faith of laypeople, frequently despite the objections of the institutional church.

When we think about the meaning in front of the text of Mary, we must first think of the generations of popular devotion to the mother of God. We will also look at how patriarchal structures have used the Virgin Mary to promote purity as the ultimate virtue, to denigrate women's bodies and women's sexuality and all that this denigration has entailed from the lack of sexually active women in the list of saints to the fetishization of motherhood. All of that is ahead. But I am choosing deliberately to start with popular devotion as meaning in front of Mary because this devotion is not an afterthought. For the vast majority of Catholics worldwide, devotions, simple prayers, and home practices are the first and most constant way they learn their faith. Frequently passed down from and by women (grandmothers, aunts, etc.), popular religious devotions are a central feature of Latinx theology but are by no means limited to Latinx cultures. We begin with the devotion of the people because too often laypeople's belief systems and practices are relegated to the end of theological books, as if doctrines came first. But in the case of every doctrine, every teaching, every devotion, people's faith and their prayer comes first. Let's look, then, at how people pray to Mary.

We can't cover every national virgin or patroness in the Americas, much less the world. Because we are in the United States, I think it's most fitting to focus on devotion to Our Lady of Guadalupe. Not because she's the only Virgin revered by Latinx Catholics, who are rapidly becoming the majority of the Catholics in the United States, but because Guadalupe is a very early apparition narrative, there's a lot of scholarship about it, and it illustrates the "in front of the text" meaning that is so rich in Marian devotion.

When it comes to Marian apparitions or other popular religious beliefs, our tendency is to start with the wrong question. Namely, we ask, "Did that really happen?" As in, did Mary really appear to this person, this many years ago, and did she really say and/or do those things? How can we believe something so bizarre? The truth is, the historical reality of private revelations like these (apparitions or other spiritual experiences that happen to one person or a few) is impossible to prove. But more important, when we focus on the "did it happen" aspect, we neglect the far more consequential question: how did the experience shape the practice of Christianity in that particular historical context?

The apparition of Guadalupe in what is now Mexico in the sixteenth century has become a cornerstone of Mexican cultural identity. The narrative of the apparition appears in Spanish and in Nahuatl, an indigenous language, as the *Nican mopohua*. It tells the story of Juan Diego, an indigenous neophyte (someone in the process of converting to Christianity) who sees a mysterious woman on a hill called Tepeyac (where previous indigenous communities had worshiped Tonantzin, a goddess). After several interactions and the miraculous cure of Juan Diego's uncle, Juan Diego eventually convinces the bishop, Juan de Zumárraga, to build a temple for Guadalupe at Tepeyac instead of in the center of the colonial town. He does this by revealing the image of Guadalupe miraculously present on his tilma, or cloak.

The image of Guadalupe and devotion to her fills Mexico and the southwestern United States in churches, cathedrals, even tattoo parlors and taco shops. Her image was displayed on the flag that accompanied soldiers to battle for Mexican independence from Spanish rule in the nineteenth century. And, at the turn of the twenty-first century, when Juan Diego was set to become a saint, investigations into whether he existed or not were protested by the people. Because in the end, it didn't matter if he existed or not. He exists for the Mexican people, for all people for whom Guadalupe is important. What matters is the meaning in front of the text: centuries of Christianity blending with indigenous and medieval Spanish cultures in one icon of the faith of the so-called new world.

One way to understand much of what is going on in devotion to Guadalupe is to look at the image itself. Housed in the Cathedral of Our Lady of Guadalupe in Mexico City is a tilma, a piece of clothing worn in some indigenous cultures that resembles a cloak. The image appears to be a young woman with a vaguely indigenous look about her, hands clasped in prayer, her eyes downcast. Scholars tell us there is much more happening than we might see as twenty-first-century U.S. residents. In fact, the image contains a good chunk of the gospel message: that the almighty God became human through a virgin.

If we start from the woman's hair, we see that it is loose, which indicates that she is a virgin. In the cultures of the Aztec Empire (the "Aztecs" were multicultural) unmarried women wore their hair loose while married women wore them in braids. To non-Spaniards, the hair on the woman immediately indicates that she is not married. And yet, she is wearing a black sash, which indicates that she is pregnant. We have an unmarried pregnant woman who looks indigenous. The pattern on her dress gives the final clue. Over her womb lies a flower that is the symbol of the almighty god, Teotl. The image tells a great deal about the Christian message without words—or, rather, without the words of the colonizers. Instead, it uses indigenous language and imagery to convey the special nature of Jesus and of Mary.

Lest we think that this image would have survived, and that devotion to it could have succeeded, without the approval of the institutional church, we should also look at how the image echoes European Christian devotions. The woman is standing on the moon, and her outer cloak is covered in stars, which echoes the image of the woman in Revelation 12. She very much looks like a Marian image, and the Spanish colonizers gave her a name that belonged to a Marian devotion in southwestern Spain. That Guadalupe is a dark-skinned Madonna as well. In sum, the image on the tilma blends indigenous imagery and European religious devotion into a hybrid figure that can contain the fervent prayers of the community coming to be as a result of Spanish colonization.

Spanish colonization was brutal in the Americas. It involved physical violence (killing, torture, maiming, rape, family separation), cultural violence (the outlawing of indigenous languages and the destruction of indigenous histories), and spiritual violence (the desecration of indigenous sacred sites, books, and statues and the outlawing of beliefs and practices deemed "pagan"). Much of this violence continues into the present, with the erasure of the intricacies of indigenous culture and the suppression of historical accounts of the violence suffered all over the Americas. There are no silver linings, nor should we look for any, in such rampant brutality. In the context of all that violence, however, this image and devotion emerges. This image somehow makes a middle way for Christianity to flourish amid heartbreak and bloodshed. This image still holds power, inspiring movements for social justice into the present day.

The Guadalupan image has been credited with saving communities from natural disasters along with countless cases of personal healing of bodies, minds, and relationships. Communities devoted to Guadalupe exist throughout the southwestern United States and Mexico. We see evidence of these in shrines and in churches, as well as in church groups of Guadalupanos and Guadalupanas throughout the United States. Pope John Paul II declared Guadalupe the patroness of the Americas in the late 1990s.

Of all the global apparitions of the Virgin Mary, Guadalupe is perhaps the most consequential, particularly in our historical context. Other devotions that are popular in the United States include the Immaculate Conception, Our Lady of Lourdes, Our Lady of Fatima, and the Immaculate Heart of Mary. Any of these would make fascinating topics for further study, particularly if one examines them through a hermeneutical lens: What is it about the historical and social context that led people to interact with the figure of Jesus's mother in this particular way? How did the resulting devotion calm fears, fuse cultures, or elevate people's spirits?

The Danger in Front of the Text: Mary Soaks Up the Culture

Not all the meaning in front of Mary, the meaning we make of her, is benevolent, however. Because the meaning in front of the text includes the horizon of the reader, or in this case the culture that is looking at Mary, then it stands to reason that patriarchal, misogynist cultures will create sexist meaning for Mary. Bearing in mind that the vast majority of theologians and all clergy have been male for most of the church's history, we can safely assume that the patriarchal views expressed in culture (which we looked at in chapters 1 and 4) would also be visible in depictions of Mary.

Patristic theologians like Tertullian juxtaposed Mary with Eve, where Eve was sin incarnate and therefore Mary was her opposite, grace incarnate. Marian feasts began to proliferate in the liturgical calendar. The Eastern Orthodox churches have celebrated the Feast of the Purification (or the Presentation, or Candelmas) for many centuries. But, in the years after the Council of Ephesus, Marian titles and feasts grew exponentially. The thinking behind this multiplication of honors for Mary is summed up in a Latin phrase: *potuit, decit, fecit*—since God could (*potuit*) bless Mary however God wanted to bless her, therefore God should (*decit*) and did (*fecit*). There was no honor that could be denied her. She quickly became the most important person for Christians after Jesus. After all, she was his mother, and that made her our mother, the mother of the whole church and indeed the mother of the whole world. All manner of dignity and compliments had to be afforded Mary because God would want the mother of God's son to be regaled with all kinds of honors. Queen of Heaven! Peaceful Dove! Morning Star! All these terms, any that could be considered lovely or good or queenly, were applied to Mary. The traditions of chivalry and courtly love played into how Christians imagined Mary in the Middle Ages: as a queen, we owed her all our honor; we were to fight on her behalf against all others to preserve her position.

Brick by brick, thinkers built Mary a pedestal and placed her at a height that was completely unreachable for women. She is a virgin, pure as snow, and yet also a mother. Untouched by sin or by men (or by sex, obviously), she suffered quietly and placidly the gravest injustice and pain: the death of her innocent son. God rewarded her quiet suffering by making her the queen of heaven and by sparing her from earthly death. The church celebrates this honor in the Feast of the Assumption, which began rather early, in the sixth century. According to this doctrine, Mary did not die but fell asleep, according to a belief called the Dormition; then her body was taken to heaven, as had happened to Jesus in the Ascension. In addition, Mary had to be amazing from the start of her life too, because she was chosen to be the vehicle of the incarnation. Thus, the church in the ninth century came to teach that she was not only spared death but spared original sin (a concept Augustine had popularized in the fourth century). While a common misconception is that the Immaculate Conception marks the moment of Mary's pregnancy with Jesus, in fact it marks the moment Mary was conceived in her mother's womb.

With the special nature and elevated status of Mary came a growing belief in her power to intervene before God on behalf of human beings. There's a bit of an inverted correlation here: as the church's image of Jesus becomes more that of a just judge, more of an angry God, the image of Mary becomes more powerful as well, as a docile, merciful figure who can ease God's wrath against sinners. We see this in the Hail Mary: "Pray for us sinners, now and at the hour of our death." Popular beliefs about Mary's power included the image, which some readers may remember from the movie *My Big Fat Greek Wedding*, that Mary was the neck that connected the body of Christ (the church) to the head and that could turn the wrathful Father/Son toward sinners in mercy instead of harsh judgement.

As time goes on, with so little biblical material to rely on, Mary becomes a repository for theologians' ideas of "good womanhood." Who, after all, could be a better woman than the one God chose to bear "his" son? Of course, as we have seen, "good womanhood" is often determined by patriarchy and policed by misogyny. Mary thus becomes a repository for male fantasies about what good womanhood ought to be: submissive, quiet, acquiescent to the demands of the all-powerful, all-male God embodied by her son. Less than God but more than regular women who could never meet the standard of virgin motherhood (or of that much docility, frankly), Mary is trapped on a pedestal made by a male-dominated tradition. That pedestal becomes a prison for Mary and for our understanding of Mary since we forget key moments in her life (she dared to ask the angel a question, she sang the very political Magnificat) and replace them with an image of purity and docility that reflects men's imaginations more than women's realities.

Understandably, then, feminist theologians have complicated relationships with Mary. On the one hand, a powerful female figure imbued with even semi-divine qualities might be seen to elevate the status of women. On the other hand, with all the honors and impossible characteristics foisted upon the image of Mary, it's little wonder that Mary Daly referred to the Virgin Mother as an over-adorned Christmas tree, "killed, though apparently alive." What Daly meant was that patriarchal church tradition had removed all traces of the human being who bore Christ in her womb, replacing her with a caricature that was comforting to men and dangerous for women. Theologians such as Elizabeth Johnson argue that Mary is a model of faith, of a companion on the journey of the church as we make our pilgrimage on earth. For Johnson, Mary is one of the communion of saints cheering on the church on earth. Mary models faith for us: she grows in her faith, struggles in her life, and is rewarded in the end for her faithfulness.

Latinx theologians recognize the power of Marian devotion in the everyday lives of Catholics. We are, therefore, reluctant to play down the importance of the Virgin Mary in Catholicism. At the same time, thinkers like Nichole Flores and others have noted that images like Guadalupe or Caridad can serve as motivators for social action, for solidarity with the poor and marginalized, and this key component of Marian devotion should be emphasized over claims about purity and virginity. In communities where sexual violence and domestic violence are rampant, it is especially important to decry efforts to have women model a Mary who is viewed as suffering in silence. Suffering in itself is not redemptive, even though racist and colonialist theologies would have us believe otherwise. Similarly, we must question portrayals of Mary as completely passive and obedient, important only because of her sexual characteristics (namely, her virginity).

The figure of Mary is a locus of belief, of controversy, and even of violence done to women in our church. But by examining the meanings that the figure of Mary might have as a classic text—as we have explored in this chapter, seeking the meaning behind, in, and in front of this central character in salvation history—we have discovered much. Mary can be removed from her imprisoning pedestal, returned to the people to whom she belongs: the faithful, who look to her as a model of discipleship in a complicated, violent world.

DISCUSSION QUESTIONS

1. Research the local Marian devotion in your area, or the area of your ethnic heritage, or even an area in the world that interests you. What gave rise to devotion in that area? What preceded it? How is it different from the Mary of scripture, and why do you suppose this is?

2. Ultimately, do you think the figure of Mary is an ally or an adversary to the contemporary feminist movement? How can the figure of Mary be conceptualized as a helper and how can she be thought of as a hindrance to the cause of gender equality?

3. Are there current social, political, or historical factors that you think might lead to an increase in Marian devotion? Or will it decrease as time goes on? Why do you suppose this is?

DELVE DEEPER

Find and compare two vastly different artistic depictions of Mary. These can be in the form of paintings, sculptures, music, poetry, or any other form of art. How does the meaning behind, in, and in front of the art contribute to your understanding of the pieces?

READ FURTHER

Castañeda-Liles, Maria del Socorro. *Our Lady of Everyday Life: La Virgen de Guadalupe and the Catholic Imagination of Mexican Women in America*. Oxford: Oxford University Press, 2018.

Daly, Mary. *The Church and the Second Sex*. New York, Harper and Row, 1968.

Flores, Nichole. *The Aesthetics of Solidarity: Our Lady of Guadalupe and American Democracy*. Washington, DC: Georgetown University Press, 2021.

Gaventa, Beverly R. *Mary: Glimpses of the Mother of Jesus*. Minneapolis: Fortress Press, 1999.

Johnson, Elizabeth. *Friends of God and Prophets: A Feminist Theological Reading of the Communion of Saints*. New York: Continuum, 1999.

———. *Truly Our Sister: A Theology of Mary in the Communion of Saints*. New York: Continuum, 2006.

Rodriguez, Jeanette. *Our Lady of Guadalupe: Faith and Empowerment among Mexican-American Women*. Austin: University of Texas Press, 1994.

Warner, Marina. *Alone of All Her Sex: The Myth and the Cult of the Virgin Mary*. New York: Vintage Books, 1983.

10

WOMEN AT THE WELL OF MINISTRY

Possibilities and Obstacles

Women's discipleship, their following of Christ, takes many forms in the history of the church. We can assert without any doubt that women have served or ministered in the church in every historical period and in every context in which the church has existed. We have always done things in and for the church—both the institutional church and the people of God. Much of the evidence of this work, however, survives only in bits and pieces, just as most women's experience is lost to history, never written down or preserved. This chapter will look at how our understandings of ministry have been fluid over time, how women have participated in the church's work, what biblical precedents exist for women's activity, and contemporary debates about women's roles in church work and decision-making.

Women's Work

In Romans 16, Paul introduces the messenger he entrusted with delivering his letter to the Romans. Her name is Phoebe, and Paul describes her as a "deacon of the church at Cenchrea." He uses words like "our sister" and "benefactor of many" to fill out this relatively detailed description of a woman who is clearly an important follower of Jesus. What did Paul want to convey in these words? Clearly, Phoebe was someone to be trusted and listened to. She held a position in her home church at Cenchrea that demanded respect and acknowledgment. What could it possibly mean to call her a deacon? Was she a deacon the way we have deacons in the church today? Did she sometimes read the gospel or preach or say, "The Mass is ended, go in peace"?

Probably not, but neither is the office of deacon that Phoebe held entirely different from the way we understand deacons today. The Greek word (Greek is the original language of the New Testament, not Latin) *diakonos* means "servant." In the contemporary church, deacons have a ministry of liturgy, of word, and of charity. This means that deacons have roles and responsibilities in the church's public prayer (liturgy) regarding interpreting and preaching the scriptures (word) and in carrying on the service and justice work of the apostles (charity). Paul indicates that he trusts Phoebe with the letter to the Romans. She is clearly delivering doctrine to the community, and she is a benefactress as well, so she is doing the ministry of charity. It is difficult to discern what her role in liturgy might have been since Christian worship has varied (and still does) in different times and places. Was Phoebe a deacon or a deaconess? Probably. But does that mean she was ordained and went through a process similar to the ordination of deacons today? Likely not—but neither did the men of that day. Moreover, what might her ministry mean for women's ministries (ordained and nonordained) in the church today?

Try to think of a job that has not changed since it began. It's impossible. All work changes depending on context. Even jobs that are ancient, like teaching, have varied in rights and responsibilities throughout history. Sometimes teachers were tutors in one-on-one contexts with wealthy male children only. At other times, teaching meant taking on apprentices to continue a trade, open-air discussion groups, or tutorials in medieval buildings. The goal of teaching has also varied. Is it to ensure learning for the upper classes only? To continue the status quo? Or to create a middle class? Perhaps teaching is meant to plant the seeds of liberation in communities that need it. Or to ensure that particular, difficult skills are not lost to the world. In different times and places, different actions are considered essential to "teaching." Certainly, in the years of the COVID-19 pandemic, teaching took on a whole new look and feel, as more people than ever embraced video conferencing as a pedagogical tool.

Parenting is like this too. At different points in history and within different economic classes, parenting has looked very different. Sometimes mothers are expected, even pressured, to breastfeed their children. At other times, nursing was left to women of lower classes, and women of powerful or prestigious classes would hire wet nurses so they would not have to do the work of feeding and caring for children. Nevertheless, both the mothers who nursed, fed, and cared for their own children and the ones who did not were acknowledged to be their children's mothers. Motherhood has not always included driving kids to after-school activities or weekend playdates. Nor has it everywhere included homemade meals and family dinners prepared by a woman wearing an apron and a crinoline. Fatherhood has undergone tremendous change too. For most of history, to be a father meant contributing genetically to a child's conception and publicly acknowledging that contribution. Contemporary fatherhood encompasses far more: coaching, cooking, tending to the needs of babies and small children, housework, homework help, and more. So our understanding of "father" and "mother" and "teacher" have varied historically and geographically. We don't find this odd or difficult to comprehend. We understand that as the world and technology changes, roles and jobs change.

This kind of change is also true in the church. While we may like to believe (or have been taught to believe) that "the church never changes," all evidence proves this isn't true. In fact, as my kids learned in elementary school science classes, change is one of the characteristics of a living thing. If the church never changed, it would not be alive! In a previous chapter, we looked at Frederick Cwiekowski's different understandings of church, the "blueprint" approach and the historical-critical approach. Recall that the blueprint approach claims that Jesus, in his lifetime, established the ministries and liturgy of the church as it exists in the present day, intentionally and with complete foreknowledge of how they would look. This means that, in the blueprint approach, the Last Supper as described in the Gospels is actually an ordination Mass, where Jesus laid hands upon the twelve apostles, who were the only people gathered there, and made them priests in the way we understand the priesthood today. By contrast, the historical-critical approach acknowledges that ministries and liturgy in the church have grown and changed through time, adjusting to their historical contexts as needed for the survival of the church and the varying needs of the church's communities.

Ministry changed in church history too. We know that for the first three hundred years of Christianity, communities operated in hiding, underground, sometimes literally worshiping in catacombs, because of persecution. It was an illegal religion in the Roman Empire. Thus, communication between Christian communities was spotty, difficult, and dangerous. Naturally, in this fraught context, there was not a lot of uniformity among communities in terms of how they worshiped (except through a shared meal and faith sharing) or how their work was organized. In other words, ministries (which here just means "church work and church workers") varied greatly. Some communities had catechists, deacons, and presbyters. Others had presbyters, deacons, and widows. Some had none of these. The earliest communities of Jesus's followers likely met in each other's homes, so the host (charged with preparing and serving food and presiding at the table) might have been male or female. Variety was the name of the game for many centuries in the Christian community. So, when Paul calls Phoebe a *diakonos*, he means that she is one. But what that role was, is, or might be in the future, is more difficult to discern.

We will return to debates about what women deacons were or might be in the future of the church later in this chapter. For now, let's zoom out a bit to consider what we mean by "ministry" in the church. *Ministry* is just another word for *service*. There are many ways in which the church provides services to the world. The church runs charities for immigrants and refugees, schools, homeless shelters, hospitals and clinics, universities and trade schools, orphanages, and many more social service organizations. All of these are ministries affiliated to different degrees with the institutional church. They might be run by a diocese, a religious order, a group of Catholics. There is also church ministry itself, which is all the work that is done to keep the church running: liturgy, training and upkeep of clergy, and maintenance of parish buildings. Someone needs to sew and embellish altar linens and priestly vestments and keep them clean. Someone must keep parish accounts, appointments, and sacramental records.

All of this "church work" is vital to the mission of the church. What might be surprising is that for many years most of this work was done by women. Today, women are often the majority of the staff of any parish, employed as directors of religious education, parish secretaries, even pastoral associates who do everything except celebrate Mass. They do high-level work at the diocesan level, too, up through the Vatican curia and in international religious organizations. From elementary school classrooms to orphanages, movies portray women religious as teachers and caretakers (sometimes not very nice ones) for a reason: women religious have long been at the forefront of the church's ministry to children and to the poor. It makes sense that women would be given this role since caretaking fits with patriarchal norms for women's roles in society. In fact, Christian women have long been charged with feeding the hungry and helping migrants. Scholars such as Bonnie Bowman Thurston, author of *The Widows: A Women's Ministry in the Early Church*, have made a biblical and historical case for the category of "widows" as a distinct, named ministry in the early Christian communities. This ministry, reserved for mature women, ensured that people did not go hungry and that goods were properly distributed to those in need.

In a 2005 letter titled "Coworkers in the Vineyard of the Lord," the U.S. bishops gave a name to the workers who had been laboring (paid and as volunteers) in parishes and Catholic ministries: Lay Ecclesial Ministers (LEMs). LEMs, said the bishops, are appropriately trained laypeople who work alongside clergy in public leadership roles in the church. As of 2015, there were approximately 38,000 LEMs who did at least twenty hours of paid work a week.[1] This works out to about a quarter of all parish staff in the United States and nearly half of all workers involved in ministry at all. Of these LEMs, 80 percent are women. What this means is that the vast majority of the work of parishes, schools, church-run hospitals, and the like is being done by women, right now, this very day. It is easy to think that the clergy (priests, bishops, deacons) are the ones who keep the church going or that they are the most important people in the church's survival. But the plain truth is that without laywomen, the church simply could not function.

My own experience in Catholic schooling illustrates this. My elementary school was run entirely by laywomen, with the (not very strict) oversight of the parish's pastor. The overwhelming majority of the school teachers and staff, with the exception of the maintenance staff, were women. My all-girls Catholic high school was run by the sisters of the Immaculate Heart of Mary (IHMs), who made up some of the teaching and administrative staff, but the majority of the teachers, coaches, and staff were (and still are) laywomen. My mother is a parish secretary, and the entire parish staff, with the exception of the priests and permanent deacons, are women. In short, women do the work of the church—the teaching and accounting, the scheduling and washing, the mending and childcare, the outreach and mutual-aid organizing. Every day, they make consequential decisions about the life of the parish and therefore about how the church fulfills its mission.

If women do all this work, why can't women be recognized by being ordained? Many of my students and people I meet who are unfamiliar with Catholicism are puzzled by women's exclusion from ordination. Once they hear the data that shows that 80 percent of paid church workers are women, they are perplexed as to why the church would allow women to do everything except be ordained. So what are the reasons the church gives for excluding women from the sacrament of ordination?

The Battles over Women's Ordination

Second-wave feminism and the Second Vatican Council both collided to change the lives of Catholic women in the 1960s and 1970s. Feminist movements brought women into the workforce in great numbers, aided by the widespread availability of contraceptives and women's renewed desire for participation in public life and careers. Women were not only heading into the workforce, but (mostly white) women were also heading to colleges and universities, embarking on career paths in numbers that had not been previously seen. In the Catholic Church, the end of Vatican II ushered in a renewal of the Mass so that it no longer had to be in Latin but could be in the language of the area. The priest no longer faced away from the congregation, and the congregation was encouraged to full and active participation in the liturgy and the mission of the church. As part of this, many advanced degree programs in theology, most of which had previously been off limits to women in the United States, opened their doors to train women and confer master's degrees in divinity, theology, scripture, morality, and more. Some PhD programs admitted women for the first time. Women became lectors at Mass and eucharistic ministers as well. With this added visibility came uneasiness: if women could do all this, why couldn't they also be priests?

Beginning in the 1970s, some mainline Christian churches, such as parts of the Lutheran and the Anglican churches, began to admit women to ordination. Seen as a consequence of the growing women's movement and as a natural development in the understanding of doctrine, these Christians allowed women to serve publicly as ministers and still do. Some Anglican churches in the United States even ordain women as bishops. Faced with increasing pressure to allow Catholic women to be ordained (after all, they were in graduate programs and received the same training alongside men who would be ordained), the Catholic Church offered two responses. The first, *Inter Insignores*, was written in 1976 by the Congregation for the Doctrine of the Faith (once called the office of the Inquisition) and approved by Pope Paul VI. Nearly twenty years later, in 1994, Pope John Paul II authored an encyclical, *Ordinatio Sacerdotalis*, reiterating the reasons for excluding women from ordination and declaring that the question was closed and that future discussion of the matter basically amounted to dissent. Both documents lay out three major arguments against ordaining women: from scripture, from tradition, and the iconic argument. We will look at each of these in turn, but scholars have debunked the first two, so we will spend more time on the iconic argument than either of the others.

The argument from scripture flows from the understanding of the church critiqued by Cwiekowski as the "blueprint" approach. This argument claims that at the Last Supper, which was an early Eucharist celebration, Jesus ordained the twelve apostles, all of whom were men, to carry on his ministry of word and, most important, of sacrament: the consecration of the Eucharist. At various points in the Gospels Jesus addresses the Twelve and gives them particular powers: to bind and loose people from their sins (forgive), to spread the gospel, and to "do this in memory of me." From those passages, the hierarchy surmises that Jesus did not intend to ordain women, for had he wanted to, he would have. There's no passage in the Gospels where Jesus ordains Mary Magdalene, for example, or his own mother. The work we associate with priests in the present are prefigured in the Gospels, in Jesus's directions to his (all-male) disciples. Therefore, the church cannot ordain women now because it is not something Jesus did.

The argument from tradition runs in much the same way. The central claim is that the church has never ordained women in all its history and therefore the church is not presently at liberty to just decide to ordain women. It goes against hundreds of years of stable tradition, upends the wisdom of the church fathers, and is unprecedented in theology. The church is simply unable to go against tradition in this fashion. It's not possible.

Unless, of course, the blueprint approach isn't valid. Let's look at scripture. An argument about Jesus's intent to ordain only men presupposes that Jesus intended to ordain anyone at all. Is that a safe assumption from what we know of the Gospels? By all accounts, Jesus's earliest followers thought his second coming was imminent. Setting up a ceremony to ordain ministers seems like something one would do to ensure the legacy of Jesus's message long into the future. But if the earliest Christians weren't expecting a long future, but a quick end of the world and final coming of the reign of God, why would they ordain a class of men to specific roles? Second, scholars have convincingly argued that the Twelve is largely a symbolic group, meant to echo the twelve tribes of Israel for those Jewish readers who would be reading the Gospels. We know that Jesus had many more than twelve followers, and any of them might have been present at the times when Jesus spoke about binding and loosing sins or even in the Upper Room. We have no attendance sheet from the Last Supper, which, again, scholars have argued is a symbolic scene meant to echo the Passover meal and situate Christian liturgy in the Jewish framework. This does not mean that the Last Supper didn't happen, but rather that specific details, like the location, the time it took place, the guests, and so on, were probably added for rhetorical reasons. Jesus did, undoubtedly, instruct his followers to "do this in remembrance of me." We have evidence of that command in very early texts that predate the Gospels. It seems that all the earliest Christians were moved to remember Jesus in the breaking of the bread in house churches and underground communities. Given what we know about the varieties of ministries and structures of the earliest Christian communities, can we really make the case that what is depicted in the Gospels is ordination? Or does it make more sense to say that in his lifetime, Jesus gathered followers who, upon his death and the delay in his second coming, developed ways to remember Jesus that were rooted in his life and ministry, including and especially by remembering him through table fellowship and mutual aid? This view is more consistent with Cweikowski's historical-critical approach.

The final argument against women's ordination is the trickiest because it isn't directly tied to scripture or tradition but makes a theoretical case against ordaining women. The so-called iconic argument claims that women cannot be ordained because they do not resemble Jesus. As Pope Paul VI said in *Inter Insignores* (1976): "The supreme expression of this representation is found in the altogether special form it assumes in the celebration of the Eucharist,...: the priest, who alone has the power to perform [the consecration] then acts not only through the effective power conferred on him by Christ, but *in persona Christi*, taking on the role of Christ, to the point of being his very image, when he pronounces the words of consecration" (5).

When a priest says Mass, and especially at the moment of the consecration, he is said to be *in persona Christi*, or in the person or guise of Christ. In order for the sacrament to be effective, or to work, the congregation must understand that the priest in that moment (and in the moment of absolution in the sacrament of penance, and other times) is a vessel of Christ's grace and a stand-in for Christ. So the argument goes that it would be difficult for a congregation to look at a woman at the altar and understand that she was, as the priest is supposed to be, standing *in persona Christi* because she is a woman and Jesus was a man. *Inter Insignores* says in the following paragraph: "The priest is a sign...but a sign that must be perceptible and which the faithful must recognize with ease." And later: "When Christ's role in the Eucharist is to be expressed sacramentally, there would not be this 'natural resemblance' which must exist between Christ and his minister if the role of Christ were not taken by a man:

in such a case it would be difficult to see in the minister the image of Christ. For Christ himself was and remains a man."

The iconic argument hinges on the idea of "natural resemblance." Sacraments make sense to us because we can understand the relationship of the thing to what it signifies: the waters of baptism are a sign of rebirth, for example. Like all symbols, there must be an easy-to-grasp relationship between the invisible reality that is being indicated (rebirth/cleansing from sin) and the physical reality we experience (water). The argument Paul VI is making above claims that the congregation at Mass would find it too difficult to make the connection between a woman saying the words of consecration and Christ because Jesus was a man, and that is who we should be imagining saying, "Do this in memory of me."

Let's explore this because, on the surface perhaps, it makes some sense. Imagine your local priest. What does he look like? Is he old or young? Does he have hair or is he bald? What color is his skin? His eyes? Is he joyful, sad, mourning, angry? Now picture Jesus, or what we know of him. Jewish, Middle Eastern, died around the age of thirty-three. Do you know many priests who naturally resemble a thirty-three-year-old Middle Eastern Jew? Do we ordain old men? Black men? Latinos? Do we require men to leave the priesthood if/when they lose their hair? What if they lose a limb? Of course not. We instinctively know that men of all races and all ages and all physiques can be priests. So the issue of natural resemblance demands that we ask where this nonnegotiable resemblance is located. We can begin to see why some feminist theologians (who will remain nameless) began to make a joke based on the natural resemblance argument: "If you want to be like Jesus, you've got to pee like Jesus."

Since the church feels at liberty to ordain men who do not resemble Jesus in any way except with regard to their external genital organs, we might wonder why it feels constrained when it comes to ordaining women. When little girls or women are baptized, they are recognized to put on the persona of Christ and take on his roles of priest, prophet, and king. That is, we use the same words to baptize a new Christian, regardless of their sex. There is no special rite for women. Furthermore, if a woman is martyred, that is, killed for the faith, she is said to be *in persona Christi*—which raises the question: why can she stand for the person of Christ in one situation but not another? Martyrs of any sex bear a natural resemblance to

Christ, as they died for Christ. There's no asterisk beside the names of women martyrs like Perpetua or Felicity indicating that they are "sort of" *in persona Christi* because they are fully so. In infancy and in death, women can resemble Christ. But what about when we are living, thriving, serving the reign of God? A living woman cannot. It is too great a discrepancy to overcome, according to the Vatican.

Is that it, then? Should women just resign themselves to living outside the resemblance to Christ, even though we may embody it in baptism and martyrdom? I've often found that when I reach an impasse or difficult crossroad in a situation, I rely on art to be my guide. So I offer you now this poem titled "Woman's Body" by Frances Croake Frank:

> Did the woman say,
> When she held him for the first time in the dark of a stable,
> After the pain and the bleeding and the crying,
> "This is my body, this is my blood"?
>
> Did the woman say,
> When she held him for the last time in the dark rain on a
>   hilltop,
> After the pain and the bleeding and the dying,
> "This is my body, this is my blood"?
>
> Well that she said it to him then,
> For dry old men,
> brocaded robes belying barrenness
> Ordain that she not say it for him now.[2]

Many Catholic women have felt, and still feel, called to ordination. They are excluded from the sacrament of orders based on arguments from scripture and tradition that don't hold up against scholarly scrutiny and on the basis of an iconic argument about a natural resemblance that is quite thin. They work in and for the church in all manner of ways, doing the majority of the church's labor. They teach and console; they organize and nurse; they are paid and volunteer workers in the church. The clamor for women's ordination continues to grow, despite Pope John Paul II's assertion in his 1994 letter *Ordinatio Sacerdotalis* that forbidding women's ordination was not only infallible but that the people of God were no longer allowed to discuss it (4).

Scholars quickly reacted to the letter, particularly the claims about infallibility. Though we cannot devote too much attention to these controversies, it is enough to know that many scholars disagreed about whether the ordination of women was a matter of faith or morals or whether it was, instead, a question of discipline. If it were about faith and/or morals, the pope might speak infallibly on it, but he chose not to do so. Questions about eligibility for a sacrament tend to fall into the realm of church discipline, however, which means questions about how the church is organized or run. The doctrine of infallibility, established at the First Vatican Council in the late nineteenth century, does not really pertain to questions of church discipline, as the church acknowledges that these kinds of matters are subject to change depending on varying kinds of necessity or contexts.

The faithful were also clearly divided on whether the topic was closed for discussion. As any parent will tell you, pronouncing something off-limits rarely achieves the goal of making that thing anything but more intriguing. Similarly, the discussions of whether and how women's ordination might happen have continued in the Catholic Church. Some priests have led ordination ceremonies for women, and these men were laicized (dismissed from the priesthood) almost immediately—a consequence rarely imposed on bishops and priests who were found to be child predators. But the yearnings of women who feel the call to priesthood persist. Groups like the Roman Catholic Women Priests movement exist today, populated by women and men who feel that the institutional church's failure to recognize their calling and their ministry should not hold them back from serving the people of God.

What about the Diaconate?

The election of Pope Francis in 2013 caused a great stir in the church. He is the first pope from the global south and the first Jesuit to be elected pope. Francis's approach to the papacy has been one of patient listening to the needs of the church and the world. He is particularly attuned to the needs of the global south, as he is from

Argentina. When, in 2019, Francis convened a synod on the needs of the Amazon peoples and Pan-Amazonian region, many understood that his closeness to these concerns stemmed from his geographic background. One matter that was sure to come up at this meeting of bishops was the lack of clergy in the remote region of South America. Several proposals for providing ministers of the Eucharist to the Catholics in the Amazon were discussed, though none gained significant traction. Nevertheless, the synod and Francis's pontificate in general have reignited discussions about the nature and purpose of the diaconate, including the possibilities for reintroducing women deacons in the church. So far, two commissions have been convened by Francis to study the possibility of ordaining women to the permanent diaconate.

If we want to understand where this movement originated and where it might be heading, we must first understand what the diaconate really is. A deacon is not a junior varsity priest, nor is a deacon always a person on their way to the priesthood. The diaconate, as church historians know and as the commissions demonstrated, has existed in the church longer than the ordained priesthood. And for half of the history of the church, women were part of the diaconate and participated in the ministry of the deacon. This ministry is in service to the word, to liturgy, and to charity. Deacons can preach, they can proclaim the gospel and baptize, and they can and should see to the material needs of people in the parish.

These ministries have a long history in the church. We have scriptural evidence, for example, the story of Phoebe in the letter to the Romans mentioned early in this chapter. The first letter to Timothy outlines some guidelines for deacons and adds characteristics for women as well. Historian Gary Macy notes that "these passages were understood by the majority of Christian scholars for over half of Christian history to refer to women who served as deacons in the church."[3] So, even though women deacons might seem weird to us currently, for much of the church's history, they existed as a matter of course, not as an anomaly or exception.

While the exact naming of this women's ministry varied and it is difficult to pinpoint the difference, for example, between early church uses of *deacon*, *deaconess*, and *widow* for women ministering in church communities, we can nevertheless be sure that women were serving in these roles. We have similar questions about naming titles and types of service for men. Not only were women doing the work, but we have liturgical proof of women's ordination to the diaconate: actual texts that lay out procedures for ordaining a woman to be a deacon, dating from the eighth century in the Western church. Some rites use the same procedure to ordain a man or a woman, providing only alternate language or a separate blessing depending on whether the deacon was male or female. Others had separate rites altogether. Bishops presided at these rites. To contemporary eyes, they sure look like ordination.

It makes sense that the church would need women deacons too. Social rules about propriety would make it impossible for a male deacon, for example, to tend to a sick Christian woman or to see her in any state of immodest dress, as might be required in baptism. So women deacons ministered to women, and social mores were maintained.

If we have biblical, historical, and liturgical evidence for women deacons, then why is there even a controversy about ordaining women to the diaconate now? The answer begins, like so many great stories of today's church, in the 1960s at the Second Vatican Council. As part of the council's desire to return the church to its original traditions (fueled by the *ressourcement*/return to the sources movement in Catholic theology), Vatican II reinstated the permanent diaconate. This meant that no longer would deacons merely be ordained as part of their journey to the priesthood, a small layover where they got to practice at the priest's job. Rather, the council brought back the ancient order of deacons, where laymen (married and unmarried) could be ordained to serve the church in word, liturgy, and charity. The training for this ministry was open to married men, and in many dioceses their wives took part in the training alongside the diaconate candidates. This meant that the women were getting the same training as the men, but at the end, only the men would be ordained. Imagine that. Once the church stopped treating the diaconate as a brief stopover on the way to the priesthood, the question of who could take part in this ministry really blossomed. Historically and liturgically, there was no reason to exclude women.

Over the next few decades, many bishops brought the question of women deacons to a variety of popes. Sadly, the question was often muddled by anxieties about the ordination of women to the priesthood, a lack of clarity on the diaconate as a separate ministry, and a resulting fear that opening the diaconate to women would be like a floodgate, so that women priests would become an inevitability. Simply put, we aren't comfortable enough in the church with the diaconate as a separate, viable ministry on its own. Too many Catholics still see deacons as a transitory state, not a permanent one. Ordaining women to the diaconate would imply, to these Catholics, that the women were "on the way" to priesthood. Given the robust arguments against women priests made by Paul VI and reiterated by John Paul II, women deacons seemed too much to hope for.

Until Pope Francis came along. Many factors are converging that energize the conversation about women deacons in the present day. The clergy shortage is acute: there are simply not enough priests, nor enough men seeking ordination, to adequately (or even barely) serve the number of Catholics in the world. This shortage is felt most severely in poor and rural areas, where Catholics might go without the Eucharist for months at a time. Our understandings of church ministries have changed over time, and the clergy shortage crisis is perhaps precipitating another shift in how we view ordained ministry. Is it more important to us to maintain specific patterns for ordination or is the priority getting the Eucharist to Catholics who do not have access to it? A more robust diaconate, of women and men, could bring communion to rural communities and live among them, ministering to their needs and nourishing remote church communities.

Moreover, historical research and feminist scholarship is more widely available to Catholics now. The laity is more educated than ever before, and so access to historical and liturgical precedents for women deacons is at an all-time high. It is difficult to maintain the claim that women must be excluded from all ordinations, even to the diaconate, when there is such robust historical evidence to the contrary. Finally, social media has made the existence of women in ministry far more visible. Without conflating women priests and women deacons, it's easy to see that the rising visibility of women priests (and married priests) makes claims about the ordained priesthood as some kind of unchanging reality in the church seem weak.

For now, we do not know what the conversations about women

deacons in Rome will bring. We do know that the first commission found no reason to bar women from the permanent diaconate. We also know that the work of the church is done mostly by women and that women have done this work as ordained ministers and nonordained ministers for the majority of the church's history. Our understandings of specific roles in the church—be they deacons, or priests, or widows, or fellow-workers, or bishops—have changed and evolved over time. It is quite possible that we are amid just such an evolution today.

Conclusion

From the moment that Paul entrusted Phoebe with delivering his letter to the Romans to the present day when women do the majority of parish labor, we can claim with some certainty that women's ministry has been a constant feature in the church. What we call this ministry and how we recognize it has as much to do with the surrounding context of sex roles and stereotypes as it does with what the church needs. As we think about the present and future of women in ministry, we must ask: If the majority of LEMs are women (and they are), then why not ordain them? If they are doing the work of the diaconate, what is the difference with having the bishop recognize their training and their work? The church is making slow progress toward this goal. Most recently, the Vatican allowed for the formal installation of women as lectors and acolytes although they have been fulfilling these tasks for decades. These baby steps toward integrating women into official ministerial roles point to a future where including women in the diaconate becomes inevitable.

What happens next? The specter of the iconic argument against women priests looms large here. Can a case be made that once Catholics see women in liturgical vestments at the altar, the imaginative leap is done and we can get comfortable with women leading worship in nondiaconal (i.e., priestly) ways as well? Once we see women in priestly garb near the altar, proclaiming the gospel, or preaching, can the Vatican still confidently say that the people of God cannot make the symbolic connection between a woman and the person of Christ? Or will the church discover that "natural resemblance" is more a matter of what someone does than who someone is?

DISCUSSION QUESTIONS

1. What pressing social issues do you think the church should be attentive to? Some examples might be ecological concerns, drug addiction, or gun violence. Are there areas for ministry that you think the church should expand or others that should be discontinued?
2. Some have suggested changes to ordination in order to make it more functional in our contemporary context. Suggested changes include the ordination of older married men, or making ordination a temporary thing, like the peace corps, where people could enlist for five- or ten-year terms. What structural changes do you think would have the most effective impact?
3. Write a letter to the Vatican about how you, or a group you belong to, envision ministry in the church. Who should do it? What does ministry look like? Do only the ordained have ministries, or should all ministries involve ordination? What does the sacrament mean in your life, particularly in the context of church work broadly understood?

DELVE DEEPER

Look into the role that medieval abbesses had in their communities and compare this to the role of bishops and the USCCB today. Are there comparisons to be made between the role of abbesses, anchoresses, and other medieval church women to women who do church work today?

READ FURTHER

Edwards, Jennifer C. *Superior Women: Medieval Female Authority in Poitiers' Abbey of Sainte-Croix*. Oxford: Oxford University Press, 2019.

Hahnenberg, Edward P. *Ministries: A Relational Approach*. New York: Crossroad, 2003.

———. *Theology for Ministry: An Introduction for Lay Ministers*. Collegeville, MN: Liturgical Press, 2014.

Macy, Gary. *The Hidden History of Women's Ordination: Female Clergy in the Medieval West*. Oxford: Oxford University Press, 2007.

Thurston, Bonnie Bowman. *The Widows: A Women's Ministry in the Early Church*. Philadelphia: Fortress Press, 1989.

Wijngaards, John. *Women Deacons in the Early Church: Historical Texts and Contemporary Debates*. New York: Crossroad, 2002.

Zagano, Phyllis, Gary Macy, and William T. Ditewig. *Women Deacons: Past, Present, Future*. Mahwah, NJ: Paulist Press, 2011.

PART 3

A WOMAN'S PLACE IS IN THE CHURCH

The final section of this text is where the rubber meets the road. In parts 1 and 2 we examined the theoretical underpinnings of feminism and feminist theology, and we learned about how women have interacted with primary sources like scripture. This section looks at how feminist theologians have used their training and knowledge to reformulate theology against the grain of patriarchal religion. We begin with a look at how women religious have shaped resistance to patriarchal norms throughout the history of the church. Then we take up the themes of God-talk, church, and spirituality.

11

(RE)SISTERS

Nuns, sisters, women religious—whatever you call them, these women in vowed religious life have specific connotations in our culture. They figure in our social and cultural imaginations: whether because our grandparents watched Sally Field play "the flying nun" on television in the sixties, or our parents laughed with Whoopi Goldberg disguised as a nun in the *Sister Act* movie franchise of the 1990s. We often hear tales of Catholic schools run by terrifying women in habits with rulers wielded as weapons. Nuns even make up a subsection of the horror genre, exhibited in haunted houses or horror movies like *The Nun* (2018) or *The Conjuring 2* (2016). More recently, as details of decades of sexual abuse covered up by the church have emerged, we have seen women religious portrayed as abusers, as in the case of the Magdalene laundries in Ireland, and as more complex figures, as in the movie *Doubt* (2008). Women religious have also taken an important place in the political life of the United States, with Sr. Simone Campbell's organization, the NETWORK lobby, launching the "Nuns on the Bus" initiative, raising awareness of progressive political causes in the nation.

Who are these women who are referred to as sisters, nuns, women religious? Regardless of what we call them, they belong to communities of women who live apart from the world and dedicate their lives to prayer and contemplation. As I've mentioned throughout this text, most images we have of women in the church were created by and for a patriarchal culture. The images we internalize reflect men's ideas about women, men's hopes for women's behavior and demeanor, men's expectations of deference and submission from women. We saw in some of the biblical portrayals of women that what men claim as "women's nature" and how women actually behave in scriptural narratives can be radically different.

The same is true of our ideas about women religious. In trying to understand these women's lives and their place in the church we must ask, as we do with any stereotype, whether the idea we have inherited about scary, violent nuns is based in reality or whether the stereotype serves the patriarchy's goals of keeping women under control. This chapter examines the institution of vowed religious life in a variety of historical contexts, including the present day. We will encounter several exemplary sisters, women religious, nuns who look and act nothing like Sally Field, Whoopi Goldberg, or a horror movie villain. While the world of religious life is varied and complex, this chapter's central claim is that communities of women religious have, throughout Christian history, provided a place where women had a say in the direction of their lives and therefore were a place where a woman could not only become a "sister" but a "re-sister."

Historical Development

Communities of women religious originated in the monastic movement of the early medieval era. As Christianity became more prominent in the Roman Empire, eventually becoming the empire's official religion, some Christians resisted the union of religion and political power. Faced with people converting for political gain, these Christians fled the world and formed disciplined, self-sustaining communities where the focus was on prayer and worship. In the sixth century, St. Benedict of Nursia founded a community of monks (and, according to tradition, his twin sister, Scholastica, founded one of nuns), now known as the Benedictines. Since then, monks and nuns have been a vital part of Christianity.

Monasticism has taken on many forms in the centuries since the Benedictines were established. Not all communities are completely cut off from the world, nor do most communities rely on charity, as some early mendicant (begging) orders did. While they were originally a refuge from the world (founded on the principle of *fuga mundi*, or flight from the world), monastic communities have, like everything else in Christianity, evolved over time. Some monks and nuns remain cloistered, almost entirely apart from the world, in some cases interacting only through bars or railings in a room that allows visitors. Other orders, like the Sisters of St. Joseph, the Missionaries of Charity, and the Sisters of Mercy, take on active roles in education, health care, and even politics. Along the way, convents and monasteries have been centers of education and culture. Some institutions have amassed power that rivaled the influence of monarchs and popes. Others have wielded great might and then faded away. The only constant is that they have provided a place where Christian men and women could live in community, with intentionality, striving to worship God.

For women, convents, abbeys, or priories where communities of women religious lived and worked provided refuge. Whether they were fleeing arranged marriages, poverty, or abuse, convents provided shelter to women who wished to live there. Of course, convents themselves reflected the social structures of their historical and geographic contexts. Convents in the Americas owned slaves. In Europe, convents accepted the dowries of wealthy women who hoped to become nuns and relegated poorer women to roles of servitude in the convent. There was racism, classism, and exploitation within convents as well as the refuge of prayer and peace for women and the opportunity for literacy and leadership for some. In late Victorian England, houses for "fallen" women, who had gotten pregnant outside of marriage, were run by women religious and were infamous sites of horrific abuse. Nevertheless, convents were places where women could live mostly outside of male control for much of Western history. You can see the allure. In a religious community, women could hope for what the secular world would not give: a measure of self-determination, some control over their destiny. While it might seem that they were "giving up" a lot—a family of their own, their families of origin, and so on—they were also gaining access to education, a haven, and some protection from predatory men.

Many women flourished in these communities. Some, such as Mother Teresa of Calcutta, even founded their own orders, with missions, buildings, and innovative visions for women's religious life. Mother Katharine Drexel of Philadelphia used her family's enormous wealth to serve Native Americans and Black communities when other religious orders wouldn't. In so doing, women held a great deal of power, in the form of wealth, land, and influence. There are examples of women abbesses in the Middle Ages who challenged bishops, like Hildegard of Bingen in the twelfth century, whom we'll discuss shortly. Others, like Mathilde, a duke's daughter who was the abbess of Essen, wielded power and wealth that rivaled that of a king or queen. But instead of ruling over a country or territory, these women ruled over their religious communities. Claire of Assisi, Bridget of Sweden, and Teresa of Avila all founded religious orders. Marie D'Oignies founded the Beguines, who lived in convent-like conditions but did not take vows of poverty or chastity.

In these communities, women had a chance to be educated beyond the preparation for domestic life and marriage. Though not every woman in a monastic community was learned, the context opened more possibilities for a woman's life than marriage and children. Given the rate of maternal mortality and the dangers of childbirth, becoming a nun could alter a woman's life span considerably. Moreover, life in the convent or abbey allowed a woman a measure of freedom, in contrast to the bondage of domestic life, where she was essentially a servant to her father, her husband, or her male children.

By giving women access to education and freedom that domestic life did not offer, the convents were frequently criticized. As we mentioned, nuns have been caricatured in literature as cranky and mean, as hypocritical and bawdy, and even as horror villains. In real life, at times religious communities were even suspected as sites of mass hysteria. While some allegations are difficult to substantiate, we can nevertheless grant that suspicion of women's religious communities would not be surprising, given that women's self-determination has been viewed as a threat for a long time in Christian history.

Religious communities of women, then, became places where women could practice a certain measure of resistance to the roles expected of them in patriarchal society. We can identify three kinds of resistance: resistance to male control, resistance to stereotypical domestic gender roles, and resistance to broader social structures and mores. In looking at each of these kinds of resistance, we should keep in mind several things. First, the women who joined these religious communities felt they were living out God's plan for their lives, embracing holiness, and following the guidance of the Holy Spirit. The examples we will explore below didn't primarily join these communities out of spite or a desire to be contrarian, but their lives bear out this resistance.

Second, the three kinds of resistance intertwine with one another: to live outside male control is to stand up against stereotypical gender roles, which were (and still are) an inherent part of the social structure inside and outside the church. Last, while we will look at a few exemplary women here, the list is neither exhaustive nor exclusive. By this I mean that the women who are examples of the first type of resistance are also engaging in the other kinds and that many, many other women were, and are, re-sisters.

Women beyond Male Control

Women's religious communities operated outside the bounds of male control that characterized virtually every other space for much of Christian history. From the time they were born until they died, most women belonged to the men in their lives: first their fathers, then their husbands, and sometimes their sons. Marriages were arranged as advantageous business deals between families, specifically the men. In the home, men could do what they wanted to women without fear of prosecution. In the public square, women were rarely allowed any agency. In the church, women's once-lofty positions as fellow workers and heads of house churches had, by the time of the Middle Ages, been subsumed entirely to the customs of the Roman Empire where women's roles were primarily domestic and reproductive under the dominant *paterfamilias* system where the eldest male was the patriarch of everyone else, male and female, in the extended family. Women couldn't generally own property or work for a living without the permission of a male relation. Everywhere they went, women's lives were in men's hands.

Many of my students come to class under the impression that most women accepted this arrangement because they had no other options. We might tell ourselves that if we had no role models, no images of freedom from male control, we probably would just take the status quo for granted. But this is fiction. Wherever and whenever there has been widespread oppression, in this case male control of female agency, there has also been resistance. Women's religious communities provided one such place for many centuries.

By remaining outside male control, women religious were able to exercise leadership and decide their own fates and that of their communities. As a contemporary example, think of single-sex education. I went to an all-girls high school. Without male colleagues, it meant that the young women I went to school with had to fill all kinds of roles that, at least in the mid-1990s, were still expected to be filled by young men. Someone had to be the editor of the school newspaper, the student body president, the most outspoken person in class. All those people, by necessity, were girls at my high school. Out of that necessity, some girls gained the confidence to take on leadership positions, to exhibit their intellects without undermining themselves, and to discover talents that they might have previously ignored. Women's religious communities functioned similarly: women became (and continue to become) leaders within them because the male leaders were held at bay. The convents, abbeys, and priories were in many ways beyond the purview of male ecclesial and political control. Within their walls, they were self-governing women's spheres, under women's leadership and jurisdiction.

One good example of the exercise of this leadership and jurisdiction was Radegund, a sixth-century German princess. She was taken from her family as a child after a military defeat at the hands of King Clothar, who kept her and married her years later. She was one of his six wives. After he murdered her brother, Radegund ran away from her husband and presented herself before the bishop of Noyen, demanding to be ordained a deaconess. Though he tried to dissuade her, she wouldn't relent, and the bishop yielded. Radegund founded the Abbey of Ste. Croix in Poitiers. She wielded an incredible amount of power over her community, had great personal wealth, and her community was also quite wealthy. She was, by all accounts, as powerful as a bishop, if not more so (after all, she demanded he ordain her). Famous for her asceticism (self-denial), her healing powers, and her writing, Radegund's life was remarkable. The women in her community were educated to be literate, well outside the norm for the early Middle Ages. Radegund's life was about escaping male control and exercising leadership over a community of women and a region that benefitted from her presence and example.

A second example of life outside male control is Catherine of Siena. Catherine Benincasa was one of twenty-five children and lived in the mid-fourteenth century. She made a vow early in her life never to marry. Catherine staged a hunger strike to avoid marrying her sister's widower, and she engaged in severe asceticism like this throughout her life. She was also known as a mystic who frequently had visions of Christ and who felt that she had entered a sacred marriage with him. Catherine was not part of a cloistered religious community but was a Third Order Dominican for most of her life and lived in her family home as a single woman.

She traveled and wrote extensively, and her wisdom and reputation meant that prelates and politicians called on her to intervene in political and ecclesial controversies. Catherine admonished Pope Gregory XI to return from Avignon. She helped make peace between the nation-state of Florence and the pope. As one scholar noted, "She was obedient to the church, but she insisted that the pope and the church be worthy of obedience."[1] Her political and ecclesial savvy made her one of the most influential women in church history. While she did not live in community with other women, her connection to the Dominicans gave her a legitimate reason to be free from male control. She used that freedom to benefit the church in times of great upheaval and schism. In 1970, Pope Paul VI named Catherine of Siena a Doctor of the Church, along with Teresa of Avila. They are the first two women to be honored with that title.

Femininity beyond Domesticity

Women's religious vocations allowed them the possibility of a life outside male control. Whether they lived in communities in convents or in different arrangements like Catherine of Siena, connection to religious orders offered women a way out from under some patriarchal constraints. Outside the reach of male control over their personal lives, however, new kinds of roles opened for women.

Religious communities were places where nondomestic models of femininity flourished. There, women could be something other than wives and mothers. They could be scholars, scientists, activists, even politicians. They could be powerful leaders like Radegund. Religious vocations afforded women opportunities that domestic life simply did not allow them. Much like the girls in the single-sex high school, being away from male influence meant developing all manner of talents that might otherwise have been considered "for men." Whether it's managing the convent's resources or writing sacred music, nuns resisted domestic femininity and fleshed out different models of what womanhood could be. How did they manage this?

One way in which women religious were able to evade male control and inhabit new models of womanhood was by describing their mystical experiences. Many of the women I'm highlighting in this chapter were visionaries who described in detail the visions they had of God, of Jesus, of Mary, and the like. The church accords visionaries a certain amount of respect, especially if they are believed to lead holy lives in sacrifice for others. As visionaries, mystics, and holy persons, these women were allowed to operate in theological, philosophical, scientific, and political spheres typically reserved for men. Let's look at two examples: Hildegard of Bingen and Teresa of Avila.

Hildegard was a Benedictine abbess who lived in the late eleventh and early twelfth centuries. She was a sickly child who had visions and heard voices, many of which were recorded by a monk named Volmar. Despite having little formal schooling, Hildegard became an exceptional writer whose work spanned topics as broad as herbal medicine, music, and theology. She is regarded as a pioneer in European pharmaceutical science.[2] Her theological language might sound strange to the contemporary reader. For Hildegard, immersed as she was in the world of nature and plants and herbal healing, God's grace is represented as greenness and moisture. Sin, according to Hildegard, was aridity or dryness. Her writings make frequent reference to God as "the Living Light" as well as to Sapientia (wisdom, a feminine word in Latin), which she also used as a name for God. She wrote hymns and designed clothing (habits) for the nuns. Overall, she was a renaissance woman well before the Renaissance. She was a scientist and an artist, a musician and a healer, an abbess and a visionary. She conceived of God in feminine terms like Sapientia and Sophia, in ecological metaphors like greenness and moisture. Hildegard was declared a Doctor of the Church by Pope Benedict XVI in 2012.

Our second example of femininity beyond domesticity is Teresa of Avila. Teresa is also a Doctor of the Church. Active during the Catholic Reformation in the sixteenth century, Teresa was a reformer of Carmelite life, a mystic and prolific chronicler of her experiences, and a prayer innovator. Derided by her enemies and even some patrons and her own sisters as stubborn and disobedient, Teresa spearheaded a reform of her religious order that resulted in the creation of a new branch, the Discalced Carmelites. As a mystic and well-known nun, Teresa was witty and forthcoming about her religious experiences. This did not mean she wasn't, like many other women mystics, prone to extreme asceticism and mortification of the flesh—a practice that involves self-injury that was common throughout Christian history.

Teresa's renown came from her insights into prayer. She wrote mystical treatises on prayer, most notably *The Interior Castle*, where she sets out a form of Christian meditation, or interior, contemplative prayer, that is still used by many Christians today. In describing her mystical experiences, many have noticed that Teresa uses language that might be understood as sexual. While many mystics describe their union with God as intimate and a form of ecstasy, Teresa recounts an experience where she is pierced by a golden spear with fire at the tip, and she experiences a sweet pain thrusting into her heart repeatedly. This pain leaves her on fire with love of God. The erotic language led artists like Bernini to depict her mystical ecstasy as an orgasmic experience. While some critics claim that those who read Teresa as a sexual mystic are looking at her through the lens of our hypersexualized society, one could also conclude that Teresa's mysticism might represent a reclaiming of sexual language by a woman for a religious purpose. Women's prescribed roles in society prohibited mentioning sex or enjoying it in any way. Thus, Teresa's descriptions of her ecstatic experiences are transgressive and reclaim a kind of sexual agency, even if that ecstasy is experienced mystically with God and not with a human partner.

Both Teresa of Avila and Hildegard lived outside women's expected gender roles. Hildegard used her scientific knowledge and visions to elaborate a mysticism that is ecologically rich and still relevant. Teresa's innovations in prayer made her a model of spiritual renewal in the Catholic Reformation, and her erotic imagery recaptures sexual language in a way that was licit for women of her day.

Humanity beyond Injustice

A third kind of resistance allowed by women's religious communities is resistance to sinful social structures in the pursuit of building justice. All communities, including religious communities, tend to reflect the biases of their day, and convents, priories, and abbeys are no exception to this. Not every community stood up to patriarchy, segregation, or misogyny. In many parts of the world, including Ireland and the Americas, religious communities of women perpetrated violence against young people entrusted to their care. In the Magdalene laundries of Ireland, young pregnant women were kept in horrific conditions, their children either adopted out or left to die. In the southwestern United States, schools run by women's religious orders punished children who would not speak English, separated Native American children from their families, and perpetrated other forms of physical, cultural, and spiritual violence. This chapter does not claim that all women religious are guilty of these crimes, nor were they all engaged in feminist social and religious resistance. Instead, our claim here is that religious life allowed women the space to resist in times and cultures where those spaces were quite scarce.

Two examples of women who pushed back against the prevailing social injustices of their time hail from the Americas. Sor Juana Inés de la Cruz was a Mexican-born nun who was also a prolific poet. A champion of women's education, she is hailed by many as the first feminist of the Americas. Like other women of the seventeenth century, Juana did not have much formal education but was a voracious reader and self-taught writer. Reports of her intelligence and wit reveal a profound thinker and a person deeply committed to the equality of the sexes. Juana's fundamental belief was that the soul did not have a gender, and therefore all differences between the sexes were merely physical. Thus, to subjugate women, to treat them as second class, was an insult to their God-given dignity. In her clashes with ecclesiastical authorities, they saw her as challenging the Pauline teaching that women should be silent in church (1 Cor 14:34–35). Her response to this accusation, as well as to rumors that she was a sinner and a bad influence, was published as *La Respuesta* and is worth a read. In it, she uses a common trope often used by women religious: a deliberate denigration of her own gifts ("I am unable to understand the sacred texts"), coupled with repeated allusions to the weakness of her sex and her many deficiencies because she is a woman. She writes, "I, ignoramus that I am, first among all," in a tome in which she fluidly quotes philosophy, theology, and science.

The tone is almost sarcastic, today we'd say over the top, as she responds to the accusatory letter that she characterizes as "very learned, quite discreet, most holy and thoroughly loving." As *La Respuesta* goes on, however, the reader sees Sor Juana build an impressive case for women's education. She uses examples from her own life, from history, and from biblical hermeneutics. She draws on St. Jerome, St. Thomas Aquinas, and the books of scripture themselves. Her logic is flawless as she elaborates the autobiography of a woman for whom study and learning is almost compulsive. Here she is in paragraph 29: "If my studies, my Lady, were merits (and I do see them so celebrated in men), in me they would not be so because I act out of necessity." In this as in her other writings, Juana proves her worth as a writer by employing styles that were popular in her historical context to refute misogynistic beliefs that were also prevalent at the time. As a fierce defender of women's rights to education and to equal treatment, Sor Juana is indeed rightly called the first feminist of the Americas—at least the first who wrote about it.

Our second example is Henriette DeLille. Henriette was a Black woman born in New Orleans who worked to dismantle both the sexist and racist system of plaçage that was prominent in nineteenth-century Louisiana and the racism of the Catholic Church that barred nonwhite women from religious life. Henriette refused to participate in the system of plaçage, a social arrangement where women of color became mistresses to wealthy white men, enjoyed their protection, and bore their children. You might think here of Thomas Jefferson and Sally Hemings, with the added disgrace that Sally Hemings was his slave. Henriette's own mother, a free woman of color, was part of this system. The white men did not marry the women of color and often went on to marry white women and have families that they acknowledged publicly. The women in plaçage arrangements were thus neither married nor free to marry another man but tied to the whims of white men. By refusing to take part in this system of racist patronage, and instead deciding that she would dedicate her life to God, DeLille exemplified the God-given dignity of Black women in the Americas, itself a controversial assertion. After all, Louisiana's economy depended largely on the labor of enslaved persons. The fundamental racism underlying Louisiana's economy was also evident in the church. It took nearly two decades for the church to approve DeLille's petition to start a community of religious women of color. As theologian M. Shawn Copeland has noted, DeLille's life exposed the timidity of the church with respect to caring for people of color. We might ask whether that timidity has ever been overcome in the U.S. Catholic Church.

Finally, and on a lighter note, religious communities were sites of resistance where women could, for lack of a better phrase, let their freak flags fly. Women religious brought us imagery of nursing at Jesus's breast, as Julian of Norwich experienced in her visions of Jesus as mother. Catherine of Siena was fascinated by Jesus's circumcision and was said to wear his foreskin as her wedding ring symbolizing her marriage to Christ. As we read earlier, Teresa of Avila famously described her mystical experiences, where she saw and felt God face-to-face, in blatantly erotic terms, describing Jesus's sword glimmering and piercing her and joining her to Christ. Sor Juana Inés de la Cruz excoriated men's behavior, espousing a strident feminism that in no way would have been permitted of any married woman. But as a woman of learning and a religious, she was permitted to call men stupid for accusing women of tempting them without accepting responsibility for their own sexual morality. The cloistered life allowed a lot of leeway, creativity, and boldness to flourish. And, thanks to the records kept at convents and abbeys, the stories of these bold visionary women were preserved for us today.

"Re-Sisters" Today

Perhaps the most constant sort of resistance common to women religious is resistance to the oppression and suspicion of patriarchal culture, whether religious or secular. Each of the women highlighted in this chapter faced fierce opposition from both secular culture and the church they served. We have seen that communities of women religious, and even individual nuns, anchoresses (women who lived in solitude in a cell attached to a church), and other women who took vows pushed against gendered expectations. These women were educated but often framed their deep theological insights as "visions" that came to them unmediated from God, since women were not thought capable of scholarly competence. They were brave leaders but often needed the protection of a confessor or another member of the clergy in order to avoid censure. Many heads of congregations were forced into exile or to disband their communities.

But we don't need to look to the Middle Ages for examples of this suspicion and harassment. From 2008 to 2015, the United States' largest group of women religious, the Leadership Conference of Women Religious (LCWR), was investigated by the Vatican. The accusations leveled at the LCWR ranged from a claim that they placed insufficient emphasis on the Eucharist to the idea that their goals were "too feminist" and therefore insufficiently Catholic. Though Pope Francis closed the investigation with no sanction placed on the LCWR, the fact remains that when the church was dealing with the fallout from the sexual abuse and cover-up scandals, the hierarchy chose to investigate faithful women. The women of the LCWR run schools and hospitals; they include presidents of colleges and universities, of the Catholic Health Association, and of Catholic Charities. Women in the LCWR are scholars and teachers, nurses and executives. But most important, they are women of faith, who come together to discern God's will for their lives and how to make the reign of God present in the contemporary world. That aspect of religious life is unchanged from the Middle Ages, and it is this core identity that makes these women re-sisters.

What would happen if, instead of viewing these women with suspicion, the church would look to women religious as examples of faithful resistance, of fierce holiness, and of transformative love for the world? As it turns out, women religious have been doing all of these things in the present day as well. Nuns were among the first laypeople admitted to advanced degree programs in theology just before and in the wake of Vatican II. As a result, many of the first female professors of theology were women religious. Women like

Elizabeth Johnson, Margaret Farley, and Anne Carr shaped Catholic feminist theology in crucial ways. Johnson's writings range from the doctrine of God, to Mariology, to ecological theology. Farley is one of the leading voices in Catholic moral theology. Both women found themselves at odds with the church hierarchy, who investigated their theological writings, and both women defended their theology impressively. Carr was one of the first Catholic women ecclesiologists, who wrote about Vatican II, the church, and theological anthropology. Sandra Schneiders, IHM, is one of the foremost scholars of spirituality alive today. There are many other women scholars who are no longer in religious life or chose a lay path from the start, but nevertheless continue their work on behalf of the church. María Pilar Aquino, M. Shawn Copeland, and many others are among the women theologians who were in religious life at one point. They too are re-sisters. And these scholars have gone on to train generations of new feminist theologians, including this author.

Nuns are not only important in the academic world, however. They are making their mark in politics, both within the church and outside it. In 2021, Pope Francis appointed Sr. Nathalie Becquart, an Xavière sister from Toronto, as the undersecretary for the office of the Synod of Bishops in Rome. This is the highest office a woman has held in the office of the Synod of Bishops because Sr. Becquart is the first woman to have a position there. While women have been appointed to offices dealing with families and education, Francis's decision to name a woman to the office of the Synod of Bishops is significant. It shows that women can be entrusted with managing the bishops, a definite change of pace for Vatican politics.

In secular politics, nuns have been making a splash as well. Sr. Simone Campbell became well known as the leader of the Nuns on the Bus, a group of religious women who traveled around the United States lobbying for support of progressive causes like food security, living wages, and just immigration policies. As the head of NETWORK, Campbell was at the forefront of the church's most visible social justice lobbying group in Washington, DC. We can also look at Sr. Norma Pimentel, a Mexican American nun working on the border between the United States and Mexico. Pimentel rose to prominence during the immigration crises of the Trump administration. She advocates against the family separation policies enforced by the U.S. government. As the director of Catholic Charities of the Rio Grande Valley, Pimentel oversees centers that provide humanitarian aid to refugees and other people in crisis on the border. Given the violence and instability of Central and South American countries, the numbers of refugees have been steadily increasing even as our country's willingness to grant asylum and shelter has lessened. Nevertheless, Pimentel continues to provide for vulnerable asylum seekers and travels the country advocating for the rights of immigrants and refugees.

There are so many women religious who have and who continue to make a mark on the world with their brave resistance to institutionalized misogyny, racism, and indifference. Although contemporary women have a great deal more say in the shape of their lives, and we are free to marry or not, to have children or not, to have careers or not, religious life remains a viable option in the Catholic Church. Though numbers have dwindled since the sexual and cultural revolutions of the 1960s, many women find meaning and purpose in religious life, find sustenance in the community it provides, and find God there too. While in the past women may have fled to convents because of fear or defiance, in our contemporary context women are drawn to religious life for other reasons, including finding a supportive single-sex community where they can live out their vocations. In addition to their prophetic voices on issues like immigration, social welfare, and health-care access, women's religious communities are at the vanguard of imagining different ways of being church. As one nun mentioned to me, in a conversation about Pope Francis possibly appointing a woman a cardinal: "The religious orders have been training women to exercise that kind of leadership for generations. There are already many, many women who are prepared to take on the work of a cardinal."

Whether they are fleeing the world or opening their hearts to the world more fully, women's call to religious life has consistently served as a site of resistance in the church. Nuns, sisters, abbesses, anchoresses, and other vowed women eluded male control over their lives, forged countercultural examples of womanhood, and stood as prophetic signs against social injustice. Even with fewer women entering religious life, partnerships between younger women and vowed religious women continue to flourish, as in the Nuns and Nones project, a community of intergenerational spiritual accompaniment begun in 2016. What we see in many contemporary religious communities is prophetic for the church as a whole: a willingness to embrace new partnerships, new ways of approaching a life of faith and a commitment to justice, and the openness and patience to visualize the missions of their founders in the hands of women and men who may never take vows themselves. If we can look at Teresa of Avila, Henriette DeLille, or Catherine of Siena as women who embodied the church they wanted to live in, we ought to continue to look to the nuns, the (re)sisters, as models of the church we want to be.

DISCUSSION QUESTIONS

1. Have you ever met a nun or a woman religious? Are there women in your life who do not conform to domestic norms or other norms associated with femininity? How do they do this?
2. Look up information on the Nuns and Nones project, or other intergenerational intentional Catholic communities. Would you ever join a community like this? What is appealing about these communities, and why might someone be drawn to this life?
3. In many ways, the sexual revolution and feminist movements have achieved a level of independence for women that render things like medieval abbeys obsolete as places to find refuge from male control. Do you think nuns have a role to play in the world today? What is that role?

DELVE DEEPER

Research the life of one of the women mystics mentioned in this chapter: Julian of Norwich, Hildegard of Bingen, Teresa of Avila, Mathilde of Essen, Scholastica, Catherine of Siena, or Sor Juana. Who would you cast in a movie about their life? What would the driving plot be?

READ FURTHER

Copeland, M. Shawn. *The Subversive Power of Love: The Vision of Henriette DeLille*. Mahwah, NJ: Paulist Press, 2008.

Cummings, Kathleen Sprows. *New Women of the Old Faith*. Chapel Hill: UNC Press, 2009.

Cummings, Kathleen Sprows, and Jeffrey M. Burns, ed. *Preaching with Their Lives: Dominicans on Mission in the United States after 1850*. New York: Fordham University Press, 2020.

de la Cruz, Sor Juana Inés. *The Answer/La Respuesta, Including a Selection of Poems*. Translated by Electa Arenal and Amanda Powell. New York: Feminist Press, 1994.

Gonzalez, Michelle. *Sor Juana: Beauty and Justice in the Americas*. Maryknoll, NY: Orbis Books, 2014.

Hilkert, Mary Catherine. *Speaking with Authority: Catherine of Siena and the Voices of Women Today*. Mahwah, NJ: Paulist Press, 2009.

McGuinness, Margaret. *Called to Serve: A History of Nuns in America*. New York: NYU Press, 2013.

Pratt, Tia Noelle. "'I Bring Myself, My Black Self': Sr. Thea Bowman's Challenge to the Catholic Church." *Commonweal*, November 2020.

Williams, Shannen Dee. *Subversive Habits: Black Catholic Nuns in the Long African American Freedom Struggle*. Durham: Duke University Press, 2022.

12

RENAMING GOD AND ONE ANOTHER

Images of God and Our Human Existence

This morning I went out for a run and, as I usually do, put on a favorite podcast to keep me company. The opening "icebreaker" question for the panel was: "Is God a woman?" Now, this is a feminist podcast, so I expected a variety of intriguing answers. Moreover, the panelists are comedians and political commentators. They did not disappoint. One panelist thought God was "genderless." Another claimed God was a woman but a "ladder-puller"—the kind of woman who suffers at the hands of patriarchy and therefore thinks everyone after her should suffer as well so she pulls the ladder up after she's reached the top. The panel made some hilarious points and some excellent ones about biblical and popular understandings of God, of womanhood, of pregnancy. As a fan and as a theologian, I was naturally formulating my own answer as I ran along the path. Was Ariana Grande right? Can we say that God is a woman?

This shouldn't seem like a very radical question, but it feels that way nonetheless. We are so accustomed in our daily lives to associate maleness with God. Sometimes that is because we conflate God and Jesus or because we automatically say "God the Father" is the first person of the Trinity. All around us, we turn and sing and pray to a God who is a divine, omnipotent *he*. We contemplate *his* creation and ask for *his* help. We fear *his* wrath and rest confidently in *his* protection.

Mary Daly, a pioneering Catholic feminist theologian in the 1960s and 1970s, famously claimed that "if God is male, then the male is god." By that she means that if we rely solely on male imagery for the almighty, omniscient, omnipresent God, we begin to associate all-powerfulness, all-knowingness with maleness. Put simply, we will start to think that qualities we consider "manly" or "masculine" are more fitting for God, so human males who embody these qualities on earth are more godly, deserving of more respect. I'm sure very few people think that all men are divine creatures on earth, but because of gendered language, somehow when we look at men we see some god-ness in them. Conversely, those traits that are more stereotypically associated with women seem somehow beneath God or alien to God. We don't have the same feeling of divinity when we encounter women or female gender words.

Years after Daly's proclamation, Elizabeth Johnson took this idea a step further. She points out that our persistent use of male metaphors and pronouns for God amounts to idolatry—we have replaced a fundamentally unknowable God with a lesser thing: a human male. To worship a God we only ever refer to or conceive of as "he" is to train our minds to think of the pronoun *him* as inherently more godlike than *her* or *them*. If idolatry is the sin of worshiping something that isn't God as if it were, or something that is less than God as if it were fully God, then only worshiping God as male, only conceiving of God as male, definitely counts as idolatry. God is beyond human understanding. To rely on he/him to the point where everything else feels strange and wrong is essentially to equate those pronouns with an unknowable God. God exceeds maleness, just as God exceeds femaleness and every other human characteristic, because God is infinite. God is neither she nor he. God is God. Our finite minds cannot comprehend the infinite, so God remains fundamentally unknowable to us in God's fullness. And let's face it, we don't worship anything less than the fullness of God.

But this leaves us with all sorts of practical problems. What are we supposed to do? We cannot call God "it," for we need a relationship with God, and it's difficult to cultivate a relationship with an "it." Should we always take turns, referring to God as he, then she, then they? Should we just say "God" repeatedly, including the clunky *God self*? What about scripture? Should we switch that out? Swap every "he" for "she" or "they" as some revised Bible translations do? Do we have the right to do something like that? After all, do we even know what God is? An overwhelming majority of theologians believe we cannot ever know God fully in this life. St. Augustine's famous line comes to mind: "If you have understood, that is not God."[1]

Analogy: The Bridge beyond the Impasse

It might feel hopeless to try to talk about God when God is someone we cannot hope to understand. But have you ever been in love? Or even infatuated with someone? Right now, those of you in college have a roommate who is going through this experience. In those early days of falling in love, the lovers can do anything. Anything, that is, except shut up about it. Though they cannot put their emotions into adequate words, they keep trying. And trying. Though it's impossible to explain to others what it is about the beloved that is so amazing—it's their voice, no their height, no their face, their eyes, their vibe—nevertheless, the endless attempts at expressing just what is so perfect about their crush just keep coming. Maybe you've rolled your eyes at this phenomenon, or maybe you are cringing right now thinking about yourself acting this way recently. You need not feel too embarrassed, though. Nearly everyone has been there. Part of the power of relationship, of feeling truly known and seen, is a compelling desire to share that feeling.

Centuries of scriptural and mystical texts, theological discourses, and the lives of saints prove that the same is true of our relationship to the divine. Even though God is fundamentally unknowable and beyond the reach of our language and our artistic expression, we nevertheless feel compelled to write, to sing, to paint and draw and dance the depths of our love for God, and our sense of God's love for us. Like the early bloom of love, our relationship with God overtakes us and we simply can't help but express it.

So if we can't help but talk about it, how should we do it? If Augustine's words above about God forever eluding our understanding aren't enough to scare us off, then how can we speak about God correctly? Or, if not correctly, then with the least amount of error? The answer lies in the concept of analogy.

Many years ago, standardized tests like the SAT or the ACT had a section in the verbal part of the test that required students to complete a series of analogies. An analogy is a comparison that expresses a relationship. The relationship expressed by an analogy is not an exact one, therefore it includes a measure of similarity and dissimilarity. Instinctively, we know what analogies are. For example, I'm confident that if I said, "Cat is to kitten as dog is to..." you would know to say "puppy." None of the four nouns in that analogy is, strictly speaking, the same as another. But it's clear what the analogy is trying to communicate: that the relationship between cats (mature animals) and kittens (immature animals) is like that between dogs and puppies. Kittens and puppies are alike in that they are both immature animals, but they are not the same. Neither are dogs and puppies or cats and kittens the same. They are in different stages of development. But despite having four dissimilar creatures in the comparison, the analogy expresses a truth about the relationship between baby animals and adult animals.

Aquinas is probably the most famous theologian to apply analogical thinking to the divine. For him, all our understanding of God was based in analogy because our understanding of God, who is infinite, must be expressed using human language and imagery, which is necessarily finite. In order to speak rightly of something infinite using finite language and ideas, then, we must make use of analogy, and we must understand that we are approximating God, but not necessarily describing God, with our language. As Johnson notes in her work interpreting Aquinas's analogical theology, our language is the finger that is pointing at the moon (which is God). Language and imagery are never to be confused with the moon itself.

Pseudo-Dionysius, a sixth-century writer and mystic, said the same thing in a different way. For that author, God is beyond our comprehension. All our statements about God, according to Pseudo-Dionysius, conceal more than they reveal. For example, we frequently state that God is love. But when we say "love," we are referring to our human experiences of love: romantic love, familial love, sexual love, a friend's love, the love a community has for its own members, even unconditional experiences of love. But God is beyond even that since all our experiences of love are finite and limited, but God is infinite, unlimited. Therefore it's more accurate, in this line of thinking, to say God is "not-love." This doesn't mean that God is hate or indifference, but rather that God's love is beyond any human experience of love.

Now let's try it with the word *good*. Yes, God is good. But what do we mean when we say good? *Good* has so many meanings for us. Is God a good kid? A good student or good athlete? A good mood? A delicious meal? A fun time? All of these notions of goodness are rooted in our human experience. We use *good* to mean obedient, kind, talented, upbeat, delicious, and fun. But God is beyond any of those characterizations. Pseudo-Dionysius would say in his *Mystical Theology* that it's closer to the truth to say that God is "not-good," as in "not good in the way we understand goodness, but way beyond that." For this thinker, it was important to think in images about God, but also to know that our images fall way short of God's full reality. Because we can only ever know what we know, what we experience, what we have words for, and God is beyond all of that.

Despite the poverty of our language, we are compelled to speak about God. To do this we use linguistic devices like analogies. They are all over our prayer, our scriptures, our liturgy. God is our rock, our father, our hope. Less frequently noticed, though also in scripture, God is a mother hen protecting us, a woman groaning in labor, a woman rejoicing over finding a lost coin, and a beautiful lover. All of these are analogies. That is to say, calling God "father" is analogical, even if Jesus referred to God as "Abba" or "dad." Calling God a "rock" is analogical as well, in what is likely a more obvious way to us, because we know that a rock is a thing, that it is not alive, but that the image is meant to convey strength, stability, unwaveringness. In the biblical Song of Songs, the relationship between God and humanity is portrayed like the relationship between two young lovers, seeking each other out constantly, unable to get their fill of one another. This does not mean that God is a stag or a gazelle, or that we have a sexually charged relationship with God—though some female mystics like Teresa of Avila spoke that way. Perhaps it means that the closeness between God and humanity is like the pull of young love or like the excitement of infatuation.

Is God a Woman? Theological Anthropology

Let's return to the idea that opened this chapter. If our language for God is all analogical, if it all contains some dissimilarity along with similarity, then can we say with Ms. Grande that "God is a woman"? Does it feel weird to do so? It might. And it is worth it to explore why we experience more discomfort with using feminine images and images drawn from women's experience to talk about God. To do that, we need to wade into the waters of theological anthropology, which has long been an entry point into feminist theology. Before we can ask, "Is God a woman?" we need to ask, "What is a woman?" And "Are women people?"

Theological anthropology is that branch of theological inquiry that investigates what it means to be a human being considering what we know about God through revelation. Central to the discipline of theological anthropology is the notion of *imago Dei*. Taken from Genesis, this is the idea that humanity is made in God's image. Theological anthropology asks the following questions: What are the consequences of being made in God's image? What might it mean for us, for God, that we share a likeness? If to be made in God's image means we bear a resemblance to God, where does that resemblance lie, given that humanity is so varied? Is it in our capacity for rational thought or for loving relationship? Is it in our ability to imagine what's possible? Is it in the feeling of responsibility we have toward one another? Do some humans bear a closer resemblance to God than other human beings?

This last question is where feminist theologians really began to make inroads into mainstream/dominant theology. After all, many theologians, such as St. Augustine, believed that women were not completely in the image of God, at least not outside of a relationship with a man.[2] If we consistently, and persistently, refer to God using only masculine pronouns and male language and imagery, is it any wonder that women will seem to resemble God's image less? And if they do, what are the implications for female participation in church life and leadership? We know the answer in the restriction of ordination to priesthood to men only because, the thinking goes, the priest at Mass is another Christ, and Jesus was biologically male—but Christ is only one person of the Trinity, so does that thinking split the triune God into genders?

In my undergraduate classes, I usually assign a chapter from Elizabeth Johnson's magisterial *She Who Is: The Mystery of God in Feminist Theological Discourse* and then give students the following homework assignment. For the next two to three days, initiate conversations about God with your peers, roommates, friends, and family members, especially older family members. In these conversations, you should refer to God using only feminine pronouns (she/her) and/or images drawn from women's lives and experience (mother, daughter, sister, etc.). After you have these conversations, make note of the reactions to your language shift. Then, spend some time reflecting on your own feelings as you did this exercise.

Overall, students are very nervous heading into the assignment and somewhat surprised when it's done. Mostly, the students' families, especially grandparents, are resistant or sometimes hostile to the idea of using feminine pronouns for God. The peers tend not to notice or just to shrug it off. But my favorite reactions are those of the students themselves. "I had a hard time remembering to use *she* instead of *he*." "Honestly, I felt really strange using this language." The students' reflections on their own feelings are the central point of the exercise. The objective, of course, is to point out what we mean by analogical language. If you feel very comfortable using male pronouns for God but very uncomfortable using any other pronouns, dig into that discomfort. Where does it come from? Why does it make you feel weird to call God "she"? It may be merely a habit, and making new habits is always a bit awkward. But there may be a deeper, more insidious reason at work, which is that we don't associate womanhood, or female identity, with the divine. Somehow, in some way, it seems to demean God to refer to God using non-male pronouns. To me, that says that we've internalized something very dark indeed: that there is something inherently demeaning about not being a male.

This deeper reason, the often-subconscious association with womanhood as demeaning or somehow subtracting from God, ties our theology (god-talk) to our notions of theological anthropology. Until we learn, until we are taught that women and men image God in equal (and equally paltry) ways, we will continue the cycle of viewing God as more male than any other gender and maleness as somehow more fitting for God than any other gender. And that will continue to reinforce patriarchal social structures, which rely on viewing women as less-than.

What children learn about how human beings are made in God's image (from the creation story in Gen 1) frequently gets combined in popular retellings with the story of Adam and Eve (the creation story in Gen 2—3). In this second story, as we saw in the first part of this book, Eve is associated with bringing sin into the world, and therefore all women are viewed as culpable for sin in some way. Eve is set up as an antagonist to God's plan for humanity. It makes sense, in that framework, to say that God is more like Adam than Eve because Eve is seen as working against God's plans, as disobeying God, almost as a foil for God.

Feminist theologians recognize that until we broaden our understandings of grace and sin and break the association between Eve-women-sin-temptation, we cannot hope to understand that women are as much in God's image as men. And until we understand that fundamental equality among human beings, we cannot overcome the idolatry of our dependence on a male God. Ultimately, if we believe that women are less-than, then imagery that is feminine or that uses women's experience will be seen as demeaning God, as making God less than powerful, less than omniscient, less than divine. Until we see people of all genders as powerful, as knowledgeable, as nurturing and just and merciful and wrathful and protective, we will continue to rely on stereotypical gender roles to describe who God is (and who God is not).

What about the Goddess?

In the early days of second-wave feminist thinking, many scholars of religion entertained, and even embraced, the idea of replacing the worship of God for the worship of the Goddess, a female divine figure. Women were starved for an image of the divine that represented their experience, their knowledge and expertise, and their way of being in the world, and God's association with maleness was alienating. A solution was to worship the feminine: the Goddess. Books like Rosemary Radford Ruether's *Gaia and God* sought to reclaim the feminine divine, the association with ecology inherent in feminine imagery. They also wanted to repair the devaluing of womanhood and of the earth that they viewed as going hand in hand. Other reasons for worshiping the Goddess included attempting to heal those who had suffered violence and abuse at the hands of men. For abused women and children, maleness was sometimes associated with pain, violence, or neglect: nothing we would want to associate with God. Goddess worship also celebrated women's bodily functions of menstruation, birth, nursing, and caretaking. It served to overcome the invisibility of older women in our beauty—and therefore youth—obsessed culture. The Goddess embraced women's power and agency, their sexuality and will.

This alternative imagery is important if we are to expand our theological and analogical imaginations. Recall the importance of sitting with the idea that God is feminine—a goddess, if you will. Any discomfort students felt was meant to reveal how inadequate all our language for God ultimately is. In centering goddess worship, however, second-wave feminists also found that they were decentering many of the authoritarian, hierarchical, and patriarchal trappings that came with worshiping a male God. If instead of a male God we worshiped a Goddess, then men's will was not the ultimate stand-in for the divine will on earth. Many spiritualities that center Goddess worship focus on collective energies, on communal rituals, and on celebrating nature. This fundamentally destabilizes a patriarchal culture that prizes individual achievement, singular male saviors, and the forces of "civilization" that are meant to tame the natural world for human use.

Ultimately, Goddess worship did not gain traction in the Catholic Church. We might attribute this to the conservative backlash that came after the reforms of the Second Vatican Council or to the persistently patriarchal structure of the church. Whatever the reason, the papacies of John Paul II and Benedict XVI, which together spanned from the late 1970s to the early 2000s, were not a time when interest in the Goddess was high among average U.S. Catholics. This does not mean that quasi-divine feminine figures did not, and do not, hold importance for Catholics, however. Indeed, it would seem as if some primal human need to worship figures in masculine and feminine forms is difficult to suppress.

The most obvious example of this is the prominent place of Mary in Catholic devotion. All over the world, Catholics express devotion to the mother of God in a variety of ways, places, and languages. She is revered under a variety of names and is said to have appeared on nearly every continent. In Latin America especially, images of the Virgin Mary abound, and devotions are as diverse as the cultures that make up the Americas. One of the historic criticisms of Catholicism is that she's worshiped as divine, but she's not. While official church teaching claims that Catholics do not offer worship (the Greek word is *latria*) to Mary, but rather devotion (*dulia*), in the case of Mary a special kind of super-devotion (*hyperdulia*) was distinguished in order to aptly name what is going on when Catholics pray to her. Mary is the super-saint, the saint-above-all-saints, the mother of God who can, in some people's minds, tell Jesus what's what. She has been revered as the *Theotokos* (God-bearer) since the fourth century and as the neck that turns Jesus, the head of the church, to look more mercifully upon us.

One of the main problems feminist theologians have had with Marian devotion has been its focus on Mary's perpetual virginity. This devaluing of sexuality is one of the aspects of patriarchal God worship that Goddess theologians were trying to overcome. Carol Christ notes in an essay in *WomanSpirit Rising* that "the Virgin Mary, the positive female image in Christianity does not contradict Christian denigration of the female body and its powers. The Virgin Mary is revered because she, in her perpetual virginity, transcends the carnal sexuality attributed to most women."[3] Catholics are encouraged to offer praise and devotion to Mary because of her exemption from all sexuality, her lack of need for it, and her complete submission to the divine (male) will. Since Mary is viewed as asexual or even antisexual, devotion to her does not threaten patriarchal male-God worship. In fact it reinforces the idea that "regular" women, for whom virginity and motherhood cannot coexist, embody the kind of tempting carnality that Eve brought into the world.

But in a global church, where so many different people from so many different cultures revere Mary, we must ask whether this nonsexual, submissive figure is in fact universal or whether she is particular to some European cultures. After all, every religious devotion, every religious belief, arises in a context and lives in a context. It is possible that some contexts where indigenous worship of gods in male and female form was common adapted veneration of Mary in context-appropriate ways. Let me give you an example from personal experience.

In 2016, I was part of a delegation of Catholic scholars who visited Peru to study with Gustavo Gutiérrez, a seminal figure in Latin American liberation theology. The trip took place in early August and began in Cuzco, where we were to get acclimated to the altitude in preparation to see Machu Picchu in the following days. When we arrived in Cuzco, a group of us headed into the central square to see the basilica. We were lucky to happen upon a Marian celebration that was in full swing, with prayers and music inside the cathedral and food and other vendors ready as people spilled out into the square. As a scholar of religion, and in particular as someone who had by then written a fair amount about Marian devotion, I was overjoyed at our luck. Inside were a variety of groups dressed in a mixture of European and Andean-indigenous clothing. The music featured panflutes, drums, and stringed instruments like charangos. There was dancing inside, along with different groups praying in different parts of the cathedral. The Last Supper depicted behind the altar featured a dish of guinea pig (cuy), which is traditional in Peru.

The feast the community was celebrating in the cathedral that evening was dedicated to Maria Asunta, the Virgin of the Assumption. Traditionally this is celebrated all over the country in the first week of August. But this evening Cuzco was also celebrating Pachamama, the indigenous Andean Mother Earth goddess. It was impossible to tell, in the varied celebrations and devotions that occurred simultaneously in that cathedral, what was a specifically "Marian" (i.e., Catholic, Spanish-introduced) devotion and what was an adaptation of indigenous rituals to a colonial religion and colonial religious space. One vivid memory I have is of a group of men playing music who processed with a statue of the Virgin through the cathedral doors, placed her on her altar (it may have been one of the side altars in the cathedral), and then retreated, playing Andean music and dancing out of the cathedral backward, so as "not to turn their backs to Our Lady," as I was told by a Peruvian observer. How much of this overlaps with the virginal submissive Mary depicted in, for example, the Immaculate Conception? It is tough to say.

The pontificate of Pope Francis has seen its share of controversy around indigenous images of Mary, particularly one that was brought to Rome during the Synod on the Amazon in 2019. Some conservative activists were offended by the image, which resembles a pregnant indigenous woman. These activists claimed that it was a pagan image of the Pachamama and that Pope Francis was endorsing this pagan goddess worship. Some extremists stole the statue and threw it in the Tiber. These men were celebrated by culture warriors in the United States. Of course, other depictions of Jesus's mother with indigenous features and pregnant exist, most notably the image of Guadalupe that is revered in Mexico and all over the Americas. These images reflect the contexts in which they arise, they mirror the people in the communities that give rise to them. A Mexican Mary looks Mexican, just as Korean depictions of Mary look Korean. This is nothing new. What is new is the vehemence with which some Catholics reacted to the presence of an indigenous-looking Mary in Rome. To them, it was impossible to believe that the woman in the image represented the mother of Jesus. She had to be some other deity.

If my experience at the Cuzco cathedral taught me anything, it is that people find ways to worship God in feminine forms all over the world in ways we may never fully know about here in the United States. This is a good thing, not a bad thing. After all, our hope as Christians is that God will be worshiped all over the world, in every language. The Feast of Maria Asunta in the Cuzco cathedral was a celebration of the mother of God in Peru. People in colonial and indigenous dress, as well as jeans and tee-shirts, gathered to pray to Mary, to give thanks and veneration in word and song, mixing indigenous music and using Spanish and Quechua lyrics.

Were they worshiping a goddess? Or the divine in feminine form? Perhaps. That is a place where the Holy Spirit is at work. Latino theologian Orlando Espín theorized that Guadalupe was more accurately understood as a manifestation of the Holy Spirit, not of Mary, Jesus's mother. I believe that the celebration of Maria Asunta on the feast of the Pachamama similarly embraced a variety of understandings of what Catholics do when they venerate Mary. On the one hand, they are devoted to her and ask her intercession before her son. On the other, she serves as an outlet for the human need to see the divine in human forms that celebrate the image of God in all of humanity, not only male humans. The desires of a patriarchal church to ensure that Mary is venerated officially in only one way (as a submissive ever-virgin) do not always overlap with the will of the people of God to see the divine in more than male forms.

Reconstructing Our Metaphors

In chapter 3 we looked at feminist theological method. We identified three steps: deconstruction of problematic symbols and images, searching the tradition for alternatives, and reconstructing these symbols and images in a more liberating way. The images we use for God are no exception. If we are to take women's lives and their interpreted experience seriously, our reliance on male imagery for God needs to be interrogated and dismantled. Not because we should never use male imagery for God, but because when we rely on only one image of God, it becomes like the comfortable sweatpants we reach for again and again. Or our old, beat-up sneakers that just slide on with no effort. Eventually, wearing worn-out sneakers hurts my middle-aged back, even if they are comfortable in the moment. If, instead, I wear the many and varied things in my wardrobe, nothing loses its luster as quickly, and my back is thankful too. All of this is to say we shouldn't become so reliant on one subset of images that we slide into that set without thinking, thereby blinding ourselves to the necessary distinction between our language and God's reality. Instead, we should make use of the many and varied images for God contained in scripture and tradition, culled from centuries of experience and imagination, that allow us to think about God in complex ways and invite us to appreciate the infinite mystery of the divine.

The historian Carolyn Walker Bynum has written extensively about the use of maternal imagery to refer to Jesus in the Middle Ages. This was particularly popular in the visions of Julian of Norwich, but even before Julian, Bynum traces maternal language about Jesus especially to Bernard of Clairvaux, a founder of the Cistercian order of monks. Medieval monks and nuns used motherhood imagery to talk about their work as leaders of abbeys. What's most interesting are the aspects of motherhood they choose to focus on. The first is sacrifice. Just as mothers sometimes die in childbirth to bring life to their children, Jesus's death brings life to those who follow him. A second aspect of motherhood that these medieval thinkers utilize is nursing or breastfeeding. Whether it's the church being nourished by Christ, the people of God being nourished by preaching and teaching, or fellow monks nourished by the care of their abbot or abbess, the go-to imagery is that of a nursing mother, her breasts, her milk. Bernard stresses both the ability and the duty of the mother to nourish, and aligns this with Jesus's role of nourishing the church with his body, the Eucharist. Of particular interest is Bernard's understanding of the demands of motherhood on women's bodies: he compares the duty of nursing to the work of running an abbey. In contrast, he talks about the joy of sitting in contemplation as the joy of a bride kissing a bridegroom. Bernard, Julian, and their contemporaries understood the value of feminine, maternal imagery for God, especially for Christ.

Once we realize that our go-to image of God comes very close to maleness, the process of deconstruction, which is the first step in feminist theological method, has begun. Remember that what we are deconstructing isn't maleness or masculinity, though those should certainly be subject to investigation, as we have done earlier in this text. Rather, what theologians seek to deconstruct in this method are images, doctrines, or themes that bolster patriarchal structures and enable misogynistic thinking in theology. Thus, the object of our deconstruction in this chapter has been the maleness of God when that maleness is tied so closely to the divine that it seems inseparable. The close association between maleness and God causes us to overlook God's infinite nature and fundamental unknowability. It obscures the fact that all human beings are made in God's image and likeness and can therefore adequately represent God. Most disturbingly, when we rely too much on maleness, we commit the sin of idolatry, as Elizabeth Johnson warned. We've decided God is male and thereby made males into gods. Once we have identified this problem we can move to searching the tradition for alternatives, which is the second step in the method.

There are many places to search for alternatives to the male image of God. In this chapter we looked briefly at scriptural alternatives such as the parable of the woman with the lost coin, the Book of Song of Songs in the Old Testament, and several other feminine biblical images for God such as the mother hen or the woman in labor. We examined the role of Mary in Christian devotion. We have also searched the history of feminist thinking to consider the possibility of the Goddess emerging in Catholicism and how Goddess-thinking might look in a Catholic key. All these places provide fertile ground for reimagining our image of God.

Perhaps the most important step in feminist theological method is the third: reconstructing the problematic image, doctrine, or theme in a more liberative way. In our work of reconstruction, the goal is key. Why bother reconstructing problematic images at all? Should we not just get rid of them? When it comes to Christian faith, we ultimately need images, we rely on them, in order to cultivate our relationship to the infinite Divine. Our goal, then, should be to beware of images that support oppression of any kind and to support images that remind us of the fundamental truth of Christianity: that God loved the world enough to become part of it. Humanity reflects God's image in all its variety of presentation, of orientation, of identities. Just as we have deconstructed God-as-male, we would do well to deconstruct God-as-white, God-as-colonizer, God-as-member of any structures of domination. What we put in that image's place matters just as much.

Ultimately, we cannot say "God is a woman" with Ariana Grande and leave it at that. Similarly, we cannot take Irenaeus's words "the glory of God is man fully alive" at face value since he probably did intend to include only men. We must look at the rich kaleidoscopic variety of humanity and say: God is this, God's is reflected here. In the poor, in the migrant, in the orphan, in the forgotten, the excluded, the marginalized: God's glory is *that* person, fully alive and thriving. God is glorified only to the extent that these forgotten ones in our midst are thriving. This is important for our ethics, yes, but also for our language and our imagery. If we cannot imagine the God of Jesus Christ in the form of the most marginalized in our midst, we cannot love them. And if we cannot love them, we, quite simply, cannot call ourselves people of faith.

DISCUSSION QUESTIONS

1. Replicate the experiment described in this chapter: spend a weekend using only feminine pronouns and language for God. Change out prayers, daily conversation, and so on so that all references to the divine are in the feminine. It may

be necessary to initiate conversations about God with people you know: friends, parents, even grandparents. Keep a journal of reactions to your experiment. Be sure to note your conversation partners' reactions, but also your own. How does it feel to think of God only in the feminine? What difference did it make in your weekend?

2. Visit your local art museum (or do a virtual visit if there isn't one near you) and look at art depicting goddesses. What do they look like? What is celebrated in the goddess? What contexts do these images emerge from? Do you think there is room in Christianity for images like this?

3. Are there nonbinary images for God that we could put into use? Can you rewrite a prayer or hymn such that it is nonbinary? Try it out ona group of people and get reactions.

DELVE DEEPER

Many theologians and mystics have explored the idea of a feminine God. Research the visions of Julian of Norwich and her language regarding Jesus as Mother. Explore how femininity and motherhood have changed in the centuries between Julian's life and ours (maternal mortality rates, expectations of mothers versus fathers, etc.). Has anything remained the same?

READ FURTHER

Bynum, Caroline Walker. *Jesus as Mother: Studies in the Spirituality of the High Middle Ages.* Oakland: University of California Press, 1984.

Christ, Carol P. *Rebirth of the Goddess: Finding Meaning in Feminist Spirituality.* New York: Routledge, 1998.

Christ, Carol P., and Judith Plaskow, eds. *WomanSpirit Rising: A Feminist Reader of Religion.* San Francisco: Harper San Francisco, 1992.

Daly, Mary. *Gyn/Ecology: The Metaethics of Radical Feminism.* Boston: Beacon Press, 1990.

Johnson, Elizabeth. *She Who Is: The Mystery of God in Feminist Theological Discourse.* New York: Crossroad, 1992.

———. *Women, Earth, and Creator Spirit.* Mahwah, NJ: Paulist Press, 1993.

Julian of Norwich. *Showings.* Translated by Edmund Colledge and James Walsh. New York: Paulist Press, 1977.

Lightsey, Pamela R. *Our Lives Matter: A Womanist Queer Theology.* Eugene, OR: Pickwick Publications, 2015.

Ruether, Rosemary R. *Gaia and God: An Ecofeminist Theology of Earth Healing*. San Francisco: HarperOne, 1991.

13

RETHINKING THE PEOPLE OF GOD

Throughout this text, we have made extensive references to the church, to how the church functions, and how it is perceived. But when people say "church" they might be referring to a variety of realities. *Church* can mean something like a denomination (the Roman Catholic Church throughout the world), but it can also mean a building or a community that is more ecumenical—made up of Christians from lots of different denominations. They might be referring to their local church community or to the institutional, visible aspect of the church. In the Catholic case, this is the hierarchy, and very often when people say, "The church teaches...," or, "According to the church...," they mean the hierarchy of the church. You may have heard it when people say, "I disagree with the church on this." But church is a far more expansive concept than any of these—it's all of these and more. This is why there is a subset of theology that devotes its work to studying the church.

Ecclesiology is the branch of theology that focuses on the nature and mission of the church. Ecclesiologists seek to understand what the church *is* (the nature) and what it is *for* (the mission). Another way to look at it is this: we can examine the church *ad intra*, how it functions inwardly, its internal structures and rules, whether these are ethical or theologically relevant to the church's work. Some church *ad intra* matters include whether women should be ordained, how the magisterium communicates, how Mass should be celebrated, all the way down to what salaries and benefits are offered to church employees and whether those are fair wages. We can also examine the church *ad extra*: the outward-facing church, its mission in the world, its work within secular society, and its relationship to that society. Some church *ad extra* matters include whether and how church officials should involve themselves in national politics, how the church should respond to particular crises like migration or ecological disaster, and how the church functions as a sacrament of salvation in the world.

So what would a feminist understanding of church, both *ad intra* and *ad extra*, look like? Such a reality calls for a lot of dreaming, I think. Perhaps we should start with what we do know. The hierarchy of the Catholic Church, because of its all-male composition and near-total decision-making power in church matters, remains one of the most thoroughgoing institutional examples of monarchy, aristocracy, and patriarchy in existence today. Religious and secular commentators who are trying to illustrate what a patriarchal society or institution looks like will point to the leadership of the Catholic Church as an obvious example. While Pope Francis made some strides to include women in important posts in the Vatican, the visible decision-makers in the church are all men, and only men vote for the pope. This is true at the global level (the Rome-based hierarchy that governs the universal church, names bishops, disciplines priests and theologians, etc.) and at the local level, where parishes are administered by a priest, usually the pastor. It's common for a parish to see a wave of staff resignations or firings whenever a new pastor is assigned to their community. The pastor is the religious authority and also the boss in church offices. This is why when a new pastor comes in, sometimes everything about a parish changes.

The fact that power is concentrated in the hands of men while women are relegated to the margins of power in the church's structure and governance means, quite simply, that the church is fundamentally patriarchal. As such, it is at odds with feminist goals. But remember how expansive the concept of church is. There is comfort in knowing that the church is more than just the institutional face. The fact of the matter is that women do the majority of the church's work as school administrators, directors of religious education, teachers, and administrative workers. Feminists have our work cut out for us: to make sure the decision-makers in the church reflect the reality of the church's daily life. There is opportunity here.

If the church *ad intra* is explicitly patriarchal, what about the public-facing part of the church, the church *ad extra*? This too suffers from the sin of sexism. Just as the internal structures of the church are dominated by men, sidelining women, so too the way the church operates in society can harm women. How can this be, given the excellent charitable work the church does all over the world? In addition to religious work, like liturgy and sacraments, and the charity work it does, the institutional church is also involved in education and health-care, spheres that require its involvement in the political sphere. Though church officials aren't usually involved as elected officials, nevertheless the institutional church influences local and national politics. The Vatican is its own country, of course, and has a seat at the United Nations. This position comes with a fair amount of power, so it is important to know how the Vatican uses that power. While the pope's voice carries a lot of moral authority in the world, and Pope Francis, like many of his predecessors, has used that voice to advocate for migrants, for the poor, and for ecological causes, the Vatican's voice at the United Nations has also advocated against the availability of contraceptives and against family planning in the name of being "pro-life." The church's voice has also not been strong in advocating for the human dignity of the LGBTQ community. When the Vatican uses its voice and its support for particular causes, it lends those causes a certain moral weight. And here we are just looking at the contemporary era. The problems with the church (both *ad extra* and *ad intra*) are far more serious, and deeper, when we consider the church's complicity and participation in colonization, slavery, and other forms of spiritual and cultural violence.

With a legacy that includes colonization, enslavement of human beings, and residential schools for indigenous children, can an institution like the church ever be a force for the full flourishing of human beings? Is the church hopelessly patriarchal, kyriarchal, and oppressive? Or can we identify theological touchpoints where the patriarchal/kyriarchal force rests in order to reimagine these touchpoints so that they support a more inclusive, liberating community?

It's easy to point out that the church is a sexist institution both in its internal functioning and in its public-facing role in society at large. But we must look deeper and ask why this is so. Is the church patriarchal because it has taken root in patriarchal societies, or because it emerged and flourished in patriarchal cultures? Is it sexist because its theology views women as less than men? Perhaps it is a combination of these factors. In the remainder of this chapter, we will look at the theological underpinnings of the church's sexism. We will then search for alternative theological images for the church, as well as more inclusive ways of studying the church—methodological shifts in ecclesiology that help us to conceive of the church in more inclusive ways.

Pronoun Trouble: The Bridal Church

The first and most obvious theological touchstone for the sexism of the institutional church comes from the language we use to refer to it. In the previous chapter, we discussed the problematic association of God with maleness. This is not unrelated to the problem we tackle here, which is the persistent femaleness of the church. Why do Catholics call the church she or her? It might make sense in, for example, the Romance languages, where all nouns are gendered in some way. So in Spanish, the church is *la iglesia* and in Italian it is *la chiesa*. Both these nouns are in the feminine, so they take feminine articles (the *la*). English does not work like this, and yet, in prayer and in music, we repeatedly hear the church referred to as a woman, a she. Does the church have pronouns? And if the church did have pronouns, would she/her/hers be the preferred ones?

I can think of two reasons why the church is repeatedly referred to in the feminine. The first is a translation issue—if the word for church in Greek (*ekklesia*) and in Latin (*ecclesia*) were both feminine nouns, then translations that are striving to stick to the original words would logically translate the pronouns referring to the church as "she" or "her." This reason implies that there isn't something fundamentally feminine about the church, just that the translators had made a decision to stick very, very closely to the words in the text rather than extrapolating for clearer meaning. If they were doing the latter, then "it" would make sense since the church is a collective noun that includes males and females.

A second reason, also rooted in scripture, presents a more theologically ingrained notion of the church-as-woman. In chapter 2 we discussed the nuptial metaphor for the church, the notion that the church is Christ's bride. There, we explored how this metaphor no longer holds, given that contemporary ideas about marriage, based on romantic love and envisioned as a partnership of equals, does not signify what the metaphor intended to convey, which is that Christ is the head of the church, its boss, its loving but governing authority. There can be no presumption of equality between Christ and the church, but modern people don't think of marriage as a union of people who are fundamentally unequal. That's what marriage was in the first century, not in the twenty-first. So, as we argued in that chapter, the nuptial metaphor, while poetic and biblical, no longer means what it is supposed to mean and might in fact be misleading as people assume that the intimacy between Christ and the church amounts to a relationship of equals. It's just not a clear way to depict the relationship between God and the church.

The nuptial metaphor is rooted in scripture, most notably in Ephesians 5. There, Paul infamously urges wives to be subject to their husbands and husbands to love their wives. Antifeminists love to highlight this passage as some sort of biblical confirmation that patriarchy is divinely ordained. But let's look at the text. Husbands should love their wives "as Christ loved the church and gave himself up for her, in order to make her holy by cleansing her with the washing of water by the word, so as to present the church to himself in splendor, without a spot or a wrinkle or anything of the kind—yes so she may be holy and without blemish" (Eph 5:25–27).

In the broad context of this chapter, Paul is asking the Ephesians to turn away from their pre-Christian ways and instructing them in the proper way to set up Christian households. To do this, he relies on the image of marriage between Christ and the church, but you can see right away that it is not a modern marriage between equals but rather one in which patriarchal values are entrenched, such that women are "subject to" the men in their lives. This makes sense, as it was the common arrangement for marriages of the time—had Paul referenced a marriage of equals founded on romantic love, it would've made no sense to his audience.

But let's look at the broader ecclesiological point as well. In exhorting husbands to love their wives as Christ did by giving up his life, Paul then goes into deeply symbolic, eschatological imagery about baptism and the relationship of baptism to salvation. This is why he says that Christ makes the church holy (in giving himself up for the church) by cleansing the church with "the washing of the water" (a reference to baptism). Tying Jesus's sacrifice on the cross to the baptism by which people become part of the church makes plain that Paul is talking about salvation here, not about Jesus and the church being in an intimate romantic relationship.

Importantly, the pure church, unblemished and unsullied, "without a spot or a wrinkle," is not a reference to the virginity of the bride or to something that is a requirement prior to relationship with Christ. Indeed, it is Christ who purifies the church—an action that can be interpreted only as eschatological, which means that it is ongoing but not to be finished until the end of the world. Like the final judgment, the separation of the sheep from the goats, this pure church is not something that can be accomplished except at the end of time and in Christ. This is a very strange marriage. Here, purity (and salvation) is found only in and through relationship. Purity is not a condition that must be preserved in order to enter into a relationship, as purity culture dictates.

Both the literal translations of the feminine nouns for church and the theoretical understanding of the church as Christ's bride contribute to the persistent imagining of the church as female in Christian liturgy, prayer, and scripture. But there is a third reason that continually reinforces the idea that the church is feminine: the persistent use of male pronouns and imagery for God.

We outlined in chapter 12 the variety of reasons that God has been persistently imagined as a male figure. If we think of God as masculine, it makes some sense that the church, which is not God, is imagined as feminine. This is especially true when we recall the hierarchy's commitment to the notion of gender complementarity. Building on Genesis's assertion that God created humanity "male and female," the ideology of gender complementarity, championed by many popes and bishops but none more than John Paul II, extrapolates from biological difference to differences in psychological makeup and, most important, in social roles. Complementarity makes it seem that the gender binary is a foundational Christian belief. Along with this comes an emphasis on heteronormativity, which is the idea that to be heterosexual is normative, or required, and any other sexual orientation is deviant or disordered. Finally, complementarity claims that what one person lacks is made up for in their fated mate. Gender complementarity is pervasive in many streams of Catholic theology. It is given as a reason why women cannot be ordained. It is relied on when discussing women's "special" nature. It is claimed as a reason why motherhood is essential to women's nature. Indeed, gender complementarity informs theological understandings about marriage, about sexual ethics, and, yes, about ecclesiology as well. Gender complementarity relies on masculine and feminine stereotypes, so men are aggressive and dominant while women are submissive and nurturing. God is initiatory; the church is responsive. God is powerful; the church is dependent. God is male; the church is female. The clergy, which is a stand-in for God on earth, must be masculine to guide, lead, and teach. In this concept of ecclesiology, laypeople, because they are not clergy, are necessarily feminine and receptive, obedient, assenting even if they are male.

Of course, realizing that the initial theological premise (God's maleness/masculinity) is not supported by scripture or by theology should go a long way to curbing our desire to see the church in some sort of gendered polarity to God. If the foundation is cracked, the building can't stand. But it hasn't. Instead, we must go deeper into our understanding of God-as-male and to precisely what sort of maleness is at the heart of this image to grasp why God's maleness and the church's femaleness necessitate and reinforce each other.

The male-God/female-church polarity makes sense in a similar way that the nuptial metaphor made sense at one point in history. It has to do with the imbalance of power between the two entities. We believe that God is all-powerful (omnipotent) and all-knowing (omniscient), two things the church is definitely not. Moreover, we believe that all of creation, which includes people and obviously also the church, is utterly dependent on God for its existence and sustenance. That belief is rooted in our understanding of creation.

But what if we thought about power in a different way? As we currently understand it, God's power is characterized by a near-total capacity to dominate, to override human wills and hearts (see the character of Pharaoh in the exodus as a prime example). God's power is absolute, and human capacity for acting depends on God's generosity or on God "allowing" us to act, to think, to choose.

Jewish theologian Judith Plaskow points out that this concept of God as "dominant Other" to humanity has had dramatically bad consequences for our intra-human relationships. In her book *Standing Again at Sinai*, she writes, "If the image of God as male provides religious support for male dominance in society, the image of God as supreme Other would seem to legitimate dominance of any kind. God as ruler and king of the universe is the pinnacle of a vast hierarchy that extends from God 'himself' to angels/men/women/children/animals and finally the earth."[1] As long as we envision God as supreme ruler, as king, as authoritarian, controlling, ultimate power, we legitimate those sorts of power relationships on earth. We will continually envision power as some sort of domination, even if well-intentioned domination. And indeed, this is how we are taught power is wielded, or at least was, historically. We have, however, moved away from authoritarian, dictatorial models of power in many spheres of human life. Let's look at two examples.

Our first example is political. Plaskow points out that we continue to call God the divine ruler and the king of the universe even though humans have moved away from these models of power in their political lives, preferring democratically elected forms of government in many parts of the world. Societies reject the notion of a person ruling by divine right, and political philosophers have long critiqued the idea that "might makes right." But we persist in our emphasis on almighty God's power, wielded however God wants, because God also has absolute freedom, where human freedom is necessarily limited, like every aspect of our lives, because we are finite. Can we think of God using power, or having power, in a different way? A way that is more attuned to life-giving understandings of power that we have come to embrace politically?

A second example comes from parenting. A few generations ago, children were viewed as completely dependent on parents and parents as exercising complete control over children. The purpose of parenting was to mold the child into an ideal (or at least passable) citizen who could follow rules and keep order. The methods used to do this were often violent and/or coercive. Children would misbehave and parents would spank or hit them as punishment. This was common even in schools, where teachers and administrators were seen to be acting *in loco parentis* (in the place of parents). My children still recoil in horror when they hear that their father's high school practiced corporal punishment into the 1980s. But adults were doing what they thought they were supposed to do: bending children to their will, training them to be productive members of society in the way that they (the parents) were probably trained to do.

Now, I am not saying that every family was like this or that there aren't important cultural differences to be accounted for. What I am saying is that in the twenty-first century, we view our roles as parents and educators differently. While the goals remain the same (raise good humans), the methods are quite different. The lessons of intergenerational trauma have taught us that violence rarely begets anything but suffering in the children on whom it is inflicted. We have learned that teaching is best accomplished by invitation and encouragement, not coercion and punishment. Discipline, rather than being something purely external and based in fear, is something that can be cultivated in the self. Parents, then, are hoping to raise their children to be self-sufficient, to be good contributors to society, and to be able to make their own decisions about what is right and wrong not out of fear of punishment or pain, but out of a desire to do what is right.

These two examples illustrate that we are largely abandoning the notion of coercion (power-over) as a model in favor of more voluntary models (power-with or power-sharing). I know that as a parent my role is to nurture the good I see in each of my children, to provide for their individual needs in an effort to see them grow into the singular beings they will be. Similarly, our hope for democratic governments is that they will derive authority from a mandate of a plurality, a majority of our fellow citizens, such that they can work productively on behalf of the common good.

Why not try to envision God as that kind of parent that invites us to the good without coercion, instead of as a scary, all-powerful, potentially violent Father? Interestingly, the bishops of the Second Vatican Council initiated this transition in the ecclesiological sphere at the Second Vatican Council. While they didn't offer a repudiation of the maleness of God or of gender complementarity (let's not get too excited), they nevertheless made important strides toward redefining how the church wields power in the world. In *Dignitatis Humanae* (The Declaration on Religious Freedom), the council disavowed coercion as a tool for conversion, affirming instead that true faith cannot be brought about by force. You read that correctly: the same church that ran the Inquisition in Spain, which was literally devoted to forcing Jews and Muslims to convert by torturing them until they did, that very church declared in 1965 that true faith cannot be achieved through manipulation or violence. Because of the church's commitment to the dignity of every human being, coercion is seen as unacceptable, even in the service of saving souls, said the church that colonized the Americas. If this sort of turnaround is possible in the ecclesial sphere, then surely a turn away from other toxic understandings of power and gender can happen too.

So it seems the church, at least in the mid-1960s when former colonies were becoming independent nations in Africa and Asia, was beginning to make a turn away from power-as-domination and to power-as-invitation. Let's look now at some other images of the church, put forward by feminist scholars and scholars of color, that can help us reimagine the church as something other than a force of domination in society.

One Alternative: A Discipleship of Equals

Elisabeth Schüssler Fiorenza, a German American feminist theologian, has written extensively on the biblical and extrabiblical evidence for a different sort of church community than the patriarchal hierarchy we have inherited. Her vision of the church is one of a discipleship of equals, ushered in by Jesus himself and attested to in the Gospels, particularly the Gospels of Mark and John. Schüssler Fiorenza pays particular attention to the literature of the New Testament and the writings produced by the emerging Christian church communities. These communities were internally diverse and marked by persecution. They were struggling to survive in a hostile Greco-Roman world and growing apart from the matrix of Judaism in which Jesus and his earliest disciples lived. In this difficult context, Schüssler Fiorenza identifies competing desires: fidelity to Jesus's vision of an egalitarian society where there is, as Paul writes in Galatians 3:28, "neither Jew nor Greek, slave or free, woman or man" or some level of accommodation to the patriarchal outside world. Whether this accommodation was intentional or a byproduct of being part of Greco-Roman culture, in taking on the structures of the patriarchal household, which was the basis for power structures all over the Roman Empire of the late first century, some early Christian communities made the path for their own survival. This accommodation included concentrating teaching authority in men, ensuring that widows were regulated and not paid for their work unless strict qualifications had been met, and limiting the power of women to teach only other, younger women. This ensured that women never had authority over men, which is mirrored in the Greco-Roman paterfamilias model of male leadership.

Still, Schüssler Fiorenza argues, a different model of church is possible, one rooted in Jesus's own vision of radical equality and egalitarian power sharing. This model finds its basis in the demands of altruism and love preached by Jesus during his ministry. Furthermore, it finds expression in the varied roles women took on as presiders in house churches and as missionary disciples, as Schüssler Fiorenza points out when she highlights the work of Phoebe and Thecla. Phoebe, a deacon, is mentioned in the New Testament explicitly, in the letter to the Romans. Other women, like Prisca and Nympha, are mentioned in the letters of Paul as leaders of house churches, as we saw in chapter 8. Thecla appears in an extracanonical text (a text not included in the Christian scriptures but nevertheless known and studied by biblical scholars and those who study Christianity in antiquity) named the Acts of Paul and Thecla. Schüssler Fiorenza reminds us that this text portrays Thecla's authority as a woman missionary of some standing who is commissioned by Paul to teach the word of God.[2] All told, Schüssler Fiorenza amasses a great deal of evidence that women were important leaders in early Christianity, serving alongside men to make Jesus's vision of a community of equals a reality. By teaching, preaching, and presiding at house churches, women in early Christianity defied, for a time at least, the patriarchal order expected in the Roman Empire. Because of this, they met with resistance, eventually women's roles were marginalized, and women were excluded from leadership.

Schüssler Fiorenza's point is this: it doesn't need to be this way. She wants contemporary Christians to rediscover the egalitarian vision of church presented in scripture. While the patriarchal order won out historically, and maybe even enabled Christianity to survive in a hostile environment, nevertheless the vision of a discipleship of equals cannot be eradicated from the Christian tradition. Indeed, now that we are leaving behind notions of power-as-domination, it seems the perfect time to rediscover and create a model of church based on egalitarian power structures.

Kinship and Kin-dom: Isasi-Díaz's Church as Family

Let us turn now to a Latina theologian that runs with this egalitarian vision: Ada María Isasi-Díaz, a Cuban American theologian who described herself as a *mujerista*. By this she meant something different from mainstream/white liberal feminism, but also different from Latina feminism and chicana feminism. She saw her work as one of midwifery, supporting the effort to bring forth the insights of Latinas in the United States, the grace of their daily lives, in an effort to mold Christian ethics in a liberating direction. Throughout her theology, Isasi-Díaz remained committed to her community, Latinas especially, and her writing reflects this by integrating bilingualism and neologisms regularly. Her understanding of the church is no exception. Drawing on liberation theologians' understanding of God's reign, as well as on the insights of the Second Vatican Council and the Latinx theology of which she was a pioneer, Isasi-Díaz's preferred metaphor for the people of God is the kin-dom.

To understand this, we must once again rewind to the development of the metaphor she is reacting against, namely, that of the kingdom of God. While most theologians today will confirm that the kingdom of God and the church on earth were never meant to be understood as the same, nevertheless in the era of theological manuals (prior to Vatican II), the predominant metaphor for the church was the "perfect society." This was meant to indicate not that the church was sinless but that the church, specifically because of its hierarchical structure, was perfectly ordered: everyone had a role, and the roles made sense. For everyday Catholics, however, the notion that the church was a perfect society really did mesh with sinlessness and perfection to some degree. As Isasi-Díaz points out, the notion of the kingdom of God became spiritualized to such an extent that it was viewed as existing only in an otherworldly or heavenly realm. It almost became synonymous with heaven. The church, in the meantime, was the entry point for this kingdom, which is one reason why the maxim "outside the church there is no salvation" was a widely held belief.

With the sinless kingdom of God removed to the heavens, and the church on earth peopled with sin-prone human beings left to be its gateway, corruption and abuse was never far from the church's reality. As Isasi-Díaz notes, "Though it repeatedly claimed that its role was only religious, the church throughout its history has legitimized and supported those who have social, economic, and political power."[3] Like Schüssler Fiorenza, Isasi-Díaz expresses a desire to return to Jesus's vision for God's reign. This vision, which she shares with liberation theologians from Latin America, desires to return the reign of God to a reality with real human possibility, not something beyond our earthly reach. Rather, the reign of God is something that Christians can and should be working toward, through enacting justice wherever possible, attending to the poor, healing the sick, and and so. In order to revise the metaphor of the kingdom of God, which Isasi-Díaz sees as sexist, elitist, and patriarchal in addition to being overly spiritualized, she focuses on Jesus's understanding of shalom, the fullness of life. She equates this fullness with mujerista notions of liberation that are holistic—material and spiritual, social and political, personal and communal.

Isasi-Díaz proposes the metaphor of the kin-dom—a synonym for family without being synonymous with the nuclear family, which she recognizes can be limiting and individualized when used to mean only immediate blood relations. Rather, her notion of kin-dom and familia are expansive, meant to include chosen family as well as those brought into the familial community through the practice of *compadrazgo*. This "godparenting" practice in Latinx communities combines family and friendship ties in religious and social rituals of sponsorship and care. For example, in many Mexican and Mexican American families, children will have separate sets of godparents for their baptisms, their confirmations, the celebration of their fifteenth birthdays, and so on. These ties are sometimes financial, sometimes also spiritual, always familial in the sense that godparents are considered family.

The emphasis on expansive notions of family makes sense to anyone familiar with Latinx theologies. From its earliest days, Latinx theology has emphasized a communal rather than individual anthropology, in contrast to the dominant notions of humanity as singularly constituted by individual choices. For theologians like Roberto Goizueta, humans are born into a preexistent, unchosen web of relationships (familial, communal) that constitute our humanity. It is little wonder, then, that Isasi-Díaz's notion of church, based on Jesus's vision of life to the fullest, is couched in the language of family writ large, of kinship. This family is a place of support and obligation that promotes self-worth and works toward the liberation of all from oppression in its many forms. In moving away from the broken metaphor of kingdom that denotes dominance, Isasi-Díaz ushers in a liberating image that rests on what she calls "the infrastructure of interdependence"[4] we see in expansive families. Ultimately her notion of church seeks to "create an institution where we can be ourselves in a safe way, where our well-being is of primordial importance, where a new order of relationships excludes all exploitation and abuse."[5] This is God's family, a beautiful vision of what the church might be.

Methodological Shifts and Future Possibilities

We have much work to do if we hope to transform the Catholic Church's internal structures and external work away from patriarchal misogyny and toward a liberating, inclusive community. The obstacles to this transformation are clear: persistent patriarchy, clericalism, sexist theologies, and social norms that support these unjust systems. But along with these obstacles, there are reasons for hope: resistance movements, innovative ecclesial communities, a push for the restoration of women to diaconate ministry. In all these things, we can discern the possibility that a methodological shift in how we do ecclesiology might help our efforts toward an inclusive community along.

In the work of theology, including in ecclesiology, our methods for investigation are just as important as our language, our images, or our scriptural grounding. For centuries, all of theology proceeded according to a deductive method: there were "truths" that were universal and knowable, and from those truths, scholars deduced how they functioned in the world. So, since we know that God is all good, we must then figure out how and why evil exists by deducing either that God permits it or that there is some other reason. In the middle of the twentieth century, as a result of scholarly shifts in Europe and the United States, theology began a sort of reorientation to a more inductive approach, starting from what was knowable and then asking questions from there. But ecclesiology never really made that turn, and ecclesiologists tended to remain focused on, for example, certain characteristics of the church that were central to belief and to figuring out how those were evident in the church as we experience it.

Elsewhere, I have suggested that narrative methods, especially the incorporation of diverse and divergent stories of church, can be the building block of ecclesiology in the contemporary age.[6] Ecclesiology is, after all, the work of telling the church's story. To do this well, we must first listen and be attentive to the stories already taking place in the church. We can attend to how we tell the history of American Catholicism or to who gets to shape that story as a protagonist and who gets relegated to supporting roles. We should also pay attention to demographic shifts in the church to ensure we are telling the church's story in a representative way that doesn't marginalize those who don't have influence or power. We can also pay attention to art and aesthetics in order to understand people's sense of faith. In each of these ways, the method of ecclesiology shifts from one that begins with preexistent truths to one that begins with listening to the reality of the people of God and their experience of church. By making that methodological shift, our job of telling the story of the church becomes easier and more accurate.

The first and most important step in turning to a narrative method in ecclesiology is to adopt a posture of listening. After all, as Catholics we believe that the Holy Spirit is always already at work in the people of God. So we should make every effort to listen, to pay attention to where the Spirit might be guiding the church. As a concluding exercise to this chapter, let me suggest three places where I think feminist ecclesiologists should be particularly attentive: alternative religious communities, the movements for women's ordination to the diaconate, and Pope Francis's Synod on Synodality.

Alternative ecclesial communities have a long history in the church. They are as old, at least, as the monastic movements and hermitages that began to flourish as soon as Christianity became the official religion of the Roman Empire in the fourth century. For as long as there have been Christians, the church has contained different sorts of communities, some quite countercultural (like mendicant religious orders), where people could live out a vision of Christianity that was authentic for them. Some examples of contemporary communities like this include Catholic Worker houses of hospitality. A movement started by Dorothy Day, whose cause for canonization is ongoing, these small, independent communities consist of Catholics living together with homeless persons, offering hospitality, food, and other services as needed. The houses aren't organized in any hierarchical way, nor are they governed by any central office. Their main organizing principle is devotion to God and direct service to the poor and marginalized.

While houses of hospitality have been around since the mid-twentieth century, new groups have emerged in the twenty-first century as well. One small group I find promising brings together women religious and young people who might be described as spiritual seekers. These young people, who identify mainly as "spiritual but not religious" or "unaffiliated" are invited to live in community with women religious, many of whom are aging. Through faith sharing and working together for justice, the sisters and the seekers have forged new bonds, renewed their faith, and mutually supported one another.

A second ecclesial story worth listening to centers around movements to restore the ordination of women to the diaconate. While women deacons existed in the church into the Middle Ages, changes to the theology of priesthood and the understanding of the sacrament of holy orders led to the exclusion of women from any kind of ordination. Late in the twentieth century, scholars took up this cause again, combing through the historical record and liturgical evidence of women's service as deacons. Vatican II restored the possibility that men could be ordained deacons permanently, not merely as a stepping-stone to the priesthood. Why should women not be allowed what married men can do, particularly if we have clear evidence that this ministry existed for hundreds of years in the church? Eventually, Pope Francis brought together a commission to study the restoration of women deacons. Many grassroots organizations have taken up the cause, hosting listening sessions, leadership training, and appealing to Rome for swift action.

Interestingly, the notion of ordaining women to the diaconate does not have the support of all feminist theologians. For some, like Schüssler Fiorenza, ordaining women to a flawed patriarchal system does little to reform that system. Instead, it just incorporates women into a dysfunctional model of church. Moreover, says Schüssler Fiorenza, anything short of making women bishops relegates them to service work in the church. This is work that women already do. Instead, what feminists like her advocate is for women to be incorporated into decision-making roles, not merely consultative or service-oriented ones.

To that end, Pope Francis has offered some hopeful solutions. He elevated women to second-in-command positions in key offices in the Vatican, including naming French sister Nathalie Becquart to the position of undersecretary for the Synod of Bishops. With this appointment, Francis ensured that, for the first time, a woman has the right to vote at a synod (a meeting of the world's bishops). The meeting at which Sr. Becquart exercised this historic right is crucial to this new, listening style of ecclesiology. This is because Pope Francis called this synod to be on the topic of the church's synodality. In other words, the pope called a meeting to talk about how the church listens and discerns the way forward not as individuals but communally, as an assembly. To make this happen, local churches and dioceses as well as national bishops' conferences created avenues for listening to Catholics in their communities about the problems faced by the people of God and possible solutions. Any synodal process begins with listening to the people and continues with summarizing, consolidating the insights gathered at the listening sessions, and presenting them to the Vatican for discussion and discernment.

That listening and discernment must include female voices in a deliberative role. Feminist theologians have long recognized that the church is patriarchal in a thoroughgoing way. Many have worked to reform the institution, others have left, and some have reformulated how they relate to the institutional church. By recognizing the shelf-life of metaphors like nuptiality and kingship and by suggesting both new images and new methods, we can envision a church that is inclusive, liberating, and transformative for the world. When we make this vision a reality, the church can become a true sacrament of salvation in and for the world.

DISCUSSION QUESTIONS

1. Are there communal spaces or communities of people that feel like "church" to you? Can you think of places or communities that give you a sense of shared identity and purpose? List as many of these communities, locations, causes as you can.
2. Some feminists believe that merely ordaining women will do little to cure the ills of clericalism in the church. What do you think? Must church structures change before women are ordained? Which ones? What changes would make it more likely for the ordination of women to succeed?
3. What do you think will change in the church as more women are added to the offices in the Vatican? Are some criteria more important than others when choosing whom to appoint to these positions? If you were an adviser to the pope, what would you suggest he look for?

DELVE DEEPER

Your college or university might have intentional or living-learning communities. Research what the purpose of these communities is. When did colleges adopt this model of learning and why? What are the benefits to schools and to students? Are there parallels with church communities? If you could design an intentional community in your context, what would it be like?

READ FURTHER

Brown, Raymond E. *The Churches the Apostles Left Behind*. New York: Paulist Press, 1984.

Goizueta, Roberto. *Caminemos Con Jesus: Towards a Theology of Accompaniment*. Maryknoll, NY: Orbis Books, 1995.

Imperatori-Lee, Natalia. *Cuéntame: Narrative in the Ecclesial Present*. Maryknoll, NY: Orbis Books, 2018.

Isasi-Díaz, Ada María. *En La Lucha/In the Struggle: Elaborating a Mujerista Theology*. Minneapolis: Fortress Press, 2009.

———. *La Lucha Continues: Mujerista Theology*. Maryknoll, NY: Orbis Books, 2007.

Pilar-Aquino, Maria, and Maria Jose Rosado-Nunes, eds. *Feminist Intercultural Theology: Latina Explorations for a Just World*. Maryknoll, NY: Orbis Books, 2007.

Schüssler Fiorenza, Elisabeth. *In Memory of Her: A Feminist Theological Reconstruction of Christian Origins*. New York: Herder & Herder, 1994.

14

REFRAMING SPIRITUALITY

I have a dilemma whenever I get on a plane and am seated next to someone who is chatty. I will usually have work with me of some kind, which means reading or grading, usually on my laptop. My seatmate will inevitably ask what I do for a living.

"I'm a professor."

"Oh, wow. What do you teach?"

We have now entered the danger zone. Do I lie and say, "Mathematics"? One time I chose that path and wound up next to an engineer who asked a follow-up question. I had no answer about a subspecialty and had to come clean. I can confirm: it is extremely embarrassing to be caught lying about your profession!

My other answer to the "what do you teach" query is to say, "I teach religion or theology," and then wait. This conversation can go in a number of directions now. Some people will just nod and turn away. Those are my favorite people when I've got work to do. Sometimes I will get a theory about how religion is a scam or the church is corrupt (I agree with the latter, not so much the former). Or they will tell me about a recent supernatural experience, such as dreaming of their deceased grandmother or something they saw on *Ghost Hunters*. Occasionally I will get a question about the meaning of life or about which crystals I like best. Most often, I will hear, "Wow, you must be a very spiritual person." And here's the thing—What?? Whatever "very spiritual" means, I doubt I'm it. Maybe they mean very pious, someone who goes to church a lot, which is definitely not me. But even the intensifier there implies that there's a baseline of "spiritual" that each person has, and I'm not even sure that's true.

Of all the terms in religion and theology, maybe even in our contemporary English lexicon, I think *spiritual* and *spirituality* might be the most misused and misunderstood. The terms appear nearly everywhere: on wellness websites (whatever "wellness" means), on biographical information requests that I ask from my students ("I'm spiritual but not really religious"), on advertisements selling crystals or meditation apps or hiking trails. There is an entire genre of books called "spiritual memoir" that includes texts about eating, praying, and loving, among other activities. What does it mean to be spiritual or to have a spirituality? Is it about skincare or incense or yoga poses? Is it a journey of self-discovery, self-regard, self-absorption? Is spirituality synonymous with piety, or an inner life, or is it just code for woo-woo beliefs about magical rocks?

Spirituality has served as a kind of catch-all for "things that are important to me and larger than my life, that somehow make me happier or give my life meaning in some way." Whether its mindfulness or travel or fitness or journaling, it can fit in the category of spirituality. Even in academic circles, spirituality can sometimes become a mixture of psychology of religion, devotional studies, ritual studies, and ethnography, among other disciplines. But in the field of theology, spirituality has much deeper roots and more specific meanings.

Though it might be tempting to think of spirituality as something having to do with our feelings (of self-worth, of being loved by God, etc.) or about our attitudes toward one another or the world (mindful, grateful, compassionate, etc.), in truth, spirituality has a dimension that is emotional and affective and therefore subjective—we talk about spiritual experiences, and these are part of spirituality.

But spirituality also has an objective dimension that makes it something we can study. In this meaning, spirituality is simply about life lived according to a deeper orientation or dimension. For example, we can study Jesuit spirituality: the prayers, practices, and ways of life inspired by the life and legacy of Ignatius of Loyola, the founder of the Jesuit order of priests.

In a way, spirituality and ecclesiology are both focused on the lived reality of faith. If we think of ecclesiology as where the institutional rubber meets the road (communal faith in real life), then spirituality is that, but on a more personal level (personal faith as we live it). Spirituality is how we put our faith into action. What our faith spurs us to do in the world, how it inspires us to live. Yes, there are feelings involved in how we live in the world, but spirituality far exceeds the affective part of life. Nor is it a merely "subjective" part of life: it not only pertains to me or my preferences but, because spirituality is the way I put faith into action, is also necessarily social, involving other people.

Spirituality and Experience

Perhaps the best way to zero in on what spirituality is and how to approach it is to focus on the notion of experience. Experience as a theological category has always existed but became paramount in Catholic theology around the time of the Second Vatican Council. Experience can refer to many realities. There are experiences that are individual or personal, like your childhood, and experiences that are communal, like a concert. Some spiritual things happen to me (I feel closer to God after a sunset walk on the beach), or I understand them in a particular way. Other spiritual things I experience as part of a group, like my favorite Mass in the sophomore dorm at Fordham late Sunday nights. Sometimes the group is defined by characteristics like "all people who share similar biological traits to me." Getting your wisdom teeth removed is a common experience for those who have impacted wisdom teeth, for instance. Sometimes the group is geographic, "all people who were gathered in this place at this time." Everyone who was at the original Woodstock festival, for example, had some shared experience. Fans of Broadway shows frequently talk about seeing their favorite productions as a religious experience.

Most scholars of spirituality distinguish between the personal dimension of spirituality and the communal/social dimensions. Additionally, they stress that all spirituality is rooted in a context, which means that it expresses the values, aims, and style of a particular place and time. Context shapes experience because all our experiences occur at particular times and in particular places. It also shapes our understanding and interpretation of our experience because our context limits the language and frames of reference we have for understanding what happens to us. So Black spiritualities display the characteristics of African, Caribbean, and other diasporic community contexts. These spiritualities are also grounded in the historical experience of chattel slavery, of the middle passage, and of colonialism. Similarly, Latinx spiritualities reflect indigenous, African, and Iberian influences, depending on the contextual reality where they originate, and are also rooted in experiences of colonial occupation, violence, and so on.

Thankfully, feminist theology has, from its inception, focused on experience as a locus, a place, from where theology arises. One of the first insights feminist theology brought to light was that "human" experience was an overgeneralization. Women's experience was different from men's, and it deserved attention as a place where God was at work. We can see that feminist theology and spirituality mesh well together since they both focus on experience and the attitudes and actions that flow from that experience. As feminist theology has grown and as more women have added their voices and experience to the mix, theology and spirituality have been enriched in intercultural, interreligious, and ecumenical ways. The field has broadened to include more marginalized voices and is slowly learning to allow feminist theology to be driven by the concerns of women who are most marginalized.

Feminist spirituality centers on the experience of women, especially women who are most marginalized and excluded from positions of power and influence. What other features make up spirituality in general and feminist spirituality in particular? Let's look at three: belief, embodiment, and community.

Feminist Spirituality: *Lex Orandi Lex Credendi*

An ancient adage in Christian theology is that "the law of prayer is the law of belief." This is a translation of the Latin phrase *lex orandi lex credendi*, which means that we cannot separate our belief from our prayer. How we pray expresses what we believe, and vice versa. These two aspects of the Christian life are inseparable. But what does this have to do with feminist spirituality?

Given the number of people who identify as "spiritual but not religious," it is particularly important to nail down what we mean by *spiritual* and *spirituality*. The Pew Research Institute estimates that in 2021, about 30 percent of Americans identify as "unaffiliated" religiously, up from 16 percent in 2007. The amount nearly doubled! Analysis of these disaffiliated or unaffiliated believers, who used to be known as seekers, tells us that they reject institutional religion as corrupt. Nevertheless, they find value in a kind of do-it-yourself spirituality, taking insights from different ancient traditions (like yoga, with its roots in Hinduism) and blending these with other beliefs and practices to form an amalgam of sorts, a set of ideas and actions that brings deeper meaning to their lives. Maybe someone in your life is a regular practitioner of yoga who also volunteers with Habitat for Humanity from time to time. It might be a focus on justice or on mindfulness or compassion. Or it might be on self-actualization and a sense of fulfillment. But again and again, studies show that people who identify as spiritual but not religious aren't "nones" or "nothing in particular," as the surveys used to see them. Instead, they are forging new paths of meaning-making in a world that simply does not trust institutions, religious ones in particular.

Even in the case of those who do not fully subscribe to a religious tradition, spirituality isn't a random set of practices unrelated to one another. Think of fitness communities like SoulCycle or OrangeTheory or even CrossFit. There's a communal aspect of exercising together and some shared beliefs about wellness, empowerment, and overall health. It's not just a random assortment of people coinciding at a gym class. The community is constituted by shared beliefs. All spirituality necessarily stems from beliefs, and commitments flowing from those beliefs. It is one way we live out our values. So we can say that spirituality is notional, which means it springs from belief (religious, ethical, or otherwise). It has a cognitive element; it involves our thinking, our believing (*credendi*).

The *lex orandi*, the prayer and spirituality, of specifically feminist spirituality stems from the *lex credendi* of feminist beliefs and commitments. Feminist spiritualities, then, will spring from a commitment to women's flourishing. This can be expressed in a variety of ways. Core feminist beliefs include a critique of misogynistic institutions, religious and otherwise; a commitment to understanding compounding marginalization, or intersectionality; and the centrality of women's experience, bodies, and work. Whether through the end of stereotyped gender roles, reproductive justice, or organizing for women's decision-making capacity in the church, feminist commitments all call for action on behalf of gender justice. Prayer and ritual will foreground women's leadership capacity, their sacramental imaginations, the necessary symbiosis between humanity and the earth.

There are many examples of spiritual practices that flow from feminist beliefs and commitments. Throughout the second and third waves of Catholic feminism, groups of feminists have gathered in a variety of organizations, conferences, meet ups, and other gatherings. Early movements like the Women's Ordination Conference and a group called Women-Church have given way to associations like FutureChurch, Voices of Faith, and Votes for Catholic Women. The notion/belief that links these groups is their attention to achieving gender justice in the church. While the Women's Ordination Conference came into existence to lobby for the ordination of women to the Catholic priesthood (and still does this work), the camaraderie and sense of shared purpose that groups like WOC foster among Catholic feminists goes beyond the stated goal of the organization. These women (and some men and nonbinary persons as well) pray together, strategize together, and work together for a more just ecclesial structure, for more representative liturgical celebrations, and for more inclusive ethical teachings. Being committed to the feminist goal of critiquing the patriarchal structure of the church not only means staging protests around the globe but also includes spiritual work, relationship building, and communal prayer.

One example of this communal prayer is the Catholic Women Preach initiative. This program produces short videos where Catholic women preach on the Mass readings for each Sunday. It follows the lectionary used by the Catholic Church and invites women from a variety of racial, ethnic, and educational backgrounds, all of whom have some credential in Catholic theology or ministry, to preach the word of God. The group disseminates these videos on the internet, through a website and through various social media outlets as well. Supported by individuals as well as charitable foundations, the Catholic Women Preach community creates what it wishes to see in the church: an outlet for women's insights into the gospel, shared with a national and international community. Rooted in the belief that the gift of preaching, like all gifts of the Holy Spirit, is given to all regardless of sex or gender, Catholic Women Preach allows women the space and invites them to share their gift with the wider church. It is a form of prayer, of liturgical collaboration, that is rooted in some core feminist beliefs about women's capacity for leadership, for theological insight, and for their suitability for public prayer.

One Bread, One Body? Feminist Theology as Embodied and Contextual

Spirituality is also contextual because it is based on experience, which always occurs and is interpreted in historical and social contexts. What's more, all spiritualities are embodied—we take actions, make changes, live certain ways, and all these actions are always already embodied, an integration of our spiritual and physical selves. We cannot separate spirituality from the body. Though for most Christian history the contexts of spirituality were white European social contexts and the default body for Christian spirituality was a white male body, feminist spiritualities move beyond this constraint.

We know from our reading of feminist history and theology that women's experience has been overlooked, and women's bodies have been sources of shame rather than delight in Christian prayer and liturgy. Menstrual blood has been considered a source of pollution and impurity in Jewish, Christian, and Muslim religious traditions. Even the necessary bleeding after giving birth excluded Christian women from the sanctuary. Up until the late 1960s, Catholic women could not attend Mass after giving birth until forty days had passed. Ask your grandparents! Frequently, the mom who had just given birth would be absent from the baby's baptism. They were welcomed back into the community with a special blessing known as "churching." A particular prayer with a blessing for postpartum women was required for a woman to return to the eucharistic community. Rather than accompany women in the difficult weeks after birth, Roman Catholicism kept them away from the spiritual arena of the church.

Feminist spirituality seeks to remedy this exclusion by creating rituals that celebrate women's bodies. Writers have composed prayers and liturgies blessing menstruation, birth, and nursing. Rather than viewing women's bodies as sources of pollution, feminist spirituality celebrates the gift of menstruation and lactation and the gift of women's bodies regardless of their fertility.

Here is one example of feminist prayer, taken from a liturgy celebrating "Word Made Flesh," in *Woman Prayer, Woman Song* by Miriam Therese Winter. After an opening song, silent reflection, call-and-response prayers, and a feminist reframing of the creed, a reader prays as follows:

> Flesh of our flesh
> bone of our bone:
> God was born of woman alone,
> nursed at her breast,
> clung to her knee,
> shared thirty full years of silence
> with her,
> and broke it only for three.
>
> Women have much in common with God,
> secrets that only women share,
> of the womb,
> of the heart,
> of bringing to birth
> and sustaining life
> and becoming aware,
> a giving,
> forgiving,
> nurturing role
> intent on making whoever is broken
> whole.[1]

This prayer calls to mind the creative commonality between women's bodily experience of birth and nurture and God's creative activity in the world. I am reminded of a beautiful etching by the artist Benjamin Wildflower that depicts a Black woman seated on the floor with her legs crossed, a baby nursing at her breast. Behind her a chalice shape and cross outline the woman and above her, along the halo surrounding her head, Wildflower has included this text: "Take and eat, this is my body." Feminist spirituality sees in women's body not sources of temptation and shame, which have been the dominant images and ideas we've seen in history, but echoes of God's creativity, God's sustenance, and God's eucharistic feast.

All stages of women's lives are celebrated in feminist spirituality: girlhood, womanhood, and old age. This last category, old age, is particularly important for Latinx spirituality. Writers such as Orlando Espín have extolled the importance of older Latinas to the communal wisdom and catechetical work of Latinx Catholicism. More recently, authors have begun to explore the importance of "abuelita theology"[2] and the role that Latinx grandmothers specifically have in forming and sustaining the faith of their families and, by extension, of their communities. Cuban American theologian Kat Armas writes, "Abuelita theology helps us articulate how a marginalized, impoverished and subjugated people continue to have faith in the God of liberation, and how such faith has endured through centuries, despite the exploitation engrained in the colonizers' proselytization of the Americas."[3] Through their gentleness and proximity, as well as their commitment to a faith that sanctifies the everyday, the older Latinas in our lives model resistance and joy amid struggle. This cornerstone of Latinx theology, that everyday life is sacred, shares much with feminist theologies and is prominent in mujerista theology as well. Grandmothers and older women, often part of Latinx and Black households and nuclear families, teach children to pray, impart a view of creation as sacred, and preside at family meals and other important celebrations. They serve as models of faith and of devotion. They create spirituality that is liberating and rooted in cultural contexts.

Black and Latinx feminists don't focus only on personal embodiment, however. These thinkers remind us that embodiment has broad historical consequences. When feminist theologians talk about liberating action or liberating prayer, we must center the most marginalized bodies in our midst. These persons are frequently Black, transgender women. Feminist spiritualities must be intercultural, antiracist, and LGBTQ-welcoming. Organizations such as Dignity

USA and New Ways ministry, and even some Catholic priests, have written prayers and devotionals specifically grounded in the experience and embodiment of the LGBTQ community. Because women have historically been marginalized on the basis of their biology, the intricacies and consequences of embodiment are important.

And Also with You: Community and Spirituality

A third characteristic of spirituality is its communal nature. Spirituality must be communal because it is never only about one's personal decisions. Even hermits, who live in solitude, a popular lifestyle in the early Middle Ages, were reacting to a social reality. A decision to flee the secular world in search of God is a judgement on the possibility of finding God within the secular world. So we are always interacting with the broader community, even if we make decisions that are seemingly "personal." (At no time has that been more evident than during a global pandemic that requires all of society to mitigate the spread of a potentially deadly virus!) Since spirituality shows itself in one's decisions about how to live in the world, it is necessarily social and communal, political, not limited to the individual. The old feminist insight that "the personal is political" fits well with this claim about spirituality as well. As much as we'd like to think that how we choose to live out our faith is a personal matter, we are always already making decisions that affect those around us, the earth, the communities of which we are a part.

Feminist spirituality is a story of ever-expanding communal circles. From the earliest days of consciousness-raising groups and Judith Plaskow's "yeah, yeah" moments in meetings of female graduate students, to the abuelitas and Guadalupanas who create and sustain Latinx devotional life, to the Black Christian women who founded the Black Lives Matter movement, feminist spiritualities have been marked by inclusivity and expansiveness. Though this text has tried to limit its discussion to Catholic feminism and issues in the Roman Catholic Church, feminist spirituality has always been an ecumenical and interreligious endeavor. Perhaps because of the solidarity women have forged as members of marginalized groups, feminist prayer has long been open to traditions that were feared and marginalized, including the Wiccan tradition. Anthologies of women's prayers include blessings from Native American cultures and from self-described witches who celebrate the seasons and the solstices.

One simple explanation for this could be women's longstanding identification with bodiliness and nature in patriarchal cultures. Since women's cycles of menstruation called to mind lunar and seasonal cycles, women's bodies were assumed to be closer to the natural world, or more difficult to transcend, than male bodies. Of course, this is a stereotype and a fallacy, as all human beings are embodied. Our experience, our senses, our knowledge all come to us in an embodied way. Even God is embodied in the incarnation. Nevertheless, this closeness between women and nature has led feminist theology to move away from the dualism that says that humanity is above and apart from nature and sets women against men, emotions against intellect, body against soul. Add to this a feminist rejection of the domination paradigms that invite men to dominate women, the intellect to rule the emotions, and the soul to be privileged over the body, and you get a pretty good sense of where feminist theology stands in terms of the human-nature interconnectedness.

It is no coincidence that so many authors speak of the spiritual life as the cultivation of a garden. Alice Walker, who coined the word *womanist,* did so in a text titled *In Search of Our Mothers' Gardens.* This groundbreaking work outlined the contours of womanist spirituality through literature and inspired many other writers to appropriate the image of the garden. Gardening is a feminized task (unlike farming, which is for profit and therefore masculinized). Gardens are focused supposedly on beauty and frivolous planting. But cultivation is about using one's gifts to enable another to shine. A successful garden blooms throughout the year, with a variety of plantings serving a variety of purposes. Gardening is inclusive and time-consuming. It involves seeding even when we are unsure of growth. The spiritual life is also like this: expansive, inclusive, moving beyond the immediate gratification of the self and the now to a promised future of beauty.

The spiritual life is not, however, without conflict. Ada María Isasi-Díaz explains such conflict using the garden metaphor when describing her feminist awakening in the white paradigm of WomanChurch and then realizing that white feminists saw the garden of feminist Catholicism as proprietary, as theirs. Isasi-Díaz writes, "As long as I toiled in the garden of Euro-American feminism, I was welcomed. But as I started to claim a space in the garden to plant my own flowers, the ethnic/racist prejudice prevalent in society reared its head."[4] The realization that nonwhite feminisms were not welcome to contribute to the direction of Euro-American feminism, to its priorities and values, prompted Isasi-Díaz to cultivate her mujerista insights elsewhere.

Beyond gardening metaphors, feminist spirituality also encompasses ecological activism. The feminist desire to do away with hierarchical dualism manifested itself, among other ways, in a preoccupation with ecological concerns that is almost as old as feminist theology itself. Rosemary Radford Ruether published *Gaia and God: An Ecofeminist Theology of Earth-Healing* in 1992. Sallie McFague's *The Body of God: An Ecofeminist Theology* appeared in 1993. So when we talk about inclusive communities, about ever-expanding circles of concern, we can include not only women and other marginalized groups of people but also the earth. Nature has been exploited and dominated to serve the "needs" of humans to the point where we are doing irreparable damage to our environment. A feminist sense of the interconnectedness of communities and contexts leads us to pay attention to the needs of the natural environment, particularly now.

One example of the broadening of feminist concern to include the natural world can be found in a collective of ecofeminists of Latin America. The Conspirando Collective is a group of feminist theologians and activists from Latin America and the Caribbean whose mission is one of cultural transformation. That is, these activists seek to change people's minds, to move them from a worldview of exploiting the earth and its resources to one where the earth is revered, protected, and held sacred. Founded in 1992 and active until 2012, the group published academic articles and ran workshops and educational seminars for women and others who were interested in feminist and ecofeminist theology, in community organizing and political strategy, and in personal and social transformation. A quick glance at their journal, also titled *Conspirando*, reveals a variety of articles about healing the earth, sustainability, the value of religious life, the role of women in the political sphere. This energy around environmental concerns in the Global South (where most of Latin America and the Caribbean exist) makes sense given that the most vulnerable communities (the poor, women, children) are the ones most dramatically effected by climate disaster. Look at the aftermath of Hurricane Katrina in our country. The Lower Ninth Ward, home to some of the most impoverished residents of New Orleans, was also the most at risk from faulty infrastructure that was easily overwhelmed by a powerful storm. Ecofeminists remind us of the interconnectedness of all life and of the importance of prioritizing the vulnerable natural world as part of caring for vulnerable humans.

The communal dimension of feminist spirituality can be seen in how feminists of all backgrounds have broadened beyond even the human community to include the fate of the earth among their concerns. In many ways, the ecofeminist movement overlaps with all the characteristics of spirituality we have highlighted so far. It is rooted in feminist beliefs about the interrelatedness of all creation and the importance of scientific insights about the ecological crisis in which we find ourselves. So, notionally, ecofeminism comes from commitments to scientific inquiry and interrelatedness. Ecological feminism is also about embodiment and context, in that it recognizes that the health of the human body and human communities cannot be separated from the health of the air we breathe, the water we drink, or the land we inhabit. And ecofeminism is communal for several reasons. First, it recognizes that only communal effort will succeed in saving the planet from climate disaster. Second, it seeks to mobilize communities through political action and social activism. Third, it views the earth as part of a community of living beings that must be considered with reverence.

The (Present and) Future of Feminist Spirituality

Feminist spirituality, like all of theology, finds itself at a crossroads. For many years, the priorities, concerns, and resources of Euro-American feminists have been at the forefront of feminist theology. Blacks, Asians, and Latinas have been relegated to the margins, where they have elaborated spirituality in their voices and from the hearts of their communities. Increasingly, however, the racist structures that pervade our country have been revealed to pervade institutions like the church and the academy as well. So when we look to the future of feminist spirituality, we must recognize that women from marginalized communities will set the priorities and lead the way.

As this chapter and book draw to a close, it is worthwhile to turn our attention specifically to the spirituality of women in these marginalized communities. Womanist spirituality and Latina spirituality share important characteristics that echo the ones mentioned above. The notional, embodied, and communal aspects of spirituality are, however, intensified, accented, in particular ways in these communities. The rubber meets the road differently among historically disenfranchised people.

The first feature of womanist, Asian American, and Latina spiritualities is the matter of erasure. We cannot talk about gender justice in the church if we continually present American Catholicism as a fundamentally or primarily Euro-American community. If we are looking for examples of beliefs inspiring spirituality, the belief that Black women and men remain important parts of the spiritual life of the church and the country seems appropriate. Additionally, the lives of Black Catholics have made a difference and continue to do so, despite a lack of official recognition.

An initial aspect of Black, Asian, and Latina spiritualities is a desire to be seen and recognized as members and shapers of the church community. For Black Catholic women this means lifting up the contributions of Black Catholics in a church that participated in and benefitted from chattel slavery and that excluded Black people from ordination and admission into religious communities. A spirit of resilience and resistance to erasure characterizes the spirituality of Black feminists and womanists. Witness the work of M. Shawn Copeland to bring to light the contributions of Sr. Henriette DeLille of New Orleans who founded the Sisters of the Holy Family and is currently on the road to canonization. Or the work of historian Shannen Dee Williams to uncover the lives and legacies of Black Catholic women religious. Her book, *Subversive Habits: Black Catholic Nuns in the Long African American Freedom Struggle*, traces the lives of Black nuns in predominantly white convents in ensuring accessible education in Black communities, in the Civil Rights and Black Power movements. From the life of Sr. Mary Antona Ebo, who marched at Selma, to the activism of the Sisters of St. Joseph of Carondelet in the wake of Michael Brown's murder in Ferguson, Missouri, Williams reminds us that Black women religious have been at the forefront of justice movements in this country. While not specifically scholars of spirituality, the work of these women exemplify a refusal to be swept aside, a desire for recognition and visibility in a hostile church environment.

The value of resistance is also a driving force in the spirituality of marginalized groups. For Latinas, this looks like resistance to dominant scripts about individualism in favor of communal identities while maintaining the goal of liberation from oppressive, colonial structures. In spirituality this manifests itself as a sanctification of everyday life, of the dignity of the small moments of grace that Latinas celebrate amid struggle. For example, in many Latinx cultures it is customary to request a blessing from a grandmother or mother upon greeting. Nothing special, just a recognition of the graced relationship between family members and a sign of intergenerational respect. Many Latina theologians, including Isasi-Díaz, Jeannette Rodriguez, and Socorro Castaneda highlight the notion of struggle or *lucha* as a defining characteristic of Latina spirituality. The difficult struggle is not the point, however, but rather the setting for resistance, for celebration in the midst of difficulty, for perseverance and survival. This perseverance looks like celebration, like joy in the middle of difficulty. As Isasi-Díaz notes: "My most profound religious experiences have happened in the midst of la lucha; and la lucha is what gives meaning and joy to my life. In la lucha I find God time and again. Yes, for me la vida es la lucha: we must struggle to create community if we are to contribute to making justice for women a reality in our lives and our world."[5] As we can see, *la lucha* is the place of divine encounter, the struggle for life, not unlike Jacob's wrestling with the angel in Genesis that defines his life.

In terms of bodiliness, Black and Latina spiritualities are also accented differently. For womanists, an emphasis on the erotic as a spiritual power that exceeds mere sexual arousal is a defining feature of spirituality. From poets like Audre Lorde and writers like Alice Walker, womanist spirituality takes a celebration of erotic power into the spiritual realm. This is not merely an act that takes note of embodiment, but it is a profoundly revolutionary move. Rather than accept the hyper-sexualization of Black bodies that racist structures have perpetuated in this country, womanist spirituality embraces the erotic as, yes, sexual, but also life-giving, life-sustaining, and life-enhancing joy.[6] Kelly Brown Douglas, in her book *Sexuality and the Black Church: A Womanist Perspective*, defines human (erotic) passion as "that divine energy within human beings, the love of God, that compels them toward life-giving, life-producing, and life-affirming activity and relationships in regard to all of God's creation."[7] An embracing of the erotic as part of being embodied constitutes a kind of resistance, especially for Black women who have been sexually denigrated from the days of chattel slavery to the present. Just as Latinas utilize *la lucha* as a setting where the divine and human meet, womanists refuse to allow the erotic to be used as a cudgel against black women. Instead, they celebrate an expansive understanding of the power of the erotic, as Audre Lorde called it, to encapsulate all of our loves.

As to the communal nature of feminist spirituality, Black, Latina, and Asian spiritualities invite us to consider the community beyond as a destination for spiritual work. Earlier, we discussed feminist spirituality as communal because, as a way of living, spirituality necessarily has an effect on those around us. Black, Latina, and Asian feminists remind us, however, that community is not only on the receiving end of spiritual work but serves as a point of origin for spirituality. Again and again these thinkers remind us that the double and triple rejection on the basis of race, class, and ethnicity forges communal bonds of solidarity to which they hold themselves accountable. Ada María Isasi-Díaz is a prime example of this, describing her role as a mujerista theologian as one of "midwife" to the community of Latinas in Northern Manhattan with whom she shared her life. For Isasi-Díaz, theology did not make sense outside of these communal ties. In turn, her ties to her community of mostly poor Latinas strengthened the urgency of her calls for justice. We need look no further than the very first page of her groundbreaking text, *Mujerista Theology: A Theology for the Twenty-First Century*, for an example of what we mean. There, she outlines the goals of mujerista theology as follows: "to provide a platform for the voices of Latina grassroots women, to develop a theological method that takes seriously the religious understandings and practices of Latinas as a source for theology, to challenge theological understandings, church teachings, and religious practices that oppress Latina women, that are not lifegiving."[8] Latina feminists encounter God and live out values that benefit not only women but the Latinx community as a whole. The communal bonds of shared ethnicity and race inform spirituality as much as the transformation of unjust structures serves as a goal for spirituality.

When we look at Black, Asian, and Latina spiritualities as the future, we must not overlook that these women are already shaping the priorities of a liberating spirituality, grounded in community struggle, searching for physical as well as spiritual justice. If feminist spirituality includes a call to be expansive, it must be willing to center the historically marginalized voices and allow them to drive the conversation now. How? There are many entry points, but I am partial to narrative and storytelling as a way to build bridges in spirituality.

How does storytelling build bridges? Let's do a thought experiment. Think of your favorite story, or your favorite song, or the last movie that really made you think. What grabbed you about the story? As you recall it, ask yourself: Was it a general narrative "all Americans think x," or was it a dive into a particular character, setting, or context? Elsewhere, I've written about one of my favorite stories, "The Battle of the Virgins" by Puerto Rican author Rosario Ferré. Though I'm not Puerto Rican and have no particular devotion to Guadalupe, the story drew me in with rich characters and a compelling plot. Ironically, if we want to build community, particular narratives are the way to go. We think generalities will connect to more people. Don't generalities apply to more people than particulars? But would you rather read an instruction manual, which applies broadly to anyone who is trying to use a particular thing, or a biography, which is about a particular person? It's counterintuitive, but particular narratives bring more people together than general ones. Have you ever met someone who is a fan of an obscure show or band that you like? Insta-friends!

This is why it's so important to allow marginalized narratives to drive the conversation about spirituality: it allows us to plug in to a perspective we might normally overlook or know nothing about. Marginalized stories highlight our common humanity, they awaken us to injustices we might be blind to, and they invite us to conversion. In reading Ferré's story, I witnessed a different take on Guadalupan devotion, one that reveres Guadalupe as a fierce defender of those who know what they want, as an ally to poor women, and as a counterpoint to the asexual Immaculate Conception. I was intrigued and provoked. The story invited me to think differently about what's going on in Marian devotion. Namely, it invited me to consider that what church leaders say people are revering about Mary (her purity, her submission) might not be the whole story.

As we listen to, read, or otherwise engage one another's stories, we see God at work in women's experience, in Latinas' struggle, in Black women's liberating resistance. Spirituality rooted in conversation and dialogue brings the work of the spirit to light in places we would not think to look. This widens the circle of concern, inspires us to see the sacred in the everyday, and pushes us to work for justice for all victims, including the natural world.

Conclusion

The field of spirituality can be misunderstood and murky. As an interdisciplinary field in theology, it draws on resources from psychology, history, theology, liturgy, and sociology. As a feature of human life, it is multifaceted, touching on our self-understanding, our relationship to God, self, and others, and our desire for justice. Spirituality shapes how we live, how we set ourselves up to encounter the divine, and how we live out the consequences of that encounter.

Because women's lives, bodies, and experiences were viewed as too sinful or too frivolous for divine encounter, we have much work to do in elaborating rituals, texts, and theories of feminist spirituality. But the groundwork is there. Feminist spirituality springs from beliefs about gender justice, about the value of the body and of the natural world, about the interconnectedness of human and nonhuman life. These spiritualities are embodied in a variety of personal and communal ways. They inspire resistance to erasure, to oppression, to colonization, and to violence of all kinds. And perhaps most important, feminist spiritualities are shaped by and oriented toward communal concerns. Different bodies, different kinds of oppression and marginalization, different communities of accountability but one overarching desire for justice in the name of the God of justice: this is what constitutes feminist spirituality.

If you are among the "spiritual but not religious" crowd or are someone who identifies as a seeker—looking for depth of meaning and transcendence of the limitations of life—ask yourself how your beliefs, your embodiment, and your community shape the way you live. Are you making decisions about what you eat, what you buy, and where you do business based on sincerely held beliefs? Are you hungry for meaning that validates your embodiment and your agency as a woman, as an LGBTQ person, as a member of some other marginalized community? Do you see the divine at work in your desire for justice, for action on behalf of the victims of history? If so, you are already living spiritually. You are already responding to a divine invitation. Let us listen to the stories of the women who came before us, the women who walk alongside us, and decide what story we will make of our own life-long dialogue with the divine.

Just be careful when the person beside you on your next flight asks what you're thinking about.

DISCUSSION QUESTIONS

1. Investigate a group of activists in your area or an activist cause important to you. Does the group have a website or a social media presence? Can you identify religious language in their mission, vision, and goals? What connections can you draw between socio-political activism and spirituality?

2. In your opinion, are women better suited to environmental activism? What are the demographics of people at the forefront of environmental causes in your city or state? Why do you think this is?

3. With a partner or in a small group, share the last story, movie, or show that made you reevaluate how you live. What was the story about and why did it move you?

DELVE DEEPER

Write a spiritual autobiography. What key moments, people, texts, or experiences shape the way you understand life and the world? Where did your values come from and what are they? What influences your decisions, your priorities, your hopes and dreams?

READ FURTHER

Biviano, Erin Lothes. *Inspired Sustainability: Planting Seeds for Action*. Maryknoll, NY: Orbis Books, 2016.

Douglas, Kelly B. *Sexuality and the Black Church: A Womanist Perspective*. Maryknoll, NY: Orbis Books, 1999.

Gebara, Ivone. *Longing for Running Water: Ecofeminism and Liberation*. Minneapolis: Fortress Press, 1999.

Isasi-Díaz, Ada María. *En La Lucha/In the Struggle: Elaborating a Mujerista Theology*. Minneapolis: Fortress Press, 2009.

Johnson, Elizabeth. *Ask the Beasts: Darwin and the God of Love*. New York: Continuum, 2015.

McFague, Sallie. *The Body of God: An Ecological Theology*. Minneapolis: Fortress Press, 1993.

Price, Courtney Bryant. "Erotic Defiance: A Womanist Ethic of Moral and Political Agency." PhD diss. Vanderbilt University, 2018.

Ruther, Rosemary Radford. *Gaia and God: An Ecofeminist Theology of Earth Healing*. San Francisco: HarperOne, 1991.

Segura, Olga. *Birth of a Movement: Black Lives Matter and the Catholic Church*. Maryknoll, NY: Orbis Books, 2021.

EPILOGUE

Adding Your Voice: Reimagining the Future

This epilogue addresses the most important part of the book: you. Your voice, your insights, your context coming into contact with this material is what matters most to your learning journey and also to this author. Every aspect of theology, but especially every aspect of feminist theology, benefits from new insights and new perspectives. So as you look back on what you accomplished while reading this text, I want you to ask yourself: What would I have written differently? What did the author leave out? What would I emphasize in order to make a difference in my life and the lives of my community?

That is my first challenge: to add your voice to this important conversation about women in the church.

Here is a second challenge. If this is the first time you are hearing about feminist interpretations of scripture, or women who resist patriarchal constraints, or female deacons or Latinx theology, it is not your fault. That doesn't mean it's not a problem. The omission of women's voices, LGBTQ voices, nonwhite, nondominant voices from the theological conversation is deliberate, not accidental. Women and others from marginalized communities have been doing theology forever and have been credentialed academics in theological fields at least since the middle of the last century. If you aren't learning about these things in schools, that is a choice, not a mistake. The choice to omit women's scholarship and robust discussion of women's roles in Christianity furthers patriarchal goals. Because of this deliberate omission, each generation of scholars is forced to redo work that has already been done by their predecessors—and then forgotten. This leads to frustration and to so much wasted time and effort relearning wisdom that's already there for the taking.

Let's end that cycle here. I'm challenging you to ask why there are no women on a reading list for a course, or for comprehensive exams, or a book club in your community or local library, or movies with women directors or screenwriters in your town or campus's film festival. If you notice an all-white syllabus, ask about it. If you are invited to join a club with no members from marginalized communities, do not stay quiet. Bring it up! Erasure is the ally of oppression. The more evidence of resistance gets erased, the harder the next generation has to work for liberation. This keeps oppressive systems in place.

Let me give you an example. In 1999, I visited Cuba with my mother, who had left her homeland as an exile in 1959, when she was ten years old. While in Bayamo, her hometown in the eastern part of the island, we stayed with family in my great-grandparents' home. We were there a week, doing our best to help, to catch up on so many years of absence, and I was getting to know my extended family in person for the first time. Unlike Havana, which at that time was pretty well-stocked for supplies, reliable electricity, and water, Bayamo lacked some resources because it sits far from the capital. One thing that we did every afternoon was pick through the day's ration of rice provided by the government in order to "clean" it. This amounted to pouring the dry rice out onto the glass dining room table and picking through it, grain by grain, taking out little rocks, dust, and other unwanted bits, and then sliding the actual rice granules into bowls to prep for dinner. Growing up in Miami, I wondered why people didn't revolt against repressive governments. After all, if political dissidents were being arrested just for having opinions, why weren't people protesting on the streets?

The rice. That's why.

You can't plan a revolution if you're picking through rice for an hour before every meal. If several hours of your day are devoted to figuring out how you'll get enough food between the regular market and the black-market sellers. If you're keeping track of whether today is a "water on" day or a "water off" day. The inconvenience is deliberate because it keeps you busy staying alive and preventing you from figuring out how to thrive.

Whenever Catholic theology or church history is presented to you as a long line of European male insights, just think of a bunch of white rice mixed with rocks and dust and dirt being spilled out onto a glass-top table. And then refuse the whole system that has you picking through bits to find women's contributions to sustain you. Keep women's contributions, Latinas, Black women, trans women at the forefront of your work, so the next generation will have it at the ready. That is my second challenge.

The third challenge is to take to heart a lesson I am still working to learn, well into middle age. And it's this: learn to tell the difference between descriptive and prescriptive language. Descriptive language tells us what is or was. Prescriptive language tells us what ought to be or what should have been. Much of our suffering and oppression stems from a confusion of these two ways of communicating. And this works against us on a personal level and a communal level. To illustrate, let's take the example of traditional (or biblical) womanhood. When we hear about what it means to be a traditional woman, or to be someone who adheres to biblical womanhood, we think of a woman who is subservient to the men in her life (her father, then her husband, and eventually her sons), who devotes her life to sacrificial service at great personal expense, who always puts others above herself. In the Bible, though, few women fit this mold. Here are some biblical women: Judith decapitates Holofernes. Yael drives a tent spike through the head of the general of an opposing army. Mary of Nazareth sings about God filling the hungry and sending thc rich away empty. Phoebe is a deacon. These are women as they are portrayed in scripture. They are examples of biblical womanhood. But they are rarely what we associate with that term. Because the discourse around good womanhood is more often than not prescriptive (telling us what we ought to be like) instead of descriptive (telling us what we are like).

Too often in theological and religious circles, prescriptive language is passed off as descriptive. Someone talking about the good old days, when men were men, is actually talking about an ideal of violent, aggressive manhood that took out anger on anyone perceived as weaker: women, children, gays and lesbians, immigrants, Black people. When you hear "traditional marriage" you are often hearing descriptions of white middle-class fantasies where women gleefully did all care work and men worked in offices and came home to be served. Few people lived that "traditional" life—so is it a description of a tradition or a prescription for oppression? How many Black families in Alabama in the 1940s had a male breadwinner working in an office while a woman in an apron and a crinoline put their children on the bus and baked cookies while they were gone? For that matter, how many families of any race did—or still do—this in Appalachia? We should attune our ears to ask, "Wait, is this how things used to be for everyone? Or is this how someone wishes we were now because it suits their interest or preserves their status in power?"

In this book, I have tried to distinguish description from prescription, "is/was" from "ought to be." I have also tried to be as inclusive as possible with voices that differ from my own. This text will benefit from additions by Asian American Catholics, by Afro-Latinas, by trans scholars. Inevitably, there are parts where my own lack of subject expertise has led to some generalizations or errors of commission and omission. More can be said about decoloniality, about antiracist work, about averting climate catastrophe, about the fallout from the sex abuse and cover-up scandals in the church, or about the horror of the Catholic residential schools in North America. It is my sincere hope that in adding your voice, we continue to build the momentum for justice within the church and beyond it.

As we do that vital work, please remember to add your voice, to speak up when you see an omission, and to listen for the difference between how things are and how they should be. It's been an honor to go on this journey with you. Now, in the words of John Baptiste de la Salle, the founder of the charism that inspires my institution, I simply say: the work is yours.

NOTES

Chapter 1

1. Kate Manne, "The Logic of Misogyny," *Boston Review* (July 11, 2016): 3.

2. Judith Plaskow, *Standing Again at Sinai* (San Francisco: HarperOne, 1991), Introduction.

3. This version appeared in 1863 in the *New York Independent*, a newspaper. Scholars have noted, however, that it was changed significantly by Gage, to make Truth sound like a southern-accented slave when in fact she was a Dutch-speaking former slave from New York, and her accent and vocabulary would have differed significantly from Gage's presentation. The Sojourner Truth Project, by Leslie Podell, a student in California, highlights the differences between the two speeches (in writing and orally) and invites us to reflect on how white women have usurped the work of Black women to fit their stereotypical understandings of Black lives and to further the agenda of white supremacy. For more see https://www.thesojournertruthproject.com/.

Chapter 2

1. Frederick Cwiekowski, *The Beginnings of the Church* (Mahwah, NJ: Paulist Press, 1987).

Chapter 3

1. K. Cummings, "For Catholics, Gradual Reform Is No Longer an Option," *New York Times*, August 20, 2018.

2. CARA, "The Changing Face of US Catholic Parishes," 2011, https://cara.georgetown.edu/CARAServices/Parishes%20Phase%20One.pdf.

3. Cummings, "For Catholics, Gradual Reform Is No Longer an Option."

4. Mary Daly, *The Church and the Second Sex* (New York: Harper Colophon, 1968), 143.

5. Mary Daly, *Beyond God the Father* (Boston: Beacon Press, 1985), 19.

6. Barbara Flanagan, "Mary Daly Leads Exodus after Historic Sermon" *The Heights* 62, no. 11 (November 22, 1971).

Chapter 7

1. J. Cheryl Exum, *Fragmented Women: Feminist (Sub)versions of Biblical Narratives* (New York: T&T Clark, 1997), 173.

Chapter 8

1. Joan E. Taylor, "Missing Magdala and the Name of Mary 'Magdalene,'" *Palestine Exploration Quarterly* 146, no. 3 (2014): 205–23.

2. Claudia Setzer, "Excellent Women: Female Witness to the Resurrection," *Journal of Biblical Literature* 116, no. 2 (1997): 259–72.

Chapter 9

1. Elizabeth Johnson, *Truly Our Sister* (New York: Continuum, 2006).

Chapter 10

1. CARA Research Review: Lay Ecclesial Ministers in the United States, 2015.

2. In *Praying with Women Mystics*, ed. Mary T. Malone (Dublin: Columba Press, 2006).

3. Gary Macy, "Women Deacons: History," in Phyllis Zagano, Gary Macy, and William T. Ditewig, *Women Deacons: Past, Present, Future* (Mahwah, NJ: Paulist Press, 2011), 11.

Chapter 11

1. Eleanor McLaughlin, "Women, Power, and the Pursuit of Holiness in Medieval Christianity," in *Feminist Theology: A Reader*, ed. Ann Loades (Louisville, KY: Westminster John Knox, 1990), 113.

2. Mary T. Malone, *Four Women Doctors of the Church* (Maryknoll, NY: Orbis Books, 2017), 18–19.

Chapter 12

1. Augustine, Sermon 52, 6, 16: PL 38:360; *Catechism of the Catholic Church* 230.

2. Augustine, *De Trinitate XXII*, ch. 3, interpreted by Genevive Lloyd, "Augustine and Aquinas," in *Feminist Theology: A Reader*, ed. Ann Loades (Louisville: Westminster John Knox, 1990), 91–92.

3. Carol P. Christ, "Why Women Need the Goddess," in *WomanSpirit Rising: A Feminist Reader of Religion*, ed. Carol P. Christ and Judith Plaskow (New York: HarperCollins, 1992), 280.

Chapter 13

1. Judith Plaskow, *Standing Again at Sinai* (San Francisco: HarperOne, 1991), 133.

2. Elisabeth Schüssler Fiorenza, *In Memory of Her: A Feminist Theological Reconstruction of Christian Origins* (New York: Herder & Herder, 1994), 173.

3. Ada María Isasi-Díaz, *La Lucha Continues: Mujerista Theology* (Maryknoll, NY: Orbis Books, 2007), 244.

4. Isasi-Díaz, *La Lucha Continues,* 250.

5. Isasi-Díaz, *La Lucha Continues,* 251.

6. See Natalia Imperatori-Lee, *Cuéntame: Narrative in the Ecclesial Present* (Maryknoll, NY: Orbis Books, 2018).

Chapter 14

1. From Miriam Therese Winter, *Woman Prayer, Woman Song: Resources for Ritual* (Eugene, OR: Wipf & Stock, 2008), 77–78.

2. See Kat Armas, *Abuelita Faith: What Women on the Margins Teach Us about Wisdom, Persistence and Strength* (Grand Rapids: Brazos Press, 2021).

3. Kat Armas, "The Liberating Theology of Our Abuelitas," *Sojourners,* July 7, 2021, https://sojo.net/articles/liberating-theology-our-abuelitas.

4. Ada María Isasi-Díaz, *En La Lucha/In the Struggle: Elaborating a Mujerista Theology* (Minneapolis: Fortress Press, 2009), 18.

5. Ada María Isasi-Díaz, *La Lucha Continues: Mujerista Theology* (Maryknoll, NY: Orbis Books, 2007), 23.

6. See the work of Alice Walker, Audre Lorde, and contemporary womanist ethicist Courtney Bryant's work as examples of womanism and the erotic.

7. Kelly Brown Douglas, *Sexuality and the Black Church: A Womanist Perspective* (Maryknoll, NY: Orbis Books, 1999), 120.

8. Isasi-Díaz, *Mujerista Theology,* 1.

INDEX